Classic Cliffhangers

Volume 1
1914-1940

Classic Cliffhangers

Volume 1
1914-1940

by Hank Davis

Luminary Press
Baltimore, Maryland, USA

ISBN 13: 9781887664769
ISBN 10: 1887664769
Library of Congress Catalog Card Number 2007927361
Manufactured in the United States of America
Printed by Odyssey Press
First Printing by Luminary Press, May 2007

For everyone who eagerly awaited
the next thrilling chapter...

Contents

Opening Credits

One can't have an interest in Classic Cliffhangers or write a book about them without meeting many kind, wonderful and interesting people. I certainly did.

My old buddy Len Brown pulled out all the stops in order to lure me back into the world of movie serials. His master plan involved sending me boxes of videotapes, thus making sure I was securely hooked. And I was. Along the way I had memorable conversations with Henry Miyamoto, Martin Grams, Eric Stedman and, most recently, Eric Hoffman. I always learned something from talking to these knowledgeable guys.

The images that appear in this book were provided by many sources. I am particularly indebted to VCI, especially Bob Blair, Annita Calvert and Chris Rowe. Eric Hoffman spent hours going through his archives and lending me some of the wonderful originals you see reproduced here. Hoffman and I were introduced by our mutual friend Bea Suarez. Bea deserves a special word of thanks for her friendship and support over the course of this project. In fact, Bea was on board before I knew the train was leaving the station.

Some of the chapters in this book are based on monthly columns I contribute to *Big Reel* magazine, and I am grateful to my former editor Clair Fliess, who gave me a free hand in selecting that material. Also thanks to Gary Svehla of Midnight Marquee Press who worked closely with me during the final chaotic months of production to bring this book, as well as Volume II, to completion.

Finally, I am indebted to Adrian Booth for taking the time to reminisce about the golden era of serial filmmaking and for writing the wonderful and highly personal Introduction to these books.

—Hank Davis

hdavis@uoguelph.ca

The First Reel

The first movie serial I remember seeing was *The Galloping Ghost*. I was a kid in New York at the time, no more than eight years old. Hardly anyone owned TV sets then, so each afternoon at about four o'clock we would climb the stairs to my friend Steven's apartment and camp out in front of his tiny black and white screen for an afternoon of juvenile entertainment. I'd like to remember which channel ran this low-budget fare. My best guess is Channel 11 (WPIX) or maybe it was Channel 13, long before it became classy and joined the Public Television network. The afternoon program block consisted of one or two cartoons, usually "Out of the Inkwell," followed by one chapter of a vintage (early 1930s) serial.

That is when my friends and I discovered *The Galloping Ghost* (1931). I only remember a lot of chases in old-looking cars and a bunch of fistfights. That's all—no plot, no dialogue, just zooming cars and flying fists. Looking back, we were probably the perfect serial audience—a bunch of rowdy eight year olds who would cheer and yell at the screen. And unlike the original serial audience, we didn't have to wait a week between cliffhangers. Thanks to the wonders of television, the serial was on five days a week. I remember telling my parents what we had been spending our afternoons watching. The cartoons were fine, but when I said *The Galloping Ghost,* my mother assumed it was a scary movie and might do me some kind of psychological harm. My father quickly assured her that "Galloping Ghost" was a nickname for Red Grange.

"Is there football in it?" My father asked. I nodded quickly to end the conversation and to make sure I'd be allowed to keep watching TV with my friends. The truth is, I'm not sure I remembered seeing anything resembling football, just lots of car chases and fistfights.

But as usual, my mother was right. The movie did warp me psychologically, but not quite in the way she imagined. A half century later I still watch old movie serials like *The Galloping Ghost*. My friends left behind the wonders of the chapter play many years ago. Me, I'm still mesmerized. I don't just watch them. I critically analyze them. For the past five years I've written a monthly column about movie serials for *Big Reel* magazine. Those installments have inspired this book and its sequel, Volume II. Mom, you were right. I am certifiably warped. I continue to be enchanted by movie serials. I love their innocence, their energy and their undeniable skill, crude though it may appear today. The best serials are classic examples of early American low-budget filmmaking. The bad ones are silly and stilted, but always charming and sometimes bizarre. At the very least, they offer a window into another time and place. In some ways, it's a world many of us long to return to. For others, it's a place we are fortunate to have left behind.

Red fights to protect Dorothy Gulliver, who is being abducted by Tom London in *The Galloping Ghost.*

Because those earlier times and attitudes influenced the people we are today, it is interesting to examine them. Something that becomes both entertaining and informative. Those were the two main goals I kept in mind while writing this book. I want to entertain readers as well as encourage them to find viewing pleasure in movie serials. Lord knows that's what they were made for. But I also want to inform readers about the serial creators—people on both sides of the camera, the producers who hired them and the world in which all this movie magic happened.

With movie serials, it's perfectly OK to appreciate their art and laugh at their lunacy. Not all the laughs were intended, but that doesn't matter. This isn't a grim, serious business. Most serials were made for youthful and less sophisticated audiences. It would be wrong *not* to laugh and nod our heads in appreciation of what these skilled professionals accomplished under very trying conditions and with limited money.

In both Volumes of *Classic Cliffhangers* I have tried to include examples of the very best as well as the not-so-great serials. Both good and bad are all a part of the genre, and if we're going to get our feet wet, we may as well just jump into the lake. I hope I've included some of your favorite serials. I've probably managed to exclude a few titles you wish were here. Serial fans are an opinionated and testy lot. Once you get past *Flash Gordon* or *Captain Marvel*, hardly anyone can agree on a Top-Ten list. There are 50 titles here (1929-1940) and 50 more in Volume II (1941-1955). My goals are quite modest. I'd like to warp

the minds of a whole new audience in the same delightful way that mine was during those halcyon days sitting with good friends in front of a flickering TV screen. I'll consider it a job well done if I can rekindle the flame for readers who may have forgotten those Classic Cliffhangers.

Finding Movie Serials Today

You're in luck. It has never been easier and more economical to purchase movie serials for home entertainment than it is today. There are more titles available and more companies selling them than ever before. The digital revolution has seen to some of this, but a growing consumer base, too, has been part of the equation. But matter how cheaply someone can duplicate a DVD of an old Mascot serial, there still be an audience out there who are willing to buy it for any of this to make sense.

Before readers buy any Classic Cliffhangers, it's important to remember that movie serials were not made to be viewed the way that most are watched today. They were weekly entertainment, projected onto a large screen. Audiences had no control whatsoever. Once the moment was gone, it was gone. The filmgoer was passively bound to the theater seats. All that has changed. Serials are now viewed on relatively small screens, the remote control closely at hand. The image can be paused, reversed and examined in detail. Bleary-eyed fans forge ahead, watching episode after episode, often until boredom sets in. These are hardly ideal or fair conditions in which to experience the serials. Producers never intended the complete serial to be seen in this way. While sometimes difficult to do, readers should try to keep this fact in mind when discussing the serials from a critical point of view.

Very few sources of Classic Cliffhangers are the soulless conglomerates that handle big-time Hollywood products. Many of these companies are barely a step up from mom and pop operations. Many found themselves in the business because of their love of vintage cinema and the difficulty in finding these forgotten treasures. The following companies are worthy of your support.

VCI

Years ago, during the pre-digital era, company president Bill Blair (who passed away just as this book was going to press) told me that he viewed old public domain (PD) serials as "orphans." He saw VCI's mandate as adopting them and seeing that they found good homes. At the time, VCI was doing little more than finding rare available sources (sometimes not quite pristine) and duplicating them on to VHS.

All that has changed. VCI now produces high-end product on DVD, working from very clean elements and using digital restoration when necessary. Their releases usually contain plenty of extras as well, including interviews with actors and original theatrical trailers. Their catalogue is extensive. (1-800-331-4077 or www.vcient.com)

Alpha Video

Alpha took the world of B-movies and so-called Forgotten Horrors by storm when they came out with an extensive line of DVDs at the rock-bottom price of $25 for five items. Originally, their serials were packaged as two separate DVDs, thus effectively doubling the price to a whopping $10 — still a bargain. These days their serials appear on a single DVDs and, like all Alpha products, feature sensational cover art. Look for reliable quality without state-of-the-art digital restoration or a bunch of extras. Their catalogue is a fun place to visit and it's hard to resist impulse purchases at these prices. (1-800-336-4627 or www.oldies.com)

Serial Squadron

These products are a labor of love. The Squadron's stated goal is to rediscover and restore lost, forgotten and damaged serials. This work is labor-intensive and barely results in a break-even situation. Their list of offerings (both silent and sound serials) is relatively modest, but each of them has been treated with kid gloves. Squadron restoration is sometimes a bit more assertive than most — the addition of tinting or toning, for example. But even when original sources have been spiffed up a bit for modern sensibilities, the original versions are usually also provided, allowing the viewer to decide for him or herself. In the case of silent serials, you'll find titles here not available elsewhere, along with some dandy original musical scores created by Squadron honcho Eric Stedman. (www. serialsquadron.com)

Finders Keepers

This is essentially a small collector/researcher-based company that offers a catalogue of titles not generally available elsewhere. One never knows what will be found here, and their offerings extend well beyond movie serials to other pop culture obscurities. They were the source of both silent serials covered in this book, and also provided a number of rare later titles we'll be covering in Volume II. (www.finderskeepersvideos.com)

Other collector-geared sellers include: **Grapevine Video**, which specializes in silent fare (www.grapevinevideo.com), **Sinister Cinema**, which has an impressive list of vintage serials and B-movies (www.sinistercinema.com) and **Millcreek Entertainment,** which offers mass-market packages of public domain films, including a collection of a dozen serials on a DVD Megapack. (www. millcreekent.com)

Classic Cliffhangers

Introduction by Adrian Booth

I have found great joy in reading Professor Hank's serial books and I am delighted to have been invited to write this Introduction. These serials were truly a gift to thousands of American boys and girls, especially during the awful depression of the 1930s and the period beyond. For a nickel, the kids could sit all day in a warm movie house and, even if they couldn't afford the popcorn, they had magic! And still do!

Reading this book has been like a warm old-home week, meeting friends like Frankie Darro; Grant Withers; my favorite henchman: Charlie Middleton (*the* Ming); Ralph Byrd (*Dick Tracy*); David Sharpe (my double in *Daughter of Don Q*); the fine actor Lionel Atwill (who almost suffocated me in *Captain America*); Clayton Moore (*The Lone Ranger*); Bruce Bennett, Kirk Allyn (*Superman*); Noah Beery, Jr.; our serial master Bill Witney and, of course, the Duke: John Wayne.

When I was a very little girl I was allowed to go and see a serial on Friday after school because they showed it in a neighboring church (my mother's church forbade movies). The first serial I ever saw was *The Green Archer*. Scary, scary, scary! When the Evil One fed the poor mother through a barred hole in the basement wall—near panic! And yet I think it was then that the Hollywood butterfly settled in my heart. Little wonder that I loved this genre all my life. With Professor Hank, I love the "abiding innocence" of our serials. There was good and there was evil, and the bad guys always bit the dust.

The Prof's humor tickles me; it's like popcorn (buttered). "Between Mascot serials," he writes, "and vintage Disney, a generation of kids probably grew up thinking that mammals like Rin Tin Tin could do trigonometry." Flash Gordon being a eunuch: that I find hilarious! And the three Daredevils (of the Red Circle) seem to be playing a perpetual game of leapfrog. All Gene Autry wants in *The Phantom Empire* is to "aw shucks" his way through life. Queen Tika? She has all kinds of parlor tricks, like raising the dead. I tell you—popcorn!

And here's some popcorn of my own. In *Deadwood Dick* the Prof calls me a "scream queen" and well he might! Don Douglas and I are on an old breakaway wooden platform; the mayor and his townsfolk have scrambled off because there is a cattle stampede heading straight for our breakaway. The director (James Horne), the cameraman and all the crew are safe in their barricade behind a line of wooden horses, but Don and I have to climb down seven narrow steps, break through the red, white and blue gauze hanging on all sides, run 30 feet *under* the platform, tear through the gauze on the other side and dash 15 feet into a barn door, just missing stampede death. I lost three beautiful fake curls in that mad dash and I have a picture to prove it!

In *Federal Operator 99,* I played the bad girl. *Really* bad. After murder, arson and mayhem, George Lewis and I would go back to his apartment where he'd blithely sit down at the piano and play "The Moonlight Sonata." I'd stand

Adrian Booth with "beautiful fake curls" on the set of *Deadwood Dick*.

there listening, wrapped in my own gorgeous new fox furs, wearing long black opera gloves. Now *that's* some popcorn!

It was always great fun working with Roy Barcroft (who I called "Bearclaw") and all the stunt guys in *Daughter of Don Q*. In that role, I could do everything; I could do anything. I could play golf or fall out of a moving car. They taught me jujitsu. I could shoot a bow and arrow. I saw Dick Cavett's replayed interview with Katharine Hepburn. He asked her about the scene in *Philadelphia Story* in which Cary Grant pushed her flat on her back through an open door and she said she had no memory of it. When Cavett seemed surprised, Hepburn explained that when you do a particular part, it's like you're mesmerized. In *Daughter of Don Q,* they showed me how to shoot the bow and arrow and I did it perfectly. Afterward, one of the crew came up to me and said, "I didn't know you were interested in archery." I said, "Well, I'm not." So we tried a couple of shots. I ended up with a black and blue elbow. But I could do it with the cameras rolling. Mesmerized!

You will admire the Prof's research, often delivered with just a deft one- or two-liner. Reading this book, I learned that some relatively unknown background music in *The Devil Horse* was actually the first serial use of "The William Tell Overture," ahead of *The Lone Ranger.* Dum. Dah dah *dah!* And that World War I flying ace Captain Eddie Rickenbacker, "America's beloved ace of aces," created *Ace Drummond.*

For many a happy Sunday in the 1930s, *Jungle Jim* topped even *Flash Gordon* in the comic strip pages. Grant Withers was the dashing safari guy and what a dash! He was surrounded by a jungle goddess, a cobra, tigers, lions, a bunny rabbit and a skunk, a crocodile, flying bows and arrows, lions eating Uncle Bruce, cutthroats, Shanghai Lil, shipwrecks, an ocean bottle message and monkeys throwing rocks at leopards. That Grant heroically braved all of this makes me feel sorry that I tried to shoot him a decade later in our movie *The Savage Horde.*

Prof Hank reveals his sensitivity as we learn about the deaths of several of our heroes—Grant Withers killing himself, Dick Purcell's untimely death and Frankie Darro's sad end. I should not say "end"; they are all up "there" with the Lord—along with my beloved husband David.

And the Duke is up there too. The people's beloved John Wayne. The Prof tells us John made three serials for

Adrian (as Lorna Gray) starred with Boris Karloff in *The Man They Could Not Hang.*

Mascot and, much to my real surprise, I learned that Mascot Pictures would soon morph into Republic Studios. In Mascot's *The Hurricane Express*, planes and railroads and cars and motorcycles tear around at high speed and John Wayne "never seems to walk when running will do." Of course, you could never top the Duke. He parlayed his serial roles into some of the greatest Westerns of all time: *Stagecoach, The Searchers* and *True Grit*. John had no idea what he was getting himself into at Mascot: six-day weeks and 12 hours of shooting a day. I think the lovely Kay Aldridge and I topped him in 1942 when we made *Perils of Nyoka*. You might not believe our shooting schedule. If we had to leave for a location at 7 a.m. to shoot in the sunlight at 8, we had to be at the studio by 4:30: hair, one hour; makeup, one hour; wardrobe, one-half hour. You do the math. We might get back to the studio by 7 p.m. Then the assistant director would give us tomorrow's shooting schedule, always pages and pages. You see, we had to know the location dialogue for all 15 chapters. Nothing was shot in sequence. The different scenes from each chapter were shot in the same room or cave or an outside porch on the studio back lot or around the rocks and trees at Iverson's ranch in the Valley. *And* if the weather suddenly changed, the Assistant Director would call at 3 a.m. to give us a different set of pages from all 15 chapters for inside shooting that day instead of outside. When were we to sleep? Nyoka and Queen Vultura decided to take motel rooms across from the studio!

The Prof has gently stirred a nostalgia in me for these serials. I can't wait to see Bill Witney's *Daredevils of the Red Circle* or *The Shadow* serials or *The Green Archer*. How I wish I could find that original version [Pathé, 1925]! I'm especially eager to see *Daredevils* because Fred Toones, the black Snowflake, had his shoeshine business right under my dressing room. It is still there as you enter what was Republic Studios. I drive by now and then to show a friend or just to look and remember. I loved every day on every set, rain or shine, and I thank God for having been a part of it all. Paramount has recently acquired all of Republic Pictures so maybe you'll see Vultura peeking around a cave for you.

I have met hundreds of fans in the last few years at nostalgia conventions or through Boyd Majors' *Serial Report* or the books of Ken Weiss and Jack Mathis, and the sweet guys at Serial Squadron. These dear fans remember you after all the years, and they love you!

Blessings,
Adrian Booth Brian
Sherman Oaks, California

Classic Cliffhangers

Background

Quiet Cliffhangers or Two Silent Serials

Although this is a book about movie serials from the sound era (i.e., post-1929), we have elected to make two notable exceptions. Classic Cliffhangers cannot be discussed without acknowledging *The Perils of Pauline* (1914). It is probably the most famous serial of all time, familiar even to people who know very little about serials. Mention the genre and they'll come back with some reference either to actress Pearl White or to the title of her most famous serial. Like it or not, *The Perils of Pauline* has become an iconic phrase in popular culture.

Any serious discussion of movie serials must acknowledge a commercial and stylistic debt to Pearl White and *The Perils of Pauline*. Pauline's adventures helped set the stage for serial moviemaking over the next 40 years, taking us well beyond the silent era. In fact, when Universal began cranking out cliffhangers to serve the emerging market for films with sound, *The Perils of Pauline* was one of the first titles they chose to recycle. We have included both the 1914 and 1934 versions in our coverage.

The other silent exception is *The Master Mystery* (1918). There are three reasons for this choice:

1. It offers a chance to watch the Great Houdini at work:
2. As far as we can tell, it marks the first appearance of a robot in a movie serial.
3. It's a wonderful old serial.

Even for those serial fans who have no great love of silent films, *The Master Mystery* is an enjoyable ride. It probably won't convert anyone to the world of silent films, but it may soften one's resolve. If it actually starts you moving along this track, be prepared for a major journey. There are about 300 silent movie serials that we can name. You'll recognize that as a larger number than the role call of sound serials, which falls a bit short of 260. The major difference, of course, is that the lion's share of sound serials still exist today. Sadly, that is very far from the case with silent movie serials, as many as 90% of them are lost.

The Perils of Pauline
(1914)

Although there were serial queens before Pearl White, and heroine-based movie serials before this one, *The Perils of Pauline* is where it all seems to begin. Any fan of classic movies and cartoons has been exposed to takeoffs of the trials of Pauline. Think of a young maiden tied to a railroad track or hanging off a cliff, and you're probably thinking of a flickering image of Pearl White on the big screen nearly a hundred years ago.

The Precursors of Pearl. Before Pearl White and *Pauline*, there was Mary Fuller in *What Happened to Mary?* (1912) and its follow-up, *Who Will Marry Mary?* (1913). That same year also saw the appearance of Kathlyn Williams in *The Adventures of Kathlyn* (1913). Once *Pauline* hit pay dirt in 1914, there was no shortage of fem-centered serials, including *The Mysteries of Myra, Beatrice Fairfax* and *Perils of Our Girl Reporters* (all 1916). *The Adventures of Ruth* followed in 1919. Even Pearl White, herself, kept the pot simmering with *The Exploits of Elaine* (1914), *The New Exploits of Elaine* and *The Romance of Elaine* (both 1915). Most of these serials ran between 10 and 20 episodes, although *The Hazards of Helen* set a record that won't be broken any time soon; it ran for 119 episodes between 1914 and 1917 and starred four different actresses, two of whom were conveniently named Helen. This survey is by no means exhaustive. The simple fact is that prior to the sound era, heroines or silent scream queens were more likely than heroic males to headline movie serials. For reasons better left to pop sociology, all that changed with the sound era.

We're going to examine *The Perils of Pauline* simply because everything that comes later in the world of Classic Cliffhangers owes its existence to the success, if not the style of this most famous silent serial. Simply put, if *Pauline, Helen, Mary, Beatrice, Myra, Kathlyn, Ruth* and *Elaine* had stiffed at the box office in those quaint early days, odds are good that weekly installments of *Dick Tracy, Flash Gordon* and *Captain Marvel* would have been less likely to make their way to the big screen a quarter century later.

Racing Through the Reels. Pearl White, who did more of her own stunts than most serial actors before or since, was right about one thing. Serials did not give her a chance to act. She wanted to get out of them as quickly as possible and into some full-length features where she felt she'd be given a chance to strut her stuff as an actress. "There is no acting in a serial," she complained. "You simply race through the reels." The irony is that White appeared in over 200 films, at least some of which gave her ample opportunity to act. Yet, today she is remembered for "racing through the reels."

THE ABDUCTION.

THE ECLECTIC FILM COMPANY'S
GREAT $25,000 PRIZE PHOTO PLAY
THE PERILS
OF
PAULINE
6TH EPISODE IN 2 PARTS
COPYRIGHTED 1914 ECLECTIC FILM CO.

Hank Davis

So just what does *The Perils of Pauline* look like to the modern viewer? Unfortunately, the answer to that question is compromised by factors beyond our control. The biggest problem is that 11 of the original 20 chapters are missing in action and considered irrevocably lost. Originally scheduled to run for 13 installments, *Pauline* was a victim of its own success. To meet public demand, 13 quickly turned into 20 when audience response ensured profitable returns. Of those, only nine chapters remain.

To further complicate matters, the original form of the serial is now unknown. It originally opened on March 23, 1914, at the Loew's Broadway Theatre in New York and continued every second week until it had run its course. The serial was then edited for European (and some additional American) release in 1916. By then, World War I had broken out and the political climate had changed sufficiently to change the villain's name from Owen (in the 1914 print) to the decidedly German-sounding Koerner in the 1916 version. Apparently all versions available today contain 9 chapters struck from the 1916 version.

It is clear that additional editing has taken place and it is not even certain whether the chapter sequence has been altered. Although all of the title cards look appropriately old, they seem to come from different sources. Worse yet, some of them contain egregious and unnecessary spelling or language errors. Examples: "…explain the reasons of (sic) her sudder (sic) departure." Or "Learning the decision his ward Koerner organise (sic) another plot with the hel (sic) of his confedarate (sic) Hicks." Or "Whe (sic) learn that the heroine…" Or how about "I must have 100 volunteers in order to clear the country of the robber (sic) with it is infected (sic)…" Some of the intertitles are unintentionally funny, as when an Indian proclaims, "The white girl shall be subjected to the ordeal which should reveal her immoral (sic?) strength." Whoever has written these translations of translations has a fleeting acquaintance with the English language at best.

Perhaps the biggest surprise is that none of the chapters, as they presently appear, ends with a cliffhanger. Certainly, Pauline faces peril, but her plight is always resolved by the end of each

Pearl White with equine friends, 1914

20- or 30-minute episode. Fans of sound-era serials have become accustomed to spending the time between episodes in doubt about the fate of the hero or heroine. As *Pauline* makes clear, so-called cliffhangers were not always what they have become. In all likelihood, both the 1914 and the 1916 versions of this film consisted of a series of separate tales. They may have thrilled the audience with mid-episode peril, but when the audience went home they had few concerns about the future. In this sense, *The Perils of Pauline* is not the godmother of modern serials. Then again, nothing is for certain, as *The Perils of Pauline* has fallen victim to quite a bit of editing over the years, as the market shifted from weekly theatrical screenings to the home projector market, serviced by companies like Blackhawk or Official Films. Indeed, it is a Blackhawk negative that appears on the DVD available from Finders Keepers Videos.

Each of the nine surviving episodes follows the same basic format (we are fortunate that the first and last chapters still exist, allowing some cohesion to the overall story). Pearl White plays Pauline Marvin, the ward of rich old man Sanford Marvin (Edward Jose). She is pretty and high-spirited. Modern audiences might call her "flaky" or "air-headed." Harry Marvin (Crane Wilbur), the old man's son, loves Pauline and wants to marry her. Things are a bit odd around the edges since Harry is strangely close to being Pauline's brother. She, too, is named Marvin although they do not seem related by blood. She does, however, live under the same roof as Harry.

Old Man Marvin dies in the first reel, but not before telling the kids that he'd love to see them married. Harry is all for it but Pauline announces, "I suppose I'll marry Harry someday, but first I want to live a life full of excitement and adventure." Poor Harry. There's nothing like pouring your heart out to your best girl, proposing marriage to her, only to have her say, "Not yet. First I want to hang off some cliffs and get tied to some railroad tracks." Actually, she makes clear to him that she wants her "absolute freedom for one year," which no doubt endeared her to a generation of nascent feminists.

The third central character is Owen/Koerner (depending on whether you see the prewar or wartime print). Koerner was played by Paul Panzer (who looks uncannily like Mel Brooks). Old Man Marvin leaves Pauline a sizable fortune, with the stipulation that the money stays with Koerner until Pauline settles down and marries Harry. Then, and only then, can the kids sail off into a life of the idle rich. Until then, Koerner gets to manage the money as he sees fit. Why Old Man Marvin would consider a deal like this makes little sense. Obviously, he hasn't had the benefit of seeing Mel Brooks in *Blazing Saddles* or *Young Frankenstein*. But even so, Koerner seems the very embodiment of avarice and sleaze. Sadly, the old man sees none of it. Once he departs in Chapter 1, Koerner spends each episode plotting against Pauline so he can lay claim to her inheritance. Since she is embarked on a life of empty, carefree pleasure and physical risk, he has boundless opportunity.

So, for example, Pauline hears about a car race and decides to enter. Once Koerner learns of her plans, he bribes a mechanic to disable the brakes or the steering mechanism or to throw some tire snares on the road. It is then up to Harry to save her and for Koerner to pace around, pulling his hair and crying "Curses! Foiled again!" at the end of the chapter. And so it goes. Car races, air balloons, horse races, speed boats. You name it — she does it. And Koerner, with a seemingly endless supply of gypsies, snakes, rats, fires and floods, tries to sabotage

Pearl White

her efforts.

Although this is an early silent film, the acting style is more accessible when compared to the typical silent film. Some of the performances actually border on being "modern," or at least not excessively mannered and old fashioned. The work by Francis Carlyle as Hicks, Koerner's old chum and sometime-accomplice, is particularly effective. Pearl White, too, is quite engaging. In the first chapter, when someone suggests she climb into a balloon basket for a photo, she finds the idea so appealing that she literally jumps off the ground with excitement. Her vulnerability is already well established. Now we see the innocence and enthusiasm as well. It's

pretty obvious nearly a hundred years later why she and this serial so intrigued the public.

One similarity between *Pauline* and many later serials is the fact that the chief villain operates undetected under everybody's nose. Just how long this subterfuge can go on without arousing suspicion is anybody's guess. In later serials, the answer was usually between 12-15 episodes. Here, it persists for 20 original chapters, although we only get to watch nine of them.

One of the most obvious differences between the way that *Pauline* was filmed compared to later work from the 1930s, '40s and '50s is the "honesty" (for want of a better word) of the shooting process. When these folks want to locate a scene on a boat, they bring the whole company down to the seashore and climb aboard. When it's a burning building they want, out come the matches. The contrast between later cinematic techniques and this direct approach is refreshing, to say the least. Obviously, part of the difference reflects technology. If money could be saved 30 years later by a process shot using rear-screen projection, then why

Hank Davis

Classic Cliffhangers

not use it? When it came to fires and explosions, Republic Studios was king of the miniatures. The results may have looked good on screen, but most of those buildings that blew up or blazed away were just inches tall. When Universal wanted a fire, they reached into their vault of stock footage, much of which derived from newsreels. You could be certain of two things: It was authentic and it was usually quite old. In *The Perils of Pauline,* that burning building at the end of Chapter 1 is real. Period.

There's another contrast between *Pauline* and many later sound serials. The comedy here (and there is plenty of it, in the midst of all the peril) is actually funny stuff. This is real, laugh-out-loud comedy, not the cheap Smiley Burnette or Stepin Fetchit "laugh at the idiot" stuff that hardly anyone still finds amusing. In Chapter 1, Harry is desperate to save Pauline, who has sped away in an automobile with her abductors. He comes upon a clunky old horse-drawn cart going the other way. "I'll buy your horse!" he blurts to the befuddled driver and, as we all know, money talks. Soon Harry is galloping down the road on a liberated horse in pursuit of Pauline. When he reaches the burning building, it becomes clear that he needs to elevate himself to the second floor in order to save her. A car pulls up to watch the fire and, again, Harry sizes up the situation and proclaims, "I'll buy your car!" In both circumstances, he has no illusions about turning strangers into good Samaritans. He simply buys what he needs. If the price is right, he can have it all. It was funny enough with the horse; when he pulls out a wad of cash and snags the car as well, it's hard not to laugh.

If you still need spoiler alerts after nearly 100 years, consider this fair warning. At the end (Chapter 9 in the surviving print) Pauline gets saved by her pet dog, Rusty. Koerner appears to drown and Pauline tells Harry she's had enough of "this life of adventure" and is prepared to marry him at last. They embrace, Koerner sinks beneath the surface, and Old Man Marvin rests easily in his grave, knowing his two kids are together for eternity. Brother and sister, husband and wife, what the heck. They're together. Now they can spend his money.

The Master Mystery
(1918)

The Master Mystery is by no means as famous as *Perils of Pauline,* although its star, Harry Houdini is probably more famous today than Pearl White. *The Master Mystery* was filmed in 1918 and marked the first film appearance of world-famous magician, illusionist and escape artist, Harry Houdini. Keep in mind that while folks today are still familiar with Houdini's name and profession, it seems unlikely that a hundred years from now the average person will know the names of magicians and illusionists who work the fancy venues along the Las Vegas strip. The celebrated Houdini may not have broken any new ground as an actor, but his presence here elevates this serial to way above the average. Anyone who wants to put the rarity and appeal of this serial in perspective, consider this: An original theater poster for Chapter 8 recently sold at Christie's auction for $27,600.

The second thing that makes this serial special is the appearance, probably for the first time, of a mechanical man. Within 25 years, robots in serials had become fairly commonplace. But, if we're right, it all starts here. As mechanical men go, this guy is pretty perky. He's got what looks like a horizontal oil drum as a mid-section, and sports large, almost cartoonish eyes. He has the usual lumbering gait, although it's pretty funny to see him use the handrails when he walks up or down stairs. The robot (called an Automaton) is scary in the usual way robots are scary: You can't reason with him and it's impossible to know what (if anything) he's thinking. We might as well have a shark or a zombie as a foe.

The primary source for this serial today seems to have been dubbed from a restored print released in 1972, which includes a piano score. The condition of the print is surprisingly good but there are gaps. These gaps are doubly frustrating because remaining material has been misidentified on the DVD menu. Chapters 8 and 9, for example, are plainly the final two chapters. It remains unclear whether *The Master Mystery* was released as a 13- or a 15-chapter serial. There are sources to suggest both possibilities. Chapters 1-7 are complete here, so things get off to a clear start. Unfortunately, they get a bit sketchy after that. If the serial has 15 chapters, then the next five (#8–12) are missing. If there were only 13 chapters, then only three of them (#8–10) are missing. The good news—and it is *very* good news indeed—is that the final three chapters are here in their entirety. The final chapter (be it #13 or #15) includes an important revelation as well as the closing title card. The disc also contains about four minutes of fragments from the missing chapters. They're quite dark and contain no piano background, offering some glimpse of what the original restorers must have faced when they first discovered the remains of this serial. We can only appreciate their efforts all the more. The best plan is to let the material unfold in sequence and we'll have as close to a complete picture as we are likely to get some 90 years later.

Probably the most surprising thing about this landmark robot is that he is not under control of the bad guys; rather, he seems to be controlling them as his henchmen. Indeed, on a number of occasions he seems to be barking out orders to his helpers. We can't know for sure: This *is* a silent film, after all, and there are no inter-titles to indicate what the robot might be saying. There's something else about this robot that's quite startling, but we'll save that for last and give you a Spoiler Warning well in advance.

Houdini is a serviceable actor in the part of Quentin Locke (an employee at International Patents, Inc), who is actually an undercover government agent investigating patent irregularities. Houdini does exactly what his fans expected to see him do: pick locks and escape from chains and other ties that bind him. Basically, all the cliffhangers and take-outs involve just such events. There's no waiting around for the magic: Before the first chapter is over, the cleverly named Quentin Locke, a.k.a. Houdini, has already picked two locks. The take-out at the start of Chapter 3 is quite a stunner. Tied and bound in a rather Christ-like position, Houdini immobilizes his captor with a scissor-hold, then uses his toes to pick the man's pocket, retrieve the key to the handcuff and free himself. It's a cinch nothing

remotely like this has appeared before or after in movie serials. At the end of Chapter 3, Houdini is bound in a roll of barbed wire (ouch!). Then they turn the Automaton loose on him (double ouch!) and spill a bottle of acid, which runs along the floor in his direction. Needless to say, the Master is back at work in Chapter 4.

The plot involves an evil businessman whose company buys the patents to promising inventions, and then suppresses their development in order to enhance the fortunes of competitors. It's white-collar crime about a century before Enron. The chief villain, named Herbert Balcom, fears his partner, Brent, might be getting moral qualms, so he has the robot deliver a dose of the Madagascar Madness, a form of mental illness that can be induced through candle smoke! With Brent out of the way, Balcom is free to buy up and discard useful inventions. Who knows what kind of wonderful devices lie in the invention graveyard in the basement of his estate?

Spoiler Alert: It seems odd to offer spoiler alerts for 90-year-old films, but fair is fair. I'm going to reveal something mighty important about the Automaton. If you still intend to see the serial, skip right ahead to the final paragraph. If you're in the market for a bit of a stunner, then keep reading. It seems that, originally, Dr. Q (a character who goes from villain to hero in the final chapters) designed the big metal guy out of "an insane desire for revenge." Apparently, Balcom had clouded his mind. But after Herbert Balcom is killed (whoops, another spoiler!), the cloud lifts and Dr. Q reveals that, originally, he planned to insert a human brain into the metal body. He never got that far, however; and, all along, it was Balcom who inhabited the body of the Automaton! No wonder he appeared to be talking! It was Balcom running the show from inside the metal man. "Now that Balcom is dead," Dr. Q tells us, "the Automaton will trouble us no more." The words are no sooner out of his mouth than the big metal guy storms into the scene and starts wreaking havoc. It's a real stunner and part of the reason we can enjoy this serial as more than a historical artifact. Thankfully, Houdini has invented a gas bullet and brings the Automaton down with a clean shot. Everyone gathers around as they open the metal casing to reveal—Paul Balcom, the son of evil Herbert!

There's something quite notable happening here. First, early in the serial when they've witnessed the Automaton storming through the house, everyone except Houdini is ready to assume that the creature is truly a diabolical invention. But Houdini is having none of it. Ever the real-life debunker of frauds, Houdini's character announces his belief that this is nothing more than a man in a robot suit. No one buys his theory and the matter is pretty much dropped until the final episodes. But even more importantly, the idea of a robot being just another disguise that a serial villain can use to conceal his identity was never re-used in later serials. Too bad. It's a gem of an idea and it appears the very first time a robot graces a movie serial. Yet it is nowhere to be found in later work like *The Vanishing Shadow* (1934), *The Phantom Empire* (1935), *The Undersea Kingdom* (1936), *The Phantom Creeps* (1939), *Mysterious Dr. Satan* (1940), *Monster & The Ape* (1945) and *Zombies of the Stratosphere* (1952).

Some moments to watch for: A lovely exchange between Houdini and his girlfriend where they pretend to quarrel to deceive one of the bad guys who listens in on a hidden microphone. "I hate you!" she says to our hero, who continues to quietly kiss her between vocal outbursts. Later, a female villain (the wonderfully named "Deluxe Dora") says to her male accomplice, "If you leave me for another, I'll queer your game." It's hard to imagine that phrase was in vogue in 1918. There are plenty of gunshots fired here but, unlike later sound serials, nearly every one of them finds its mark. The shots are rarely fatal, but they do hit their intended victims. Another anomaly: In one of the later chapters we get to see a robot caught in a fish net! That's a technique never seen in later serials, although it's quite an amusing (and successful) way to immobilize the big guys.

By the end of the serial, all kinds of relationship problems have been clarified and resolved. It seems that almost everybody turns out to be related to everybody else. Fathers and sons are reunited; so are brothers and sisters. It's just one big happy family. There have been plenty of kisses on display throughout the serial, but they never seem to have lasted more than one second. By far the longest of these on-screen smooches occurs between Houdini and his long-lost sister, whose identity I wouldn't dream of revealing. Now that Houdini has discovered his sister and confirmed his intention to marry Eva Brent, his fiancée asks whether there is *anything* our hero cannot escape from. In an answer that even 10 year olds in the audience must have anticipated, Houdini looks at his engagement ring and replies, "Yes, one thing—this little band of gold." It's hard not to cherish the simplicity of earlier times.

Hank Davis

1929
Tarzan the Tiger

It may not be the first image of Tarzan that graced the silver screen, but this 1929 Universal serial marked a special occasion for fans of Edgar Rice Burroughs' Tarzan. If your neighborhood theater was equipped for it, *Tarzan the Tiger* included an actual sound recording of Tarzan doing his famous jungle shouts. Granted, they don't sound much like the electronically enhanced version that came out of Johnny Weissmuller's mouth beginning in the next decade, but those "Nnnn Yaaaah's that appear here must have been quite a shock to audiences back in 1929 when movie sound, itself, was still a rare and stunning achievement.

Actually, *Tarzan the Tiger,* completed in the final months of 1928, was released in two versions: a traditional silent movie and, for those theaters that were beginning to accommodate the inevitable move toward talking pictures, a "soundie" version. Although there is no dialogue in *Tarzan the Tiger*, there is a complete musical score and occasional sound effects such as screams, jungle noises and the aforementioned shouts from Tarzan. The technique required the projectionist to simultaneously run the film and play a large 78-rpm transcription disc through the theater speakers. Plainly, synchronization was in its infancy, which is why dialogue was avoided in favor of grunts, shouts and hoof beats.

Almost from the day of its printing in 1914, *Tarzan the Ape Man* seemed destined for screen adaptation. Between 1918 and 1928, there were at least seven screen appearances of the character in both features and serials—including *Tarzan of the Apes, Romance of Tarzan, Son of Tarzan, Revenge of Tarzan, Adventures of Tarzan, Tarzan & the Golden Lion* and *Tarzan the Mighty*. The number is surely larger if you include unauthorized adaptations of Tarzan-like characters in jungle settings, as well as other Burroughs fare like *The Lad & The Lion* (1917).

This serial is a pretty faithful adaptation of Burroughs' *Tarzan and the Jewels of Opar,* in which Lord Greystoke searches for the treasure rumored to lie hidden in this lost city of the jungle. While doing so, Tarzan suffers a head injury, which causes him to forget his sophisticated identity as Greystoke. The jewels of Opar (which he finds) simply become "pretty pebbles" to him.

Despite the fact that, with all its exaggerated emoting, *Tarzan the Tiger* is essentially a silent movie, it is quite engaging and by no means juvenile fare. Acting without speaking is a whole different ball game. The heroine in distress (Natalie Kingston as Jane) was making her 37th film appearance although she was barely 24 years old. Kingston also appeared in the previous year's (silent) serial, *Tarzan the Mighty*. Al Ferguson as Werper is the typical silent movie villain. If there were railroad tracks running through the jungle, you know he'd tie Jane to them. And silent movie villains really do have mustaches! The evil Werper and Tarzan's cousin, Annersley, are in cahoots, bonded by their mustaches and their plotting against clean-shaven Tarzan.

For his part, Frank Merrill does a fine job as Tarzan. Merrill was a stuntman for *Adventures of Tarzan* (1922) and had also appeared in the previous year's Tarzan serial. He is a beautiful physical specimen and when it comes time to look baffled or enraged, Merrill leaves no doubt as to what he's feeling. Actually, because he suffers from amnesia for most of the film, the character might have been billed as "Tarzan the Clueless." It's really tough when people continue to make demands based upon prior commitments that you just can't recall.

One more cast member deserves special mention—Princess La, who rules over a lost jungle tribe and lusts after Tarzan, is played by an actress named Kithnou. (Some sources incorrectly credit the part to Lillian Worth.) Kithnou, who also appeared in a critically acclaimed 1929 film called *Careers*, has an exotic look, perfect for the part of Princess La. Depending on which source consulted, the actress was either born in India or on the island of Mauritius. In any case, she is gorgeous. And, for that matter, so is Natalie Kingston. Tarzan really has his work cut out for him, trying to choose between the two. In the end he selects Ms. Kingston, possibly because of her (pre-Code) nude scene in Chapter 8. Tarzan may be a Tiger, but he's a pretty chaste one. When Jane invites him to spend the night with her in the jungle, Tarzan grabs the nearest vine and heads for the trees. "Tarzan has never known a wife," he protests as he heads into the treetops. At least he has the social skills to leave his pal, Tantor the Elephant, to guard Jane while she sleeps. And so Jane curls up next to the big dusty pachyderm for the night, while Tarzan snores chastely away above her.

When Jane awakes the next morning, she yawns, stretches and goes for a coyly filmed skinny dip in the neighborhood lagoon. Is this the forerunner of gratuitous shower scenes in *Sorority House Massacre*-type of films? Remember, this is 1929, some 50-plus years before such scenes became almost mandatory. In any case, Tarzan plainly enjoys the sight of the lady in the lake and seems to come mighty close to remembering who this swimming angel is.

The musical score by David Broekman is surprisingly effective and modern. The music runs through each 18-minute episode, which raises an interesting question. If a primitive "soundie" like *Tarzan the Tiger* features such continuous musical scoring, why was the practice all but lost in the earliest talking serials released by studios like Mascot? Typically, early talkie serials feature music over the opening credits, and then silence reigns for the next 18 minutes of action and dialogue, after which the music reappears briefly over the closing titles.

Speaking of action, there is a lot of it in this serial. It's not unusual to see Tarzan riding an elephant chasing the kidnapped Jane, who is mounted on a camel, while the evil Werper chases her on horseback. Similarly, the sets seem lavish beyond the budget of most serials. Granted, a lot of action takes place in the back lot "jungle," but when the scene shifts to a plantation or an exotic temple, this serial delivers.

Historians will be fascinated to learn that the person credited with writing the title cards for *Tarzan the Tiger* is none other than Ford Beebe, who went on to an illustrious career as the director of Universal's Flash Gordon and Buck Rogers serials. Beebe's work is largely excellent, although there seems to be a *lot* of titles. This is a much more dialogue-based adventure than expected and

some of the titles seem like overkill. For example, when Tarzan gives one of his famous shouts, a card saying "Tarzan's Jungle Cry of Victory" follows it! Thanks, Mr. Beebe. We didn't think he was ordering a pizza. Sometimes, Tarzan seems a little *too* literate. Mid-jungle, he comes out with a line like, "Where is she whom I left here—and whom I love more than my jungle friends." What a guy! He does all that vine work and then he talks like he's been swinging through Oxford.

Tarzan (Frank Merrill) rescues Jane (Natalie Kingston) from Werper (Al Ferguson)

We've all heard the term "white slavery." Ever think about it? It suggests that it's inherently different from (and worse than) "black slavery." In this movie, we actually see white slavery. In fact, Jane is nearly sold into it. It's pretty grisly stuff. A group of leering, unclean looking Arab-types stand around a platform and bid on scantily clad young white girls for purposes that don't leave much to the imagination.

Most of the animals have actual names and are either pals or enemies of Tarzan. Tantor (the aforementioned elephant) is a pal. Taglat the ape (played by someone who probably taught Ray Corrigan and his gorilla suit everything he knew) seems to have a long-standing beef with Tarzan. After Tarzan defeats Taglat, he has to deal with Taglat's brother (same guy, same ape suit, no doubt.) The brother is called "Chulk, King of the Ape People." Chulk is a great sounding name, but what on earth are ape people? It's also never clear who has named these animals. Does Tarzan go through the jungle naming everyone he meets, or does he eavesdrop on animal conversations like Dr. Doolittle and learn their actual names? In any case, it's obvious that Tarzan the Tiger is not Tarzan the Biologist when he comes up with proclamations like "Numa the Lion can never catch Fleetfoot the Deer."

Whatever its comic overtones, Tarzan has been a staple of American popular culture since his first appearance in Burroughs' novel. Plainly, the appeal isn't limited to a particular time or place. Whether played by Elmo Lincoln, Frank Merrill, Johnny Weissmuller, Buster Crabbe, Herman Brix, Lex Barker, Mike Henry, Gordon Scott or Ron Ely, the character survives endless repetition and minuscule budgets. There have been over 40 Tarzan movies (not including early silent efforts), as well as a critically acclaimed 1999 Disney version and the classy big-budget 1984 film *Greystoke*. *Tarzan & Jane* were part of the WB prime-time television schedule for the Fall 2003 season. In its 90th year, the Tarzan bandwagon shows no sign of slowing down.

Hank Davis

1930
The Mystery Trooper

There are over 250 movie serials from the sound era. For every *Flash Gordon*, *Dick Tracy* and *Captain Marvel* there are dozens of obscure titles, typically known only by collectors and historians. Some of these titles are deservedly rare, although even the worst movie serial usually has some endearing qualities. Many serials are poorly known simply because they are quite old, originally released during the dawn of the talkie era. Often they were produced by independent companies and enjoyed limited distribution. This, in turn, makes it less likely that a decent print has been preserved. Fortunately for us, it only takes a single copy in order to resurrect an obscure title.

The Mystery Trooper is such a case. Originally released in 1930 (some sources say 1931), this serial remained well hidden from general view until it was commercially released on VHS in 1997 by VCI.

All things considered, the print is surprisingly clean and offers a glimpse into the long-forgotten world of serial movie making from three-quarters of a century ago. Watching films like *The Mystery Trooper* is a little like listening to Louis Armstrong 78's recorded in the 1920s. Try as one might, it's difficult to ignore the technical defects. The music has worthwhile qualities, but the viewer keeps getting distracted by the primitive technology. This is not to say that this serial offers as much substance as classic Armstrong with King Oliver. It doesn't.

But it certainly does have value. There will never be a mainstream market for titles like *The Mystery Trooper*, but for fans of vintage Westerns and early cliffhangers, this obscure title is essential fare.

Released at a time when it was still quite a selling point to advertise a movie as "All Talking," this 10-chapter outing was produced by (depending on your information source) Wonder Pictures or Syndicate Pictures. A later reissue by Guaranteed Pictures complicates the production history further. If nothing else, *The Mystery Trooper* can boast that it was the first sound serial about the Canadian Northwest Mounted Police. In fact, its alternate release title was *Trail of the Royal Mounted*. At least seven more Mounties serials arrived before the cliffhanger genre closed up shop in 1956, but here we have the very first one.

The action takes place in "Moose Head," a great Hollywood Canadian name. To eliminate any doubt about location, one of the Mounties refers to "Those gangsters from the States," a line of dialogue that may be the most contemporary thing about this entire serial.

The Mystery Trooper includes some wonderfully alliterative chapter titles such as "The Trap of Terror," "The House of Hate" and "Day of Doom." The basic plot, similar to that of *The Green Archer*, issued by Columbia in 1940, concerns an unknown benefactor who looks out for the welfare of the good guys. In this case, the title character leaves gold nuggets to see to it that young Billy (played by Buzz Barton) and his sister, Helen (Blanche Mehaffey), are well cared for. This mysterious assistance goes beyond simple financial aid; the shadowy benefactor also shoos away the occasional wild bear who menaces the young 'uns. Why is it, by the way, that dogs and horses usually receive star billing in films but bears labor away and rarely make it into the supporting cast? The part of the wild horse is played by White Cloud. He's a beautiful animal—perhaps the most convincing actor in the serial—and his scenes are really special. The shots of him being attacked by a pack of wild dogs in Chapter 8 are actually rather disturbing. Fortunately, they were filmed at long distance.

The human actors are far less impressive. Part of the problem is, no doubt, the style of the era. Many of the actors read their lines *really slowly*, like they're dictating them to a stenographer. This isn't acting as much as telegraphing lines across a great distance, speaking as slowly and clearly as possible to audiences who lived on what must have seemed like another planet. Perhaps the worst offender is bad guy Al Ferguson, playing the typical "Lucky Pierre from Trois Riviere" character. His phony-sounding French Canadian accent doesn't help things. Ferguson was no stranger to serials, sporting a resume that went back to the silent era and stretched forward to include roles in *Captain Midnight, The Three Musketeers* and *Flash Gordon*. This is not his finest work. The best thing you can say for actress Blanche Mehaffey is that her agent kept her busy. Born in 1907, she began work as a 17 year old and had already appeared in 17 films when she played the role of Helen in this serial. She went on to appear in a total of 40 films, almost all of them eminently forgettable B-movies, until her retirement in

The MYSTERY TROOPER

CLIFFHANGER 2 DVDs

British DVD release

1938. In later years she was often credited as Janet Morgan, although as *The Sea Fiend* (1936) reveals, her name change did little to upgrade the quality of films in which she worked.

Robert Frazer in the role of hero Jack Logan is a real Dudley Do Right character. He's loyal, steadfast and true, but he's also a wimp of the first magnitude. In Chapter 7, he sets some kind of record for use of the word "dear." He actually intones, "Helen dear, o dear, are you OK, dear?" It would have been hard to work more "dears" into that single English sentence unless Bambi had loped across the set. Fraser was both a Hollywood veteran (appearing in over 200 films) and a familiar face to serial fans. From early Mascot outings like *The Miracle Rider* (1935), Frazer worked regularly—often in the role of villains—until he appeared in both *Captain America* and *The Tiger Woman* in 1944, the year of his death.

Technically, this serial is about as primitive as they come, even by 1930 standards. The dialogue is stilted and awkwardly delivered. The pacing is slow to a fault. The only mid-chapter music occurs in Chapter 5 when some Indians perform a ritual dance in a cave. Other than that, the background silence is deafening. Virtually no sound effects are looped in during exterior shots, including fight scenes. For all intents and purposes this is a silent movie with some dialogue read in, as opposed to acted. Perhaps its most memorable image (other than scenes of White Cloud) takes place in Chapter 7, when the Mystery Trooper is seen sitting alone in a cave, playing the organ. It looks like a scene from *Phantom of the Opera*.

The identity of the Mystery Trooper is revealed in the final chapter and we understand through a series of flashbacks why he has acted as he has for the past 10 episodes. In that moment, the serial achieves some measure of closure. But it doesn't know when to quit while it's ahead. Instead, in an absolutely gratuitous scene, Jack marries Helen. It's not like there's been great sexual tension between them for 10 chapters that needed resolving. And as if that hokey sentimentality weren't enough, we also see that White Cloud has been finding time around his busy shooting schedule to court one of the nearby mares. It's a wonder that the local Moose Head squirrels don't come dancing out of the trees in pairs, chattering and holding hands.

The Sign of the Wolf

It's hard to know how seriously to take this ancient serial. It appears to be legit, but the plot and characters often twist and turn in ways that suggest that *The Sign of the Wolf* might be satirizing the very genre it's part of. The only trouble with that is there wasn't much of a genre to satirize when this relic was produced in 1930. In fact, it was only about the 8th sound serial to appear. The rules were not yet firmly in place. How else to explain a Western that starts somewhere in Asia, in what looks like the Taj Mahal?

The basic plot involves a group of turbaned characters protecting an ancient secret for turning sand into jewels. The process involves a couple of magic radioactive chains that produce a puff of smoke when thrown into a small heating device. Along come two white men (Winslow and Farnum) who steal the secret along with the chains and take them back to "The Far West" (otherwise known as California). As soon as they get back home, things begin to heat up. There is squabbling between the two men over who really has the right to the secret. Both of these thieves are pitted against a visitor from Asia named Kuva (Edmund Cobb), who has come to reclaim the sacred possession of his temple. Kuva is really pretty funny: He rides a horse while wearing a jeweled turban. His strategy consists of hanging around open windows and using a blowgun to deliver ominous messages to the thieves. These tiny scrolls of paper usually contain sayings like "You will come to harm if you do not return the secret to its owners." The messages are always signed with a picture of a wolf—hence, the serial's title.

METROPOLITAN PICTURES present "KING" EMPEROR OF ALL DOGS in "The SIGN OF THE WOLF"

EPISODE 1
DRUMS OF DOOM

This leads us to the real star of the movie. Back in the days when Rin Tin Tin was a featured player with a large fan base, he had plenty of competition. Among those German shepherd pretenders was this serial's star: King, the Wonder Dog. His original publicity referred to him as King, Emperor of All Dogs. There was probably a pooch working at another studio billed as Emperor, King of All Dogs. But no matter. King is only a little puppy when he is brought from Asia by one of the two thieves (Farnum) and raised in California. Although he grows up to be a loyal pet, he also seems on pretty friendly terms with the turbaned Hindu who is trying to reclaim the magic chains. King is not quite as majestic looking as Rin Tin Tin, although he has a certain scruffy charm. The poor pooch has a problem keeping his cool during some of the fight scenes. Not knowing these are just stuntmen going about their business, King gets all wound up and tends to snap at their heels. In one hilarious scene, he is supposed to untie the good guys by pulling at their ropes. He does his job, but then he can't stop grabbing things in his mouth. He's plainly a very oral dog. In a moment of triumph, he picks up one of their hats and walks off the set. The character watches his hat disappear but wisely decides not to go after it. In the next scene, the hat is magically back on his head, obviously retrieved off–camera by the dog's trainer.

Not surprisingly, all of these actors (including King) are veterans of the silent movie era. Some show the lingering effects of this experience more than others. Perhaps the worst offender is an actor named Harry Todd, who plays Farnum. Todd

Classic Cliffhangers

is so over-the-top that his actions, indeed his character, are barely recognizable as human. He has obviously become a bit unstrung by the fact that he can produce rubies, diamonds and sapphires at will. "I can control the jewel markets all over the world," he babbles maniacally. Most of the other leading actors, including heroes Rex Lease and Joe Bonomo, offer serviceable, if somewhat wooden, performances. Virginia Brown Faire is a vintage screamer.

Film historians will enjoy watching this relic of the transitional period between silent movies and talkies. For instance, inter-titles like "Meanwhile back at the ranch" are still used to set up scenes. Music is predictably scarce. The opening titles of each chapter feature a little under a minute of rather stilted instrumental work, which sounds like it was recorded at a military band concert. Here's hoping audiences like it because that's all the music they're going to get. Different production companies had their own approach to re-establishing last week's cliffhanger before the take-out. In this serial, each chapter begins with a scene of a slave girl placing a crystal ball on a table and backing away. Actually, she backs awkwardly right into a plant. Since this scene was going to be repeated every week for about three months, you'd think they'd give the poor girl a chance to reshoot her scene and exit a little more gracefully. Nope. It's just one more reason to wonder whether the production wasn't one giant satire. No sooner has the girl backed into the potted plant than a turbaned character delivers one of his messages with a blowgun that shatters the crystal ball. A swami then emerges from stage left and reads the message, which contains a handwritten summary of the plot. It is safe to say that this technique has never been used in another serial, before or since.

Chapter 1 features a car chase involving two women driving model-A Fords. That's something we don't see every day. It's always fun to see horses (and dogs) interacting with automobiles—especially when the autos are as ancient as these. The idea of what constitutes a cliffhanger—an unresolved issue during the silent serial era—doesn't seem to have been worked out in *Sign of the Wolf*. The first chapter ends with a car going over a cliff. So far, so good. But the second chapter ends by cutting away during a fistfight. In what way is this a cliffhanger? All the fights are clumsily and unconvincingly staged—something we might never have realized had Republic not taken the choreography of fistfights to an art form within the next decade. Watch for the bear attack (both a real bear and an awkward puppet) at the end of Chapter 7. Perhaps the most bizarre scene has the Hindu phoning Ruth, the dog's owner aksing, "Let me speak to King." "The dog?" she replies, a bit taken aback. "Yes," he confirms. So she puts the phone to the dog's ear and the turbaned fellow speaks a whole string of Urdu (or perhaps gibberish) to the dog. Of course, the dog immediately leaves the house and follows the Hindu's directions to a cabin in the woods. In the end, Kuva destroys "the menace of easy riches" and the chains go up in smoke.

Many collectors describe this serial, originally released by Metropolitan pictures, as rare. It doesn't even appear as one of the 251 known titles in the 1972

Rex Lease and Virginia Brown Faire (in front seat) with Al Ferguson (on running board) and Joe Bonomo (in the rumble seat)

edition of Weiss & Goodgold's *To Be Continued*. The serial has been available on videotape issued by VCI, although in December 2004 the company announced that *Sign of the Wolf* was going "on moratorium." In short, once limited existing stock is sold, the title will again become certifiably rare. It is doubtful that this original negative will be turned into a DVD anytime soon. Although much of the VHS print is watchable (if a bit dark), there is one hilarious glitch that will require some restoration in order to make things right. Something has happened to the negative for Chapters 4 and 5. A couple of bubbles appear on the left side of the screen that, when projected, look like dancing amoeba. These little entities don't go away; they swirl wildly around the screen, interacting with the characters in all sorts of unintended ways. At one point, King appears to be chasing them across a meadow; a bit later they dance around the heads of the horses and actors. One nearly bites the hero in the rear end after he falls off his horse. The funniest moment occurs when the heroine, Ruth, goes to bed. No sooner is she under the covers then the amoeba hops up and begins to dance joyously on the covers while she sleeps. When she is awakened by a noise outside, she almost reaches out and grabs the amoeba at she gets out of bed. This unscripted weirdness continues for the entirety of Chapter 4 and undoubtedly forms the most exciting subplot of the episode. On second thought, maybe VCI should make a point of *not* restoring this portion of the negative before transferring it to DVD.

Postscript: Just as this book was going to press, Serial Squadron announced the release of a restored print of this serial (with an optional musical score, no less) on DVD. It appears that *The Sign of the Wolf* will not disappear into the ether any time soon.

1931
The Galloping Ghost

Last century's headlines produce today's blank stares. Superstars become unknowns or answers to trivia questions almost overnight. Red Grange, the star of this 1931 Mascot serial, was arguably the best college football player in history. He was also the most famous athlete of his era and the man who almost single-handedly legitimized pro-football. He was voted All American for three years running. His face was on the cover of *Time* magazine on October 5, 1925.

Today, not one in 1,000 Americans knows his name. Those who do are probably sports trivia buffs or historians. Maybe serial fans will remember him for his appearance in this early serial, which was explicitly named for Grange. *The Galloping Ghost* was his nickname, conferred by legendary sports writer Grantland Rice. Nat Levine, boss of Mascot Pictures, knew what he was doing when he signed Grange to star in this 12-chapter serial about a college football player accused of taking a bribe. Grange had already appeared in two silent movies while still a student at the University of Illinois. His appearance here coincided with his playing for the Chicago Bears, employment that would continue until Grange's retirement in 1934.

For sure, this is an exciting and energetic serial. Grange seems an earlier-day version of ace stuntman Davey Sharpe. His credo seems to be "Never walk when you can run, and never run when you can leap through the air." That agility makes this the cinematic equivalent of a page-turner. It's hard to take your eyes off the screen as Grange climbs up the walls of buildings, races down fire escapes and leaps over obstacles. But, and let's get these criticisms out of the way early, it ain't a perfect picture. For one thing—take a deep breath—Grange can't act. This wasn't as noticeable in his silent movie roles for obvious reasons. But here, he has to deliver dialogue and those moments lie somewhere between painful and laughable. Second, Grange is simply too old for the role. He does not look anything like a college student. Grange was 28 years old during the filming of this serial, at least 10 years older than he should have been as a fresh-faced college student. Worse yet, Grange looks like what they call a *hard* 28. He could more easily pass for 38 than he can for 18. When you see him lounging around his dorm room in a three-piece suit and tie with a book in his hand, you really have to suppress a giggle.

The Galloping Ghost took all of 17 days to film during the summer of 1931. It was originally scheduled to be directed by Reeves Eason, but studio boss Levine brought in a second director, Armand Schaefer, in case Eason's growing reputation as a problem drinker proved true. Eason and Schaefer were to alternate days behind the camera, a practice that became fairly standard within several years. One day Eason breezed in four hours late (his nickname was actually "Breezy!")

Red Grange is carried by The Mysterious Cripple (Theodore Lorch) while Gwen Lee helps.

and decidedly hung over. Levine fired him on the spot and promoted cameraman Ben Kline to alternate with Schaefer for the duration. Stunt coordinator Yakima Canutt was already responsible for directing the action scenes. To this day, Eason's name appears as primary director of *The Galloping Ghost*, despite the fact that Shaefer, Kline and Canutt really had matters well in hand.

The plot is standard "unjustly accused" fare, guaranteed to arouse audience sympathy. Grange's college roommate, Buddy (played by Francis X Bushman, Jr.—son of the famous silent movie star), has taken money from gamblers to throw a game. Buddy is in a jam that Red tries first to resolve, then to keep under wraps. Buddy, it seems, got drunk and married one night, presumably in that order. If word gets out, he will be thrown off the team. Apparently you can't play college ball—or perhaps even go to college—if you have a wife. And what a wife! Played by Gwen Lee, Irene is almost pure evil. It is her threat of going public with their marriage if he doesn't pay her $1,000 that drives Buddy into the hands of gamblers.

Things get complicated. When they realize he can identify them, the gamblers kidnap Buddy to keep him quiet. Somewhere along the way, he gets knocked on the head and comes to with a case of amnesia. Meanwhile Red is trying to rescue Buddy, clear his own name, foil the gamblers and get Buddy's sister (Dorothy Gulliver) to fall for him. That's a lot of subplot to keep track of, but at least it keeps the characters motivated. In his history of Mascot Pictures (*The Vanishing Legion*), John Tuska suggests that if the two female leads of this serial were any indication, "women are either vicious parasites or virtuous fools." Certainly, that is what is on display here, although in numerous silent movie serials that palette was considerably more varied.

There's one other plot complication. Theodore Lorch appears as a classic silent movie villain, scowling and all dressed in black. In fact, Lorch is so good at his job that the scenes involving "Dr. Julian Blake" actually become comic. Lorch is plainly having the time of his cinematic life. His character is referred to during each pre-chapter summary as the "Mysterious Cripple." Lorch walks with a cane and is so bent over that he is literally longer than he is high. Serial fans will see a strong similarity between Lorch's work here and John Piccori's role as Moloch in the classic *Dick Tracy* serial (1937). As if Lorch's theatrics during the film weren't sufficient, each chapter ends with about 10 seconds of his maniacal cackles. "He he he he he, ha ha ha ha ha!" goes on while we see the usual "Come back next week for Chapter 6" message. It certainly saved Mascot some musician fees if nothing else.

Some of the photography is really noteworthy. Viewers realize almost immediately that this is not a visually ordinary serial. The gridiron scenes are well shot and intercut with actual game footage. When the players huddle, the camera is placed on the ground, looking up at their faces. This worm's-eye view adds to the immediacy of the scene. The first few cliffhangers are actually quite stunning. In Chapter 1, Grange drops from a parachute and plummets to the earth, hands and legs flailing. It's a pretty impressive scene, light years beyond what most contemporary serials offered. The second chapter ends with a cliffhanger that foreshadows a highlight from Dick Tracy: A small wood boat is crushed (along with our hero?) by two tankers drifting slowly together at the pier. The third chapter ends with disturbingly real footage of Grange being run over by a cab while brawling in the street. In fact, the take-out next episode is quite a cheat. Using today's ubiquitous pause button, we plainly see Grange's body run over, footage that is nowhere in evidence when the scene is resumed the following week.

Perhaps the most damning indictment of this otherwise entertaining serial is its excessive use of "slow-cranking." The technique produces a speedup in what we see when the film is projected at normal speed. It's a gimmick that works well in occasional car chases. But it appears all too often here. Just about every action scene has been artificially sped up. Nobody walks or runs—they all walk *fast* and run *fast*. The effect looks like an endless Keystone Cops routine that undermines the grace and credibility of what is really going on.

Mascot was still feeling its way with the serial format. They weren't real big on making their audiences read. Rather than summarize previous events with

Red Grange leaps from his teammates.

scrolling titles or a series of cards, a painstakingly detailed summary is read to us (by veteran serial actor Lafe McKee) over filmed highlights. Seriously, whoever wrote those summaries was a literary giant. They couldn't have been more stylish or precise. *The Galloping Ghost* features some really unusual and effective scenes. Before it degenerates into a silent movie comedy sketch, a Chapter 3 melee filmed on a real street draws an audience of equally real onlookers. It looks nothing like a back lot segment with a handful of extras. Similarly, a car chase in Chapter 7 uses real city streets and is quite a stunner. Finally, look for Stepin Fetchit doing his usual brain-dead shtick here. Yeah, I know. You can't blame the man for the racist attitudes of the day and he was just out to make a buck, like everybody else around him. But it doesn't make those moments of so-called comic relief any easier to watch. We also get to laugh at stutterers and fearful people. Life was just a bowl of giggles in 1931.

There is enough shame thrown around this serial to keep a dozen shrinks in business. Grange is repeatedly shunned by his untrusting teammates, doubted by his coach and rejected by his girl, who also doubts him. He is told things like "You've betrayed your college!" and "You've crippled your team." Just how much can the poor guy stand? No wonder he lets go of the parachute at the end of Chapter 1 and takes his chances on the air currents over southern California. When the dust finally clears (along with his good name), Red forgives everybody and leads his team to victory. Shucks, it's OK that you doubted me for the past 11 chapters and abandoned me and treated me like dog waste. I don't blame you. Everything's OK now so let's pretend it never happened and go out there and win one for the Gipper.

The Lightning Warrior

Watching this 1931 serial from Mascot is like stepping into a time machine. It doesn't get a lot more primitive than this, just the sixth sound serial issued by Nat Levine's upstart studio. At this point in Mascot's development, it wasn't clear who would be their most frequently billed star: Walter Miller or Rin Tin Tin.

Rinty, who was edging ahead of Miller, headlines this 12-chapter serial, and does about everything but rig the lighting and score the music. It's really up to the German shepherd and the kid, played by Frankie Darro (another Mascot favorite) to save the day. Darro's character, named Jimmy Carter, endears the serial to modern audiences. Too bad he doesn't have a renegade brother named Billy.

The script (courtesy of Ford Beebe and Wyndham Gittens) is the classic stuff of Westerns: The town is being terrorized by Indians (who turn out to be corrupt white guys in disguise), as well as by a mysterious character who appears in a spooky all-black Halloween costume, complete with witch's hat. He's known as the Wolf Man, a name that would take on greater fame 10 years later in Lon Chaney, Jr.'s capable paws. This character scares plenty of townsfolks and probably kept his share of kiddies in the audience hiding under their seats.

The Wolf Man wants to get rid of the settlers so he and his gang can take over the local territory. Like countless serial villains, the Wolf Man is anonymous until the end as he barks his weekly orders and threats to a gang of not-very-successful henchmen. Trying to guess the identity of the villain is the plot device that drives this serial from week to week. Is it the sheriff? Is it Hayden, the town's most respected citizen? Who will benefit most if the settlers are driven away?

Some actors, more than others, look and sound like relics from the silent film era. The sheriff's daughter, Dianne, (Georgia Hale), looks like the heroine from a 1925 film. Theodore Lorch, who plays LaFarge, is the worst offender, with his exaggerated gestures and over-emoting that seem almost grotesque. We met Lorch earlier in the year in Mascot's *The Galloping Ghost*. The actor made up in creepiness what he lacked in subtlety.

In general, canine actors made the transition from silents to talkies better than their human counterparts. Enough can't be said about Rin Tin Tin, who was appearing in his final film (all subsequent appearances feature Rin Tin Tin, Jr.). When the humans watching Rinty utter the immortal words "I think he's trying to tell us something," they aren't kidding. As smart as this dog looks, the thing on his mind might turn out to be a dialogue rewrite or change in one of the camera locations. In one scene, Rinty hurtles his body at three bad guys standing on a precipice, knocking them into a river below. He then picks up a gun dropped by one of them and registers it with the local sheriff. Just kidding. What he actually does is carry the gun off and bury it to keep it out of action. Later, he grabs a runaway horse's reins and leads him to Jimmy, pausing to open the leg hold trap on the boy's foot. Young Jimmy can always count on his pooch. When the kid is

Frankie Darro accuses Theodore Lorch as Rin Tin Tin listens carefully.

literally hanging off a cliff, Rinty lowers him a rope tied to a horse. The horse, being of a less enlightened species, isn't sure how to complete the rescue until Rinty herds him away, thus drawing Jimmy out of the ravine. Wow. Between Mascot serials and vintage Disney films, a whole generation of kids probably grew up thinking small mammals could do trigonometry.

Some serial lunacy to watch for: In Chapter 9, one of the characters actually says, "We'll head 'em off at the pass." In this movie, everyone wears a hat. Remember, this is the Wild West, so most of the headgear is Western style, including a couple of actors in those tall witch-like hats worn by the Wolf Man. But the number of hats is still striking. It would not be surprising for Rinty to run by, wearing a baseball cap. Chapter 8 is called "The Man Who Knew," surely one of the oddest titles in movie serial history. Lafe McKee, who also plays Hayden, performs the voiceovers at the start of each chapter. McKee reads his lines in stuffy, vaguely British tones that seem better suited to Masterpiece Theatre than a vintage Mascot serial. It isn't until the voiceover at the start of Chapter 5 that we learn that "the Indians have named Rinty the Lightning Warrior." That's the first time we truly understand the serial's name.

Perhaps the most obvious clue to the age of this ancient serial is the soundtrack. It isn't simply that it has deteriorated over the years; in fact, the quality of the print available from VCI is far better than should be expected. The inadequacies lie in the original product. Like Universal's original *Dracula* (also released in 1931), there is almost no ambient sound, and that includes rough-and-tumble fight scenes. When Frankie Darro cracks a bad guy over the head with a 2 x 4, it's not only done off-screen (as usual), but there is nothing on the soundtrack to suggest that wood and skull have met. There are also no sounds of human footsteps. Indeed, there are long periods when the soundtrack is totally empty. It seems odd that sounds associated with human activity (other than talking) are not deemed worthy of recording, yet every time a horse walks by, we hear each hoof beat.

One thing the soundtrack does include to great advantage is the eerie sound of Indian drums that are used to signal the presence of the Wolf Man. Likewise, the howling of a wolf, again a

Georgia Hale in the clutches of the mysterious Wolf Man.

sure sign of evil, is one of the few sounds appearing on the audio track. The title theme, such as it is, consists of 45 seconds of very dated music that sounds like it was arranged for a band shell concert on a Sunday afternoon in 1925. That is the extent of musical support offered by Mascot in 1931.

There are lots of action sequences, some of them pretty amazing for a 1931 film. Much of this credit lies squarely at the feet of ace stuntman Yakima Canutt. A number of insights into Canutt's life and career appear in Jon Tuska's book *The Vanishing Legion*. At one point Canutt jumps his horse straight off a cliff into the water below—a sequence that would appear again in other Mascot serials. Indeed, the stunt work staged by Canutt is way ahead of its time. Unfortunately, it was also way ahead of the existing camera and sound recording techniques. Imagine how some of these scenes might have looked if the Steadicam had been around then.

In the end, the real Indians prove to be noble creatures, whose reputation was temporarily sullied by a bunch of profit-hungry white guys. As the serial winds to a close, the sheriff announces that the real Indians are "the White man's friend." Shortly thereafter, leading man George Brent (who went on to fame and fortune at Warner Bros. despite being upstaged here by the dog and the kid) finally hugs Georgia Hale. Young Mr. Darro covers his eyes with one hand and places his other hand over Rinty's eyes to save him from this shocking glimpse of depravity. A final word about 13-year old Frankie Darro and some of what fate held in store for him. Twenty-five years after he appeared in *Lightning Warrior,* Darro was cast to play (inside) Robby the Robot in the classic sci-fi film *Forbidden Planet.* Darro lost that landmark role by taking Robby for an ill-advised and nearly disastrous stroll around the set after he'd had a bit too much to drink. Darro died on Christmas Day 1976. His final appearance was in a forgettable film called *Fugitive Lovers.* He played the town drunk.

Hank Davis

The Vanishing Legion

You're going to need a scorecard to keep track of this one. Without some outside help, about the only thing you'll be sure about is that Frankie Darro is spunky, Rex is dangerous and Harry Carey is decent. Beyond that, you're on your own. Thank goodness for those weekly voiceovers that precede each episode ("Last week we saw…"). They're supposed to be "catch-ups" but don't let them kid you. Revelations is more like it. They're about the only way the audience is going to make sense of all the on-screen activities. Whoever is reading those 30-second bits knows a lot more than the viewers and soon things will be explained that could never put together from watching the episodes.

Let's back up a bit and find out what's going on in this chapter play from Mascot. Shot in May 1931 in a mere 18 days, *The Vanishing Legion* featured Harey Carey and Edwina Booth, both fresh from their appearances in MGM's highly influential *Trader Horn*. In fact, Carey's wife, Olive Fuller Golden, who appeared in *Trader Horn* also turns up here in a small role. The film also stars Frankie Darro, one of the industry's pre-eminent child actors. At $1,000 a week, Darro was probably earning more than anyone on the set but Carey. The other star to be reckoned with is Rex, King of the Wild Horses. Equine or not, Rex gets equal billing with Ms. Booth—a fact that may have galled the actress. If you have any doubts about Rex's star quality, just check out the horse fight at the start of Chapter 1. It's pretty spectacular stuff.

The other star presence here is Boris Karloff. It's hard to imagine a time when Karloff was not an icon, but this serial appeared in 1931, the same year *Frankenstein* hit the silver screen. Audiences may have known Karloff was scary, but they weren't quite sure what he looked like (the Monster's makeup all but obscured his appearance) and they certainly didn't know what he sounded like. Other than a few guttural grunts, Karloff had no dialogue in his most famous role. Nat Levine, Mascot's shrewd boss, knew better. He cast Karloff in the unbilled role of "The Voice." For $75 a week, Karloff provided an eerie harsh whisper that commanded his gang. Each message and, indeed, the first 11 chapters end with the words "The Voice Has Spoken." Karloff reads the lines with gusto and provides the serial's only element of mystery.

A few other actors in smaller roles are also worth noting. Lafe McKee appears as the lawyer Hornbeck. It is hard to imagine McKee when he wasn't in his standard role of distinguished elderly gentleman—either acting or reading the catchups at the start of Mascot serials. McKee might have been playing elderly gentlemen parts as a teenager. Bob Kortman appears as one of the bad guys. Kortman has a marvelous face—angular and craggy. It is the visual equivalent of Karloff's voice. Finally, it's fun to see two ace stuntmen—Yakima Canutt and Joe Bonomo—on display here in credited speaking roles.

The plot, as noted, is not geared to those with attention deficit disorder. We have to pay full attention and, even then, we're going to depend on those

Classic Cliffhangers

Bob Kortman is ready to bean Edwina Booth, who is helping Harry Carey

voiceovers to fill in all the dots. The story has something to do with a kid whose father has been falsely accused of a murder. Then there's a plot about an oil field whose ownership is in dispute. Happy Cardigan (Harry Carey) is trying to bring in a gusher but it seems like just about everyone except Frankie Darro and Rex are against him. Then there are these two gangs, one of them called The Vanishing Legion, who seem to be chasing everybody around for reasons that are largely obscure. And then there is the mysterious villain called The Voice, whose weekly proclamations seem to drive the plot. There's also a kindly old lawyer named Hornbeck (McKee) and his secretary (Ms. Booth) who seem to be involved in things, although we have no idea why or how.

Sorry we can't do a lot better than that. Even without understanding much of what's going on, viewers will still notice a few memorable things. The gimmick of a mysterious voice coming through one of those homemade recordings gets an early workout here. In the 1930s, audiences seemed intrigued by the idea of projecting sounds and images remotely. It shows up here and in Mascot's *The Whispering Shadow* (1933), as well as such forgettable features as *Murder by Television* (1935). Obviously, the mysterious voice over a disc routine would have been impossible two years earlier during the silent era. But serial movie writers were still using it as late as 1946 in Universal's final chapter play, *The Mysterious Mr. M.* And, of course, an entire generation grew up with it as a staple of the TV show *Mission Impossible*.

Hank Davis

As is often the case, this serial's age shows up most noticeably in the barely adequate soundtrack. Don't look for much in the way of music. There's a 50-second interlude (which comes amazingly close to Klezmer music) under the opening titles, nothing during the chapters and not even a closing theme. This is bare bones filmmaking. Most of the scenes stem from exterior location work. It was tough enough recording dialogue on sound stages in 1931. Location work was almost prohibitively difficult. Hoof beats and ambient sound seem to come and go and some dialogue was obviously looped in after the fact. There is also far too much speeded-up footage (slow cranking of the camera) here. Those herky-jerky effects, which appear during fistfights and in scenes between Darro and Rex, add an unintended element of comedy for today's audience. It's not clear what director Reeves Eason had in mind when he used them with such a heavy hand.

On the other hand, there is some pretty spectacular outdoor footage on display. Some of it is the beautiful country in and around Newhall, California, but that is not the whole story. A number of shots are composed with such grace they're almost distracting. At the least they are head and shoulders above most serial cinematography. In Chapter 2, there's a shot of Edwina's car on a hilltop near a sprawling tree. The image is suitable for framing. In Chapter 12 there are some scenes of horsemen framed through a wagon wheel in the foreground. This stuff probably went unnoticed, which is a shame. The photographer was obviously working overtime through a frenetic shooting schedule to bring some individuality to his set-ups.

Some memorable moments to watch for: In Chapter 3, Cardigan's drillers quit on him, saying, "If we wanted to fight, we would have joined the army." It's a pretty funny line. They refuse to participate in the serial's plot. Watch for scenes of Harry Carey driving a car or truck. Nat Levine was not pleased to learn that Carey had never learned to drive. Every one of those shots is a fake, either using another actor filmed from behind or filming Carey "driving" from the side, while several crewmembers pulled his car along on a rope. In Chapter 5 the effect is rather comic as Carey's car begins to move forward before he has a chance to start up the engine. In Chapter 10, Carey comments, "Well, I'll be cow-kicked by a mule." That's a pretty folksy line for an actor who was born in the Bronx. In Chapter 4, Lafe McKee tries to tell the sheriff that The Voice came over a "pocket radio no bigger than a cigarette case." "Ah, nonsense," replies the sheriff. "There ain't no such thing."

There's a real cheat of a take-out in Chapter 5. In the last episode we saw Harry Carey (or a rag doll representing him) thrown down an oil-drilling tower. At the start of Chapter 5, Carey slides the length of the rig down a rope. Not even close to what we saw last week. But, in truth, Chapter 5 may be the serial's best episode. It contains the "trial" of one of the henchmen (The Dodger) by The Voice. It's pretty creepy and very well staged. These scenes seem qualitatively different from what comes before or after. For example, there are a lot of close-ups that are quite effective. Moments like these remind you just how effective this serial might have been if production had been sustained at this level. Then again, with an 18-day shooting schedule and a Poverty Row budget, you take what you can get.

One thing that can be said about Edwina Booth, she sure is a beautiful woman. Unfortunately, she finally gets to "act" toward the end of Chapter 2 and it's not a pretty sight. She even tries to do an imitation of The Voice. At the start of Chapter 3, she

Carey and Kortman in a game of hide and seek

utters the line "I shan't annoy you any further." Simply reading that line out loud may give you some idea of the self-important, pretentious quality of her acting style. She's at it again in Chapter 6 with the line, "The Vanishing Legion is disbanded," as she slams the door. It's enough to make you wish this were a silent movie. It's almost as if the woman thinks she's in another film being made on another continent, not this rough and tumble opus set in the American West.

There are some highly unusual and evocative chapter titles in *The Vanishing Legion*. They make almost no sense although they sure are fun to ponder. Chapter 9 is called "When Time Stood Still" and Chapter 11 is titled "The Capsule of Oblivion." I have no idea what that means. In fact, most of the 12 chapter titles are a cut above the average. "The Voice from the Void" (Chapter 1) isn't bad and "Queen of the Night Riders" (Chapter 2) ain't too shabby. "The Radio Riddle" (Chapter 6) tells about the wonders of technology circa 1931 and "The Hoofs of Horror" is an apt summary of the wrap up—but more on that later. "The Doorway of Disaster" is actually a perfect summary of what happens at the end of Chapter 8. It's not so much a cliffhanger as a door hanger. The heroine is lured to Room 43, which leads not to an apartment, but to a sheer drop to the street. It's a very bizarre moment and seeing her suspended from a hanging door several stories over the boulevard below is one of the more unusual moments in this or any serial.

Purists beware: The restored version of this serial issued by The Serial Squadron features tinting. Actually, the correct name for the process used here is *toning*, rather than tinting. Visually, it's more satisfying. Usually these techniques were reserved for silent films, where the practice was widespread and seems to offend few. It's rare (but not unknown) to see a sound serial tinted/toned like this and it draws occasional fire from the same folks who view colorizing vintage black & white films as heresy. But there's another side to the argument: The toning, mostly in the sepia-range, makes viewing this serial quite pleasant and actually enhances some of the outdoor scenes. The truth is, many of these scenes *look* like old tin-

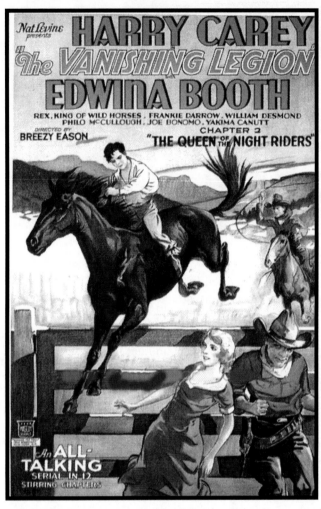

types to start with, and so seeing them come to life in sepia tones feels surprisingly natural.

There's no shortage of stock footage in this serial, including scenes from Tom Mix's *The Great T & A Train Robbery,* a silent Western from Fox. Perhaps the most obvious and awkward stock insert occurs during the final chapter, when Carey finally gets his wish and brings in a gusher. As the oil bursts from the ground on his tiny makeshift oilfield, we see a poorly matched insert showing at least 10 oil towers, telephone lines and a wholly different terrain. Was that really the best footage to be had?

By the end of the serial, most modern viewers are probably waiting for Boris Karloff to be revealed as The Voice. After all, it is his familiar voice that has driven the plot of this serial for 12 episodes. But, of course, in 1931 few people really knew how Boris sounded so there was no necessity to reveal him as the villain. The actual villain turns out to be—oh hell, we won't blow it for you. You've waited long enough to see this serial. We might as well keep the suspense alive for another few days. Interestingly, Harry Carey finds out the identity of The Voice in Chapter 10, although he doesn't share it. "Hey, we're on your side. Tell us!" we almost want to shout. But we have to wait it out for two more chapters, like everyone else.

Rex really gets to strut his stuff in Chapter 10 and it's pretty formidable. When Harry Carey climbs on the wild stallion's back, the actor doubling him, a dark-haired younger man, doesn't even come close to matching Carey. It's pretty funny: Carey needs a stunt double when he rides a horse or drives a car. But the man's warmth and folksy charm come through by the gallon. After Carey has succeeded in riding Rex, young Frankie Darro is afraid that Carey will lay claim to the horse. The older man tells him, "I wouldn't think of taking him. Rex and I understand each other, but you're the only one he loves." It's a nice line and earnestly delivered.

There's a sidebar to discussing this serial and, awkward as it is to confront, it would be dishonest to avoid it. Edward Hearn plays Frankie Darro's father. Hearn had a long, if undistinguished, film career. He had over 350 film roles, many of them small and uncredited. He also appeared in over 20 serials, including *Atom Man vs. Superman*, *The Green Archer* and *Deadwood Dick*. Hearn also appeared in some notable fare like *My Little Chickadee* (1940) with W.C. Fields and Mae West and *This Island Earth* (1955). Hearn's sexual orientation would normally be of no concern to us, except that he turns his performance here into what could pass for a pedophilia training film. In Chapter 1 alone, he spends a disturbing amount of time fondling and nuzzling young Mr. Darro. The whole thing culminates with a completely inappropriate and lengthy on-the-mouth kiss that plainly has nothing to do with his role as Darro's father. It's astonishing that nobody on the set, including director Reeves Eason, blew the whistle on Hearn. Darro was only 13 at the time so it shouldn't have fallen to him to do so. Even though Mascot didn't like to pay for retakes, those "fatherly love" scenes could have been redone with no loss in story or character development. The version of this serial issued by The Serial Squadron provides, in addition to the original release print, a brief re-edit that pointedly eliminates the excess in Hearn's performance.

We won't tell you the secret identity of The Voice but it's safe to say that Rex stomps him to death (mostly off-camera) in the final chapter. Remember the title "The Hoofs of Horror?" The Vanishing Legion, we are finally told, was on the side of law and order all along. The Voice's gang were the real bad guys. I don't know how many 12 year olds could make that distinction in 1931. It's a cinch! Even I had trouble doing it as a somewhat older viewer. It's also not clear whether there is supposed to be a love interest between Carey and Ms. Booth. The script kind of suggests it but he really looks twice her age. In fact, Booth was 26 during this film and Carey was 53. In real life, Booth's film career went nowhere after this picture, awash in intrigue about a lawsuit she instigated against MGM and a case of "jungle fever" she may have contracted the year before during the filming of *Trader Horn*. For his part, Carey went on to a distinguished career, first as a Western actor and later as a character actor of some note. He received an Oscar nomination in 1939 for *Mr. Smith Goes To Washington*. His portrayal here has elements of his best Western and character work. *The Vanishing Legion* remains essential fare for Harry Carey fans. If Edwina Booth still has a fan club, they might want to watch this with the remote in one hand. They can decide if they want to use the pause control or fast forward.

1932
The Hurricane Express

The year is 1932. Dominance in the movie serial business is up for grabs. Last year, both Universal and Nat Levine's upstart Mascot Pictures released five titles. Movie serials may be something of a diversion for Universal Pictures, but for Mascot, they represent the studio's bread and butter. Early in 1932, Nat Levine signs John Wayne, a relative unknown, to star in the three serials for the princely sum of $2,000. That includes his agent's fee. In case there is any confusion, that's $2,000 *total*, not per picture. As Jon Tuska notes in *The Vanishing Legion: A History of Mascot Pictures 1927-1935* (McFarland), Wayne had no idea what he was getting into. Each serial would require a month of filming, with Wayne committed to six-day weeks, and 12 hours of shooting a day.

The second of three serials Wayne filmed for Mascot was titled *The Hurricane Express*. The story involves a young pilot (Wayne) whose father has been killed in a train wreck caused by a mysterious criminal called The Wrecker. Wayne vows revenge against this foe, whose identity—in typical serial fashion—is not revealed until the 12th and final chapter. Not to worry, we won't blow his cover here, but we will say that the number of red herrings and false clues on display must come close to the record for a 1930s movie serial.

For most of its running time, this serial moves at an all-out pace. It simply never stands still from the opening scene until the final reel. Had the film been

John Wayne in action

Classic Cliffhangers

shot today, it might have been called *Planes, Trains and Automobiles*. Indeed, this primitive serial, shot at the dawn of the talking picture age, really earns that title more than Steve Martin's 1987 comedy. The serial spends equal time in the air, on railroad tracks and on the dusty unpaved roads of Depression-era America. In fact, in several of the early car chases, the old roadsters leave the roads and roar along railroad tracks, one wheel between the rails and the other kicking up gravel just outside the track bed. The action is everywhere: Cars chase planes, planes chase trains and, inevitably, cars battle each other down dirt roads that were not built for speed. Wherever the paved roads were in America in 1932, few people seemed to be filming serials on them. Just about every combination of planes, trains and automobiles we can think of is on display at high speed.

Wayne's character, doubled by famous stuntmen Yakima Canutt, even adds some motorcycle thrills in Chapter 5, chasing a runaway freight car on a dirt bike he commandeers. When racing metal doesn't dominate the screen, there are plenty of punch-ups with Wayne, steadfast loyal and true, slugging his way through an endless array of thugs and suspects. Often forced to fight two or three bad guys at once, Wayne seems to take delight in lifting one and throwing him at the other like so much cordwood. In fact, Wayne carries on like an early version of stuntman extraordinaire David Sharpe. He never seems to walk anywhere when running will do. Wayne wears a suit and tie throughout all of this roughneck action.

For the most part, the cliffhangers are convincingly staged and the takeouts are plausible. There are some exceptions, however. In Chapter 4 Wayne is run over by a train while he lies on the track bed, facing up. In the next episode he walks away unfazed. It's a good thing the actor didn't have a more prominent proboscis. At the end of Chapter 8, Wayne is shot in the back, but he seems to emerge without a scratch at the start of Chapter 9. But in general, nobody gets

cheated here, least of all the audience. True, no one is going to win any acting awards, but remember this is a 75-plus-year-old movie serial. Everyone onscreen works as hard as the crew working off-camera. Many of these persons, such as writers Wyndham Gittens and Barney Sarecky, and director Armand Schaefer, had notable careers in movie serials. Only the stilted narrative that precedes each chapter, read in a surprisingly bland voice, seems out of kilter. Mascot often used veteran character actor Lafe McKee in this capacity, but this is surely the work of someone else.

Some of the fight scenes show the rudiments of the kind of graceful choreography we would come to expect in serials before the end of the decade, after Mascot Pictures had morphed into Republic Studios. There is a subplot involving the use of masks that disguise the real identity of The Wrecker. It seems pretty clever at first, but ultimately we realize that it will make identifying the villain virtually impossible. The masks simply establish the fact that anybody can look like anybody else, thereby making visual cues useless.

Even in such an ancient serial, it is instructive to see cost-cutting measures firmly in place. Recycling footage is one of the most grating, now as then. Reportedly, theater owners and film distributors raised hell about it with producers. We get the first example about five minutes into Chapter 5. It's not a particularly long segment, but it is an omen that there's more to come. Another repeat appears in Chapter 8; this one lasts over three minutes. Chapter 11 is probably the worst offender for rerun footage, some of it appearing for the second or third time.

In Chapter 8, the battery goes dead in the bad guy's car. One of the villains simply says, "Oh, the battery's dead. We'll have to crank it by hand." And so he hops out of the car, operates the external hand crank under the grill, and off they go. Just when did that handy little device cease to be a fixture on American cars? Anybody who's had to call a tow-truck would agree: It sure seems like a handy option.

Although movies and stories about the railroads have a long history of commercial success, some of what we see here is a little hard to take. For example, the train that runs under the titles of each episode may look and sound romantic, but it was also an environmental disaster. Check out the coal smoke that pours from its stack as the train rushes by. Those aren't light grey or cloud-like puffs of smoke we see; that is pure soot coming out of the chimney. That thick, acrid black smoke couldn't have been doing anybody or anything any good, regardless of where they were sitting or how romantic the train looked on a movie screen. In any case, the romance of the railroads was nearly over by the time this movie was filmed in 1932. The railroad industry could feel the hot breath of aviation at its back. Planes could go a lot faster than locomotives, and were not held to a fixed course by track. It is exactly this competition between trains and planes that fuels the plot of this enjoyable early serial that, as a bonus, offers a look at an actor who would soon become an American icon.

The Devil Horse

"This is the story of a boy, a horse and a man." So begins this hokey, dated, juvenile and absolutely charming 1932 serial from Mascot Pictures. The serial offers a window on a different world. Kids were wide-eyed, innocent and quite vulnerable. Villains just dripped meanness and avarice and good guys were palpably decent; they were kind to kids and animals alike. *The Devil Horse* is also a historical landmark in popular culture in a way nobody could have anticipated when the cameras began rolling in early 1932. More on that later.

As advertised, the story revolves around three characters and they all have agendas. The boy and the horse have a lot in common. They are both wild. The boy (played by Frankie Darro) is the victim of an outlaw attack that claimed the life of his father. The scene is disturbingly graphic and does a good job of triggering anyone's fear of abandonment. The boy has been on his own since his childhood, surviving in the wilderness with few concessions to adult life or civilization. He's even forgotten how to talk.

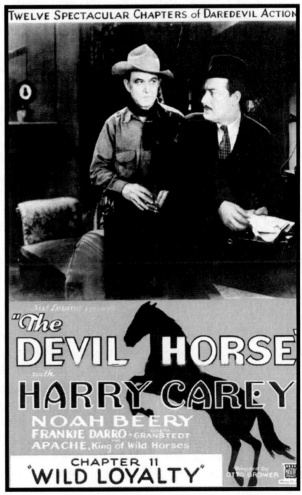

The horse has his own backstory. He began life as *El Diablo*, "the most valuable racehorse in the world." A bungled attempt to kidnap him leads to his escape. He, too, is living apart from civilization, surviving by his wits. When the boy meets the Devil Horse, the two of them hit

NAT LEVINE *presents.* „THE DEVIL HORSE"

CHAPTER II

WILD LOYALTY

it off immediately. The arch villain of the piece is Canfield, aptly played by Noah Beery. Canfield is responsible for both the boy's father's death and the attempt to kidnap *El Diablo*. Beery brings just the right touch to the role of villain. He's got that sleazy, duplicitous, fat cat persona down pat. The character of the "man" (played by Harry Carey) also has an agenda. It is his brother, a park ranger, whom Beery coldly killed during the kidnapping attempt on *El Diablo*. Now Carey will not rest until his brother's murder is avenged. His quest draws him into the lives of the boy and the Devil Horse. Carey, working on his third and final Mascot serial, is also perfect for the role. He exudes the qualities we all seek and admire in a father figure and protector.

There's not a lot of dialogue, which made things all the easier for Mascot's film crew and limited equipment. The boy hasn't yet remembered how to speak and both the horse and Harry Carey are creatures of few words. Most of the talking is done by Beery. You almost get the feeling that basic decency doesn't require language. Guys like Noah Beery use talk mainly to scheme and deceive.

The idea that wild horses would draw people into movie theaters didn't start here. There had already been a successful silent film called *The Devil Horse*. This 1926 film included a spectacular fight scene between Rex ("King of the Wild Horses") and a painted stallion. Ace stuntman and second-unit director Yakima Canutt staged the scene. The footage was recycled into Mascot's 1931 serial *The Vanishing Legion* as well as *The Devil Horse* a year later. It didn't stop there. The fight scene between horses showed up again and again in the 1930s, turning up in Universal as well as Republic films.

Frankie Darro takes a flying leap in *The Devil Horse*.

Normally, Rex, the Wonder Horse, would have played the title part. However, studio boss Nat Levine had already pushed his meager $60,000 budget to the breaking point by hiring Carey, Beery and emerging star Darro. Young Mr. Darro, appearing in his third Mascot serial, was now earning the princely sum of $3,000. Thus, an untested wild mustang named Apache got his big break in films. The only rub was that Apache was *really* wild. Unlike Frankie Darro, he wasn't just faking it for the camera. What began as a cost-cutting move ended up inflating cost, as extensive reshooting was required for the untamed and dangerous animal. Nevertheless, the serial contains some spectacular stunt work presided over by Yakima Canutt for his meager $1,000 salary.

Not all of the stunt work is attributable to Apache's grace and Canutt's skill. At the start and conclusion of Chapter 2, the horse, ridden bareback by Frankie Darro, finds himself in an impossible situation, facing twin peaks with a deep gorge between them. In desperation, Darro and Apache leap from one peak to the other, soaring over the gorge. The first time we see it; the horse and rider get away with it. The second time, their bodies fall into the ravine. What a stunt! Or it would have been, had any actor actually attempted what we see. Instead, there's a good chance we are watching a deftly staged early example of special effects. The scene is visible only in a long silhouette shot, making it likely the characters turn into hand-drawn figures as they glide from one mountain top to the other (or fall to their presumed death). The effect is actually pretty well done and might not even have been apparent were it not for the virtual impossibility of the stunt. *Something* has to be going on. The most notorious actor-to-cartoon switch is, of course, the *Superman* flying sequences in Columbia's 1948 serial. Compared to that bit of money saving hokum, the flying horse sequence in this serial looks like the Mona Lisa.

Hank Davis

Seeing the serial today, the first thing most audiences will notice, and it won't take them long, is the theme music. We can rest assured that most folks will sit forward and comment on it. "What's *that* doing here?" A good question! *The Devil Horse* uses as its title theme "The William Tell Overture." Rossini's rousing work might have languished as a piece of 19th century operatic schmaltz if it hadn't become permanently associated with a true icon of American popular culture, *The Lone Ranger*. So what *is* it doing here?

The choice of this particular title theme might have started off as another cost-cutting move by Mascot studio boss Nat Levine. Understandably, Levine opted to use some royalty-free prerecorded classical music instead of paying a composer for an original score. It was an inspired choice. The theme appears under an impressive opening shot of Apache, the Devil Horse, running toward the camera, rearing up and pawing the air. The brief title sequence is instantly memorable. Just add a few hoof beats to that *Dum*—dah dah *dah* opening and audience attention is all sewn up.

Whether he went to see *The Devil Horse* in a theater or heard about its theme music indirectly, it is clear that the message got through to a man named George W. Trendle. Trendle owned radio station WXYZ in Detroit and he had just taken a big risk. He had severed his ties with the Columbia Broadcasting Network and now needed to fill the gap created by this courageous business decision. In short, Trendle was desperate to find original programming for his station. One of the possibilities he was considering was a kid-oriented Western series that would eventually be called *The Lone Ranger*. There is some confusion in historical sources about exactly what transpired, but the sequence seems pretty clear. As far as "The William Tell Overture" is concerned, Nat Levine and *Devil Horse* beat George W. Trendle and *The Lone Ranger* to the punch. For the record, *The Devil Horse* hit the theaters on November 1, 1932, whereas the premier episode of *The Lone Ranger* was reportedly still being discussed at Christmas meetings in the offices of WXYZ. The show had its first regularly scheduled broadcast on February 2, 1933.

Frankie Darro has Harry Carey all tied up.

Unfortunately, coming in first doesn't guarantee immortality. There was only one *Devil Horse* serial and few remember it (present company excepted!). On the other hand, almost everyone knows *The Lone Ranger* from literally thousands of radio shows, television shows, serials and feature movies. Say what you will about who got what from whom. It may have started with this wonderful old Mascot serial, but it is *The Lone Ranger* that is associated with "The William Tell Overture." Rossini wrote his rousing opera in 1829. It took just over 100 years for two pop culture merchants to discover, almost simultaneously, that this music was stirring, readily available and free. In the early cutthroat days of independent moviemaking and radio drama, there wasn't a sweeter combination than that.

Shadow of the Eagle

Even if it weren't a historically important film, John Wayne's first serial for Mascot Pictures, *Shadow of the Eagle* (1932), would be a pleasure to watch. Wayne is totally believable as a stunt pilot working for a small carnival. Audiences, who grew tired of watching John Wayne play a caricature of himself as he swaggered through his final roles, would find his performance here hard to resist. This is a youthful, hungry actor—still seven years before the role in *Stagecoach* that would catapult him to public attention.

When he signed aspiring actor John Wayne, producer Nat Levine was making his movies on budgets that would barely cover the catering bills on some of today's sets. Still, the results offer some impressive moments. The carnival is an effective backdrop for the story and the point-of-view camera work on carnival rides' like the Ferris wheel and carousel, is quite engaging.

Like many early serials, *Shadow* is not really juvenile entertainment. In fact, it's quite melodramatic in places. The plot can be summarized in one sentence: Wayne works to clear the name of the carnival owner—a man who has been like a father to him. Wayne's character shares most of his onscreen adventures with the carnival strongman (Ivan Linov), the midget (Little Billy Rhodes), and the carnival owner's daughter, played by Dorothy Gulliver.

Nat Levine presents

THE SHADOW OF THE EAGLE

with THE GREATEST CAST EVER ASSEMBLED FOR ANY SERIAL, *starring*
JOHN WAYNE · DOROTHY GULLIVER
KENNETH HARLAN · WALTER MILLER
ROY D'ARCY · RICHARD TUCKER · PAT O'MALLEY · IVAN LINOW
Directed by FORD BEEBE
A STUPENDOUS CARNIVAL SERIAL IN TWELVE THRILLING ALL-TALKING CHAPTERS

Linov isn't much for dialogue, although his character spices up most episodes. He doesn't so much fight with the bad guys as he throws them around like cordwood. In Chapter 8, Linov has more than one consecutive line of dialogue. Big mistake, although it's pretty funny watching him struggle to remember all those words. Indeed, the carnival ventriloquist says to him, "I'll do the thinking; you provide the beef."

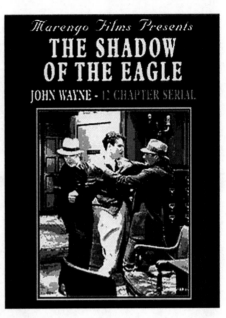

Billy Rhodes is a walking endorse-ment for little people's rights. He spends most of the serial looking like a hefty kid in grownup's clothes, puffing on a long cigar. He calls everyone (except Wayne) a "big palooka" and is quick to protest when people offer unsolicited help. "Get your hands off me, I'm not a cripple," he protests indignantly. Billy is often quite funny and adds some novel twists to the plotting. In one scene, he disguises himself as an abandoned infant in order to gain entrance to a hideout. The 37-year-old Rhodes must have loved the dialogue, much of which seems improvised. In a career that began in the silent era, Billy Rhodes appeared in titles as diverse as *Terror In Tiny Town* (1938) and *The Wizard of Oz* (1939), and continued appear-ing in films until 1967, the year of his death.

Dorothy Gulliver is quite effective as the daughter of the carnival owner and resident pretty girl. She was barely 24 years old when she made this film. Incred-ibly, it was the 69th movie in which she had appeared. Gulliver was only 18 when she became a contract actress for Universal, appearing in a series of bit parts for which she often received minimal billing. Many actors view their early serial work as something between an embarrassment and a necessary evil on the way to mainstream recognition. For Gulliver, her appearance in *Shadow of the Eagle* was one of the meatiest roles of her career. After yet another tiny and uncredited role in 1942, Dorothy Gulliver left films for 26 years, reappearing unexpectedly in John Cassavetes' critically acclaimed 1968 film *Faces*. She died in 1997.

One thing that dates many older low-budget movies is their sparse soundtrack. In the early 1930s, moviemakers who tried to cut corners often figured that dia-logue and minimal sound effects were sufficient. Technology wasn't very highly evolved yet and whatever sounds they provided seemed a massive step up from the silent films of just a few years back. Here, there is a nearly total absence of sound in most exterior shots. The deficit is glaring when these scenes involve fights or people running up or down staircases (which they do a lot here). The results simply regress into silent movie territory. Add the nearly total lack of

John Wayne, 1932

music, and the effect is quite distancing. It's hard not to react to it as an unpleasant combination of cheap and old.

As with most Mascot serials of the era, the catch-up at the start of each chapter is delivered in a voiceover (often provided by Lafe McKee), rather than by printed text. Unfortunately, the readings are done in a style sounding like an elderly British schoolmaster. Perhaps it was supposed to add a touch of class to the proceedings, but the effect seems comically out of sync with the rough and tumble content of the film.

Although some excellent stunt work can be seen, owing to the presence of Yakima Canutt, the fight scenes still leave a lot to be desired. They are awkwardly, even comically, staged. There is also a subtext here, common to many serials of the era, that the cops are all but useless. They are a bunch of middle-aged, slow moving, even slower thinking buffoons named O'Malley and O'Rourke, who couldn't catch a cold. Only the good guys are smart enough to outwit the crooks.

How many times did 1932 audiences abide the old "the name of the killer is...(gunshot)...ooohhh" (dies)? In the early '30s, that may still have been a credible plot device, but it must have gotten old rather quickly. The cartoonish fast-motion scenes of a plane writing messages on the sky are pretty silly, but an early scene of a biplane flying low enough to menace John Wayne and Dorothy Gulliver on the ground is surprisingly effective.

The factory owned by Major Evans has a big sign in front, saying "Evan's Factory." What's distressing is that nobody associated with the film caught that unschooled spelling error. There's something odd about the design of these old roadster convertibles. The drivers spend a lot of time craning their necks to look *around* the windscreens instead of looking through them. And no one ever opens the doors to these cars. They enter by scrambling over the doors and flopping into the seats.

Chapter 6 ends with a most unique cliffhanger. The carnival folk turn on John Wayne and appear to execute him by covering him in tent canvas and spiking him

to the ground. Thankfully, this is 1932 and the carnage takes place off-camera, but it does evoke some of the eerie carnie menace found in Tod Browning's *Freaks* (1932). It's scary to imagine what that scene would look like today if they were still making serials.

The cliffhanger at the close of Chapter 9 defies reason. Things have just gone remarkably well for the good guys and they escape with a contested bill of sale. As they're driving away, two thugs suddenly appear on the running board of their moving car. Where did they come from? There was no place to hide as the car was motoring down the highway. Did they drop in from the sky?

Poor John Wayne. In the last chapter he has all kinds of problems. He's supposed to remove some fake bandages from his face as he delivers his lines. Unfortunately, the bandages refuse to budge no matter how he tears and pulls at them. Less than two minutes later, Wayne nearly takes a belly flop as he races to his car to pursue The Eagle. Did director Ford Beebe allow him another take? No way! Not on this budget. But John Wayne stuck by his contract. He made two other serials for Mascot before evolving into an American movie icon that earned the right to play various aspects of his own persona for nearly a half century.

1933
The Mystery Squadron

This is as good a place as any to talk about film titles. Serials tend to have great names. More so than feature films, they were meant to intrigue and instantly engage the customer. Of course, it didn't hurt that the customer was often 12 years old. Sometimes, the titles of individual chapters were just as intriguing and quite alliterative. Who could resist a title like "The Door of Death" or "The House of Hate?" In general, silent serials had more enticing names than their later sound counterparts. Titles like *Voice on the Wire* (Universal, 1917), *The Shielding Shadow* (Pathé, 1916), *Bound and Gagged* (Pathé, 1919) and *The Third Eye* (Pathé, 1920) make you wonder what went on for 15 weeks back then. Unfortunately, in the majority of cases, we'll never know. Most silent serials appear to be irretrievably lost.

Certain words were very popular in creating serial titles. "The Adventures of…" was a dandy way to start. There are at least 14 silent and sound serials beginning with those words. Right behind "Adventures" was the word "King," which appears 11 times in serial titles. *King of the Circus, King of the Congo, King of the Jungle, King of the Rocketmen, King of the Texas Rangers*, etc. The name suggested some kind of mastery over a domain; after all, Tarzan was "King of the Jungle." The truth is, later serials, especially those issued by Republic, often cheated. "Hi, my name is Joe King and I'm a garage mechanic." And so "King of the Garage Mechanics" was born.

"Perils" wasn't far behind "King" as a way to build serial titles. "Perils" appears 10 times, and it wasn't just Pauline who experienced peril over the years. Nyoka was right there with her. Tied with "Perils" at 10 appearances is the word "Phantom." We've got all kinds of Phantoms throughout the world of serials. Some of them Creep, some are Empires, and others are Riders, Foes, Police or Fortunes. Some operate in the Air, some out West. All in all, Phantoms were big business when it came to titling Cliffhangers. The word "Fighting" was almost as popular as "Perils" and "Phantoms." It seems everybody fought: the Marines, Kit Carson, Buffalo Bill, Devil Dogs, Rangers. There were nine such titles in all. Tied with "Fighting" in the title sweepstakes was "Secrets." Filmgoers loved secrets and would pay to see them unraveled week after week. Secret Codes, Secret Agents, Secret Kingdoms.

But by far, the most popular word to grace the title of a movie serial was "Mystery." If you count cognates like "Mysterious," there are at least 28 serials out there, from early silent efforts like *The Great Radium Mystery* (Universal, 1919) or *Mansion of Mystery* (Capitol, 1927) to later fare like *Mystery Trooper* (1931), *Mysterious Dr. Satan* (1940) or the present title, *Mystery Squadron*. It's clear that audiences loved most things mysterious, adventurous, secretive, phantom-like or

NAT LEVINE
presents

BOB
STEELE
in

"The
MYSTERY
SQUADRON"

12 MYSTIFYING
CHAPTERS
of
ZOOMING
ADVENTURE

Chapter 8
The CANYON
CALAMITY

MASCOT
SERIALS

"BLAZING THE TRAIL"

perilous—and if it took three months to unveil the yarn, so much the better. As far as we know, there were no serials called "Mystery of the Secret Phantom" or "Adventures of the Mysterious King," but there's no reason to believe they wouldn't also have kept the seats warm.

Having taken this roundabout way to introduce *The Mystery Squadron,* I've got one more digression to share. This one is a bit more personal. I always thought my own name would turn up in a movie serial. Hank Davis sounds like the name of a character in some kind of B-movie. I just never assumed it would turn out to be the name of the arch villain. I had watched at least 50 serials before I chanced upon Mascot's 1933 entry, *The Mystery Squadron.* There for all the world to see is veteran serial actor Jack Mulhall appearing as Hank Davis. In Chapter 1 he is introduced as likeable, folksy and virtuous—all qualities I would happily associate with my name. Unfortunately, by the final chapter, his real nature is revealed, and he's unmasked as the dreaded Black Ace. The only comfort I can take from this comes from what some critics describe as serial logic—you take the *least* likely character, someone who just exudes boy-next-door goodness, and reveal him to be the evil villain at the last minute. As the heroes of *Mystery Squadron* aptly comment, "We thought he was our pal." And so my one serial appearance contains a backhanded compliment. Hank Davis was so decent and trustworthy for the first 11 chapters that he was the inevitable choice when the time came to identify the culprit in Chapter 12.

Hank Davis

The Mystery Squadron is really an aviation Western starring actors who usually spent their time on horseback rather than crammed into the cockpits of old biplanes. Bob Steele brings the same "ah, shucks, do-right" qualities that guided him through a lengthy career of Westerns beginning in the silent era and continuing for decades afterwards. His best pal, named Jellybean, is played by Guinn "Big Boy" Williams, who brings similar credentials (appearances in over 200 films). Somewhere there must be a "Sidekick's Manual," and it might prove interesting reading. There's little point in quarrelling with 70-plus-year-old conventions, but Jellybean's character can be pretty hard to take. At times, he makes a guy like Smiley Burnette look like a delegate from Mensa. Williams plays a character the professional IQ testers would probably label "dull normal." He's infantile, awkward, dim-witted and loyal. These are qualities more suited to a big old lovable dog than a man. And don't make the mistake of thinking of him as an overgrown boy. The truth is, most child actors in B-movies and serials are usually wise and savvy beyond their years. Williams' character is the opposite. The camera loves watching him in close-up as he struggles to understand things happening around him, often reaching conclusions long after the moment has passed. Guinn seems to have a permanent "What the...?" reaction stamped on his face. He's also a liability whenever subtlety is required. In short, you can count on his loyalty, but little else. Sad to say, but other Mascot serials of the day portray their canine and equine stars Rex and Rinty as possessing more recognizable signs of human intelligence than the character played by Guinn Williams. And the punch line is, we're supposed to find all of this uproariously funny. Whatever genetics or experiences have reduced Jellybean to the man he is, the results are paraded for our finger-pointing, knee-slapping guffaws. Think about that the next time you long for the good old days in cinematic entertainment.

Lucile Browne, the female lead, appeared in 40 films before retiring in 1938 to raise her family. Her career also focused on B-movies and Westerns, although serials kept her quite busy between 1931-1934, when she appeared in no fewer than five titles for Mascot and Universal. Ms. Browne is a beautiful woman, although her acting style is firmly rooted in an earlier decade—the heart of the silent movie era. The problem is exacerbated by director David Howard, who provides an abundance of close-ups, which only underscore Ms. Browne's over-emoting. Other actors to watch for include J. Carrol Naish, who plays a Black Ace henchman. Naish would later go on to the Villain's Hall of Fame when he starred as Dr. Daka in Columbia's 1943 serial *Batman*.

The story line of *Mystery Squadron* is typical serial fare: Stephen Gray (Lafe McKee, who appeared in many Mascot serials, when he wasn't narrating them) has plans to build a dam but they are thwarted at every turn by a team of daredevil flyers known as the Mystery Squadron. Just about everyone seems to have a reason not to want the dam built. Gray's foreman hires two old flying pals to try to keep the Squadron in check, and they have their work cut out for them. The squadron is led by the mysterious Black Ace, whose identity I have already blown in the second paragraph. Just about everyone is a suspect, and for 12 episodes we are led a merry chase in the air, as well as at the San Juan Tavern Hotel, which is as close to a 1920s "old dark house" as you can imagine in the New Mexico desert. The place is riddled with secret passageways, hidden entrances, dark corridors and sliding panels.

In Chapter 2, a mid-air crash surely claims the lives of both Bob Steele and his sidekick, Jellybean. In fact, the take-out makes the crash look even more deadly than our previous view. But with classic serial illogic, both male leads brush away the debris, dust themselves off and walk on to their next adventures. A few chapters later, Steele's car flips over the edge of a mountain in a realistic (non-model) crash that no one would survive. But, again, take-outs in the early 1930s were far more likely to involve a "dust yourself off and walk away" resolution than a "jump out just in time," which became standard fare a decade later.

Aviation was truly in its infancy, which made airplane adventure serials all the more exciting (and difficult to make) in 1933. The appearance of airplanes in a movie serial all but guaranteed audience attendance for at least three months. Mascot was certainly aware of the solid business their competitors at Universal had done earlier in the year with their 12-Chapter serial *Phantom of the Air,* and they were not to be outdone. You get a sense in Chapter 11 of just how flimsy and minimal these old biplanes really were. There wasn't much to protect the flyer or his passengers from what lay immediately outside their cockpit. This serial obviously depended quite a bit on the use of models and the special effects involving little toy planes are surprisingly good, perhaps because actual planes, still looked like large toys.

The opening titles are quite effective, both graphically and musically, but one place where the serial really shows its age is the totally inappropriate one-minute musical interlude accompanying the catch-up titles at the start of each episode. This is the worst kind of hackneyed late 1920s dance music, containing zero tension or relevance to the serial. It's like Guy Lombardo or Paul Whiteman suddenly stepped in for a one-minute dance interlude, and now back to our story.

There's a surprising amount of re-used footage in this serial, a cost-cutting ploy that became all-too common 10 years later. It starts early in *Mystery Squadron* ("Remember when we first came to town and...") and continues right up until the middle of the final chapter. Speaking of which, everything is wrapped up tight as a golf ball by the end. Gray finally gets to build his dam, Steele gets the girl, his loveable big oaf of a sidekick gets a lifetime supply of jellybeans and Hank Davis, sad to say, goes down in a flaming crash that nobody walks away from, even in a 1933 Mascot serial.

The Whispering Shadow

By the early 1930s, characters named The Shadow were becoming big business. A series of radio shows on CBS starting in the summer of 1930 introduced a mysterious character called The Shadow. Within two years the character had gone from narrator to story regular as the popularity of the radio show—sponsored by Blue Coal—continued to grow. The Shadow would finally earn a movie serial of his own in 1940, but, prior to that licensing deal, there was nothing to stop serial producers from borrowing the word "Shadow" as part of their titles.

The 1930 Universal serial *The Jade Box* features a mysterious presence known as The Shadow. He may have mastered the art of invisibility, but he was powerless to work himself into the serial's title. Perhaps he should have worked for Mascot. One year before they released *The Whispering Shadow*, Mascot had produced *The Shadow of the Eagle* (1932), and one year later Universal (finally) released its own contender called *The Vanishing Shadow* (1934). In 1936 Bela Lugosi was back with another entry called *Shadow of Chinatown*. Whether he was whispering, vanishing, flying through the clouds or hovering over Chinatown, none of these Shadows bore any similarity to the radio character. Nevertheless, Lugosi fans will sing the praises of this 12-chapter serial play. It is the first of six movie

Bela Lugosi wishes he had paid his cable bill.

serials made by Lugosi and, truthfully, the actor has never had a better chance to strut his campy, melodramatic excess. There is no parodying what Lugosi brings to this serial; he is simply over-the-top from his first moment onscreen to his last. Bela never had a part better written for his unique style, and he never had directors more indulgent than Albert Herman and Colbert Clark, who allowed him to chew the scenery without interference.

In fact, Bela seems to set the tone for some serious melodramatic excess here. This serial is essentially a silent movie that talks. This is 1933 with an eye cast firmly on 1913; you keep waiting for someone to say, "Curses! Foiled again!" With only one or two exceptions do Lugosi's fellow actors make any effort to show restraint in their performances. Bradley, played by Henry Walthall, is one of the few characters who acts in a recognizably human manner. Subtlety is an early casualty here; everyone plays for the last row in the balcony. Lugosi appears as Professor Strang—a clever name that manages to *sound* European while *looking* suspiciously close to "Strange." Strang is the proprietor of a wax museum called "The House of Mystery." It's not clear what this has to do with the plot other than providing a semi-creepy setting for most of Lugosi's skulking around. Lugosi is suspected of being the mysterious title character, who is described in the weekly opening summaries as "a sinister being." The Whispering Shadow projects his caped visage on to walls of rooms or sides of trucks and whispers one-liners to the suitably terrified characters. He's also got a method for killing people who get in his way by using a "radio death ray," whatever that is. Today it might be known as a "remote control device" but you can imagine the effect it had on audiences in 1933.

So what's going on here? Apparently the Czar's Imperial jewels are hidden at the Empire Storage Company and everyone is trying to steal them. There's the Whispering Shadow — whoever he is — as well as Slade, an escaped convict effectively played by Bob Kortman. Kortman simply looked menacing before he ever hit the makeup room. Some of the managers at Empire Storage (played by Lafe McKee and Roy D'Arcy) also seem pretty suspicious. And of course the Whispering Shadow has hired two or three certifiable thugs to carry out his plans. Then there's a dashing young man named Jack Foster (played by Malcolm MacGregor), whose brother has been killed by The Whispering Shadow in Chapter 1. That gives him plenty of motivation to chase everyone around for a dozen chapters, although one look at Professor Strang's lovely daughter, played by Viva Tattersall, gives him extra incentive.

This business of having a mysterious villain projecting his disembodied voice was pretty snazzy stuff in the early '30s. Mascot had used the gimmick two years earlier to much better effect in *The Vanishing Legion*. In fact, having succeeded so handsomely by casting Boris Karloff as The Voice in *The Vanishing Legion*, it's curious that they'd get so careless with the effect here. Suffice it to say that the uncredited actor who works the hidden microphone is not blessed with the stylish and distinctive speaking apparatus that Karloff brought to the set.

I won't say who the Whispering Shadow is. Anyone willing to view all 12 chapters of this ancient serial — at an age that I assume is considerably more than 12 years — then I'll do what I can to enhance that pleasure. However, I will tell you who the Whispering Shadow is *not*. And that, dear friend, is Mr. Lugosi. Despite all the speculation and incessant teasers, old Bela turns out to be nothing more than a well-paid and conspicuously billed red herring. The truth is, any viewer with half an ear will have figured this out for himself. The reason is simple. There is just no way that Lugosi could have wrapped his almost comically impenetrable Hungarian accent around the dialogue spoken by the Whispering Shadow. Somewhere along the line, there'd be some kind of telltale moment. Maybe something like "Don't try to find me. You *vill* not succeed." A few film notes: See if you can count the number of times someone says, "There, there" to Ms Tattersall. When a thug says, "Don't try any of your tricks," we kind of wish she'd reply, "Who else's, then?" It would have been a great exchange and

Vera Strang (Viva Tattersall) and her father (Lugosi) enter the House of Mystery.

certainly punctuated some of this dramatic excess. There are things moving in this serial, like statues and walls that are not supposed to move. The walls (watch for it in the "Collapsing Room" cliffhanger) just look funny. The statues make you wonder whether there's going to be some odd subplot about human wax figures (as in Roger Corman's *A Bucket of Blood* or the classic *House of Wax*), or whether Mascot had just found it more economical to hire down-on-their-luck actors and tell them to stand still. If you wonder what helicopters looked like in 1933 (or, indeed, if there *were* helicopters in 1933), check out the cliffhanger to Chapter 1. The miniature work is pretty laughable, but you'll still get the idea.

The uncredited theme music under the opening titles is worth mentioning. It only lasts a minute, but it is head and shoulders above much competing serial music of the period. The recorded sound is surprisingly full and the orchestration manages to set a palpable feeling of tension. Don't let anyone say that recycling footage within a serial first appeared during the declining years (post-1945) of serial production. Nat Levine's Mascot Pictures was working the movieolas overtime during this serial. Recycled footage appears as early as Chapter 5 (just how bad did they think the audience's memory was?) and continues unabated until halfway into the final chapter.

In many ways this serial is a victim of its age. Along with its "barely out of the silent era" acting style, it is also staged like an old dark house play. Characters run in and out of rooms, hit each other over the head and accuse each other of almost everything in sight. Virtually everyone is a suspect. There's lots of action but much of it feels like running on a treadmill. It just doesn't go anywhere, but it sure wears you out. The truth is, for all his campy excess, Bela is just about the only character who holds your interest. His daughter, Vera, is lovely to look at, but speaks in a fluttery melodramatic voice with a vaguely British accent. In truth, Viva Tattersall was born in Wales so the accent was no affectation. But it also provided a self-conscious touch of class to an otherwise threadbare Mascot production. Ms. Tattersall had a very brief career in film; indeed, this was her biggest role. Appearing in only eight titles (the final two uncredited), she made her final film in 1937. Six years later she married actor Sidney Toler and spent the last four years of his life with him (Toler died in 1947). Tattersall died in 1990.

As far as identifying the Whispering Shadow before being told his name in the final chapter, chances of success are virtually nil. In fact, we've only gotten as far as 1933 in our march through movie serials and it's safe to say that this is perhaps the best job of hiding a secret identity you'll ever see. The writers do such a fine job at misleading the audience, that the impulse is to cry foul when the secret is finally revealed. Seriously, this screenplay takes misdirection to an art form. And speaking of revelations, there is a whole bevy of them in Chapter 12. Be warned: You're going to need a scorecard to keep track of all the secret identities that come flying out. Bela is, of course, the most important one. You'll love it when he announces with genuine gusto, "I am the Foreign Minister of the Federated Baltic States." Huh? It's not quite clear what that means, but it does seem to account for his accent, anyway. It also seems to impress the other actors on the set, who immediately start calling him "Your Excellency."

Speaking of accents, one other actor deserves special mention. Karl Dane plays the seemingly halfwit radio operator named Sparks. Dane (real name Rasmus Karl Thekelsen Gottlieb) was actually from Denmark and had achieved some measure of success as a silent movie actor (over 40 credits dating from 1918). A large, physically imposing man (Dane was nearly 6'4"), Dane spoke with a noticeable Danish accent that limited his opportunities in sound films. By 1933, the year of this serial, acting work had all but dried up. Sadly, Dane began training to become a plumber and, in order to support himself in the meantime, sold hot dogs from a cart. On April 15, 1934 he found himself vending hot dogs outside the gate at MGM, a studio where he earlier had been a successful actor. Dane turned around, wheeled his cart home, surveyed the arc of his life, took his pistol from its holster and blew his brains out. He was 37 years old. *The Whispering Shadow* was his last film.

1934
The Perils of Pauline

Even folks who know precious little about movie serials have heard of this title. Mind you, it's probably not this version of the title they've heard of. But no matter. What they know is there was a heroine, Pauline something, and every week she was chased by bad guys, pursued by lions and tigers, left tied to train tracks or hanging off the edge of a cliff. Somehow, they recall, she lived to fight another menace the following week.

They're right in one sense. Her name was Pauline and her lifestyle was perilous, to say the least. It's just that they probably have the wrong serial in mind. The famous *Perils of Pauline* featured Pearl White and was released in 1914, deep in the heart of the silent-movie era. Originally a 20-episode film, it exists only in fragmentary form today. What we have here is the Universal remake from 1934 starring Evalyn Knapp. This version, released at the dawn of the talkie era, is in the unenviable position of being compared with a 20-year-old classic American film. To succeed, it would have to bring all the thrills, chills and energy of the iconic Pearl White version, while adding the magic of sound. Does it succeed? Decide for yourself (the results are widely available on VHS from VCI and on DVD from Alpha).

For our money, they got the title right, but very little else about this early

Robert Allen and Evalyn Knapp

melodrama elevates it to the level of memorable. It is by no means a bad serial but, once the studio brought that classic title into play, they were guaranteeing revenue but also set themselves up for trouble. For one thing, this is not even really about Pauline. Certainly, she's there, scurrying around in the middle of all the bombs and tigers and henchmen, but as often as not she needs to be rescued. And, for a heroine, she sure does a lot of screaming. In fact, she offers not one tenth of the flaky charm exuded by Pearl White in the original.

success, the blame lies not just with the ghost of Pearl White hovering over the set. Rather, it is that this is, first and foremost, a 1934 melodrama. Yes, it takes place in exotic locales and there are lions, tigers, gorillas and bad guys galore. But it is still a very dated melodrama that no amount of jungle noises or detonating bombs is going to hide. The story is fairly standard serial fare. Professor Hargrave (James Durkin) has discovered that the formula for an invisible poison gas, well known to the ancients, has been carved (in Sanskrit, no less) on a stone tablet, which was then broken in half and hidden in temples in the Far East. Joining the good professor in his quest to find the formula is his spunky daughter Pauline, along with an American engineer named Bob Ward (Robert Allen). Opposing them on this quest is the evil Dr. Bashan, played with relish and lots of makeup by John Davidson. The Eurasian Bashan looks and sounds quite menacing and may be Davidson's best role in a cliffhanger.

The setting moves from China to Borneo to India to New York. There is a cast of thousands and no expense has been spared to bring you this grand scale entertainment. Right? Hardly. In reality, this is a 1934 Universal B-movie production and no stock footage has been spared. If it's in the vault, it is there to be recycled. Jungles? We got 'em by the acre. Natives and wild animals? Just ask. Chinese street scenes? Bombs dropping? Ancient temples? They are there in all their grainy elegance, just awaiting your call. And so we are again treated to the spectacle of actors dodging bombs that dropped in another movie, running from hostile natives in a jungle that existed 10 or 15 years earlier for another purpose. These tigers and leopards and fleeing antelopes exist, not on a back lot, but in a can labeled "wild animals." To be fair, some of the footage, especially the far East street scenes, is very authentic looking. But it is also ancient and no match, literally, for the footage of Ms. Knapp and company being shot in southern California in late 1933.

Whatever the vintage of the perils, there is no shortage of them. In Chapter 1, it's an explosion. In Chapter 2, it's a storm at sea (a "raging typhoon"). In Chapter 3, it's a leopard. Before this serial has played itself out, we've seen attacks from natives, gorillas, sharks and all sorts of human predators. The real hero is Bob Ward. Pauline is there to get herself into trouble and be rescued. He character is alternately spunky, foolhardy and idiotic. Of course, we need her to be. If she

were fearful or shy, we wouldn't have much of a serial. We need her to need to be rescued. Of course, Bob obliges. He is introduced as "an American engineer," there to build a railroad through China or something like that. "Engineer" is a funny word. It might mean a nerd with a slide rule but it is also the name of a guy who drives a train. Casey Jones was an engineer, hardly a nerd. Bob Ward is closer to Casey Jones than Steve Sliderule.

Some comments about a few of the actors: Look for Josef Swickard in the small role of Consul Hadgen in Chapter 9. This actor endeared himself to serial fans in 1935 when he starred as Dr. Manyus in *The Lost City*. Canadian actor James Durkin, appearing as Pauline's father, made his first movie at age 51 after a long stage career. Once begun, Durkin's movie career was brief (four years) but active (two dozen titles) and included *The Vanishing Shadow*, another Universal serial released in 1934. Durkin died literally within months of this production in March 1934. Handsome actor Craig Reynolds worked under several aliases. He is billed here as Robert Allen, although

Evalyn Knapp on *Picturegoer*

in earlier efforts like *Gordon of Ghost City* and *Phantom of the Air* (both 1933) he appeared as Hugh Enfield. Reynolds' roles as an action hero were no sham; he received a purple heart in WWII and died in a motorcycle accident in 1949 at age 42. Evalyn Knapp made her only serial appearance here. Her credits went back to the silent era and extended to a few uncredited parts in the early 1940s, at which point her film career seems to have ended. She died in 1981, five days short of her 73rd birthday. The real veteran serial presence in *Perils of Pauline* was John Davidson. Making his first cliffhanger appearance here, Davidson went on to play roles in a dozen serials, including such classic fare as *Adventures of Captain Marvel, Dick Tracy vs. Crime, Inc.* (both 1941) and *Captain America* (1944). The man just exuded menace.

Try as you might, you won't forget the fact that this is a 1934 melodrama. Despite all the exotic locales, the interpersonal stuff still suffers from turgid pacing. The dialogue between Pauline and Bob is often priceless. Did men and women ever talk to each other this way? If so, it's a wonder that our species did not begin a decline towards extinction in 1934. And the ever-so-subtle superiority of white people in this serial is unmistakable. In Chapter 3, "Look!" says Pauline to her father, as we cut to a shot of some animals walking away. "Water buffalo," he replies. "They seem to have a pronounced aversion to white people." Huh?

Around all these deficits and annoyances, there are some surprisingly effective touches. The 15 seconds of music that plays over the closing "At this theater next week" titles is very effective and surprisingly full and tense. More of it would only have helped. On the visual front, the shadow of a snake drifting across a sleeping Pauline in Chapter 3 is well staged and didn't come out of any stock-footage can. Occasional plot devices and bits of dialogue also reveal glimmers of inspiration worthy of the best serials. For example, we learn that half of the sacred disk is hidden at the Temple of Ming Tau and is "guarded by the hand of the Destroyer." Who cares what that means; it just sounds like it belongs in a serial. When we finally meet the Destroyer in Chapter 4, it's a bit of a let down. The good news is that he's a creepy-looking 12-foot-tall stone idol that grabs at Pauline with a mobile right hand. The bad news is that, once in the Temple, it takes the gang about 20 seconds to find the idol, remove the sacred disk, free Pauline and be on their way. Sometimes brisk pacing can work against a serial.

The comic relief here comes from Dodge (Sonny Ray). As portrayed, he is a foppish, fearful, effete little buffoon who is treated none-too-kindly by any of the principals involved. In an odd scene, Dodge gets to ogle a briefly glimpsed native woman in a topless bathing scene. It's plainly too much for him but it did escape the final director's cut, suggesting that this serial was intended to be more than strictly juvenile fare. There are some sort of killer apes that provide the thrills at the end of Chapter 4. What are they? Gorillas? Large chimps? Bonobos? Guys in suits? I've watched the scene repeatedly and I am still not sure.

When the party gets to Singapore, they manage to work a shark attack into a hotel scene. How do we locate a shark in a 5-Star hotel? Simple. There's a shark pool in the lobby. Of course, Pauline manages to fall into it. Chapter 9 offers a lesson in aviation history. The gang flies to New York on a transatlantic clipper ship—a seaplane with six prop engines on a single wing. The plane takes off and lands on water, rather than a paved runway. Referring to their trip, one character announces with pride that the trip took just five days from India to New York!

Chapter 9 is called "The Mummy Walks," one of the oddest chapter names in serial history. Serials don't tend to be about mummies, and this is no exception. It was only two years since a mummy had indeed walked in a Universal feature, but here we get no replay of Karloff as Imhotep. Instead, we get the fearful servant Dodge, fallen into a vat of plaster, staggering around the corridors of a museum in a style we now associate with resurrected mummies. The effect is well done and quite funny, but it underscores the fact that the title is a cheat and this serial wants no part of supernatural goings-on. To his credit, actor Sonny Ray has his moments. The mummy scene may not even be his best. There's a brief scene at the start of Chapter 11 when he runs outside with a gun in each hand, blazing away. The guns seem to be firing themselves, and each shot sends ripples of fear across his body. If nothing else, the man was a physical comedian.

In Chapter 10, the Professor finally gets his whole formula together and decides to test it in a private lab in a downtown office building. A real mummy walking would have made more sense than this plot development. Remember, this is an ancient formula for poison gas that, we are told, wiped out entire civilizations. Now, one man is going to test it in a makeshift lab in a downtown office. When the Prof. calls in his pals for a demonstration, he announces, "This gas will kill every living thing with which it comes into contact." Then he adds, "I want you all to witness this." Fortunately for the good guys, he adds, "Stand back a little." Unbelievable. You just can't parody dialogue like this. And as far as securely guarding the formula that they have traipsed across five continents to find? Pauline stuffs it in her purse.

A small office fire breaks out in Chapter 11. That's all it takes. Cue the stock footage! Soon we have fire trucks racing through city streets circa 1921. The fire (obviously real) consumes entire buildings and plainly over-matches the needs of the plot. If you like the footage here (it *is* pretty spectacular), you can see it in any number of Universal B-movies from the 1930s and even the '40s, by which time those fire trucks must have been startling to see. When Pauline needs the police to come rescue her in the final chapter, she calls and says, "Come quick!" That is, of course, a cue for more stock footage. Amazingly, the police wagons look even more ancient than the fire trucks.

When the evil Doctor Bashan and his assistant Fang (Frank Lackteen) finally get exposed to the gas—as you know they will—they don't just die, they disappear. For some reason, this gas just seems to dissipate after killing the two main villains. It leaves no residue and has no apparent effects on any of the good characters. It makes you wonder about all those ancient civilizations this gas was supposed to have vaporized. They must have been crawling with bad guys.

Of course, *The Perils of Pauline* didn't end here. The name, indeed the very

idea, is just too iconic. In 1947 there was a Pearl White biopic starring Betty Hutton that conveniently borrowed the serial title. The film was greeted with almost universal disdain. In 1967 there was a whole-some, funny and heartwarming remake starring Pat Boone and Pamela Austin. If the very thought of such a project triggers your gag reflex, perhaps you might be more interested in the 1965 sexploitation flick, directed by Doris Wishman, called *The Sex Perils of Paulette*. Whether wholesome or sexy, it's a safe bet that we haven't seen or heard the last of Pauline (or Paulette) as we approach the 100-year mark.

The Vanishing Shadow

The dead come back to life all the time in horror and science fiction movies. It's a lot less common for the movies, themselves, to come back from the dead. Yet that is essentially what's happened in the case of *The Vanishing Shadow,* a 1934 serial from Universal that was thought to be lost forever. Fortunately for serial fans and collectors, this is one corpse that now walks proudly among us. Until very recently, the only traces of this obscure cliffhanger were a collection of lobby cards and a 70-year-old press package from Universal. They offered some intriguing glimpses of an early sound serial with more than a few traces of science fiction, which made things all the more tantalizing to collectors.

The Vanishing Shadow tells the story of Stanley Stanfield, an unfortunately named electrical inventor, whose father was driven to suicide by an unscrupulous newspaper tycoon named Ward Barnett. Stanfield vows to avenge his father, but promptly falls in love with Barnett's daughter, Gloria. Stanfield hooks up with an electronic genius, the slightly demented Professor Van Dorn, who surrounds himself in a menacing world of gadgets, not the least of which is an invisibility belt. The invisibility machine isn't perfect—it leaves a telltale shadow, which is how the film gets its name. Becoming invisible was big business in 1930s cinema. It was an achievable and relatively inexpensive special effect that held a lot of fascination for audiences.

"VANISHING SHADOW"

"ACCUSED OF MURDER!" CHAPTER 1

12 SMASHING CHAPTERS of ACTION MYSTERY! and THRILLS!

Along with the title invention, there's a pretty good assortment of ray guns, electric exploding devices and even the world's first electric garage door opener! (The remote control device sends electric rays that are visible on the screen.) But the highlight of this serial is—and there is no way to overstate how much of a highlight it is—a mechanical man. In fact, let's give him the credit he deserves. This is the first appearance of a robot in a sound serial. Within a year, robots were all over the Saturday matinees. Gene Autry battled a whole squadron of them in *The Phantom Empire* (1935), Lugosi planned to take over the Earth with an army of mechanical men in *The Phantom Creeps* (1939) as did Dr. Satan in a 1940 Republic serial bearing his name. The list goes on, but this, as far as we can tell, is where it all started.

This mechanical man is not your everyday robot. When he first appears in Chapter 1, we can see right off that he is not the usual slow-moving, awkward monster. This guy is full of energy. He almost dances through his role. Unfortunately, the big guy sort of pulls a disappearing act after teasing us in Chapter 1. He doesn't reappear until the 10th chapter but, from then on, he steals the show.

In many ways, this serial shows its age. In fact, without the delightful sci-fi elements, it is pretty ordinary melodramatic fare. The whole thing looks (and sounds) quite stagey when the characters aren't busy chasing each other around. Onslow Stevens (veteran of over 100 film and TV appearances) and Ada Ince are adequate in the title roles. Ms. Ince was barely 21 when she made this film. She seems to have disappeared the next year after appearing in just eight titles. James

Durkin acquits himself well as the almost-unhinged Professor Van Dorn. All three actors perform like they're very recent graduates of the silent era—which is not far from the truth. The actors talk to each other in ways that your grandmother might have viewed as quaint. The cars they drive belong in a museum right next to their telephones and office furniture. The street scenes, which may have been sitting around the stock footage department for 10 years, are simply ancient.

Some technical notes: This was approximately the 20th sound serial released by Universal. Things were still pretty primitive. Music only appears under the opening and closing credits. The catch-up at the start of each episode is a title card with very small print and *way* too much text—well over 100 words. There are lots of impressive electrical effects (courtesy of Kenneth Strickfaden) under the opening credits. To the relatively   uneducated viewing public of the times, nothing said science or, for that matter, science-*fiction* better than a laboratory full of strange-looking devices that arced and zapped current.

The car crashes at the end of Chapters 1 and 7 are very realistic. If those are miniatures, then the guys at Universal in the early '30s deserve some kind of award. They were sure giving the folks at Republic a run for their money. It's more likely that Universal kept some actual crash footage filed away for situations just like these. To show how old this serial is Chapter 8 ends with a silent-era type of cliffhanger. The bad guy gets the drop on the hero and says, in essence, "Turn over the deed to the ranch." Bam!—the episode ends. No plane crash or car wreck. Just a week to worry and wonder, "Poor Stanley. What *will* he do?"

The fight scenes are very poorly staged—not unusual for a pre-Republic serial. They don't even include the sounds of fists hitting their marks. In addition, the camera is slow-cranked to speed up the action scenes and give them more energy. The effect is like suddenly watching an old Charlie Chaplin film—hardly the boost in realism sought by director Louis Friedlander. Surprisingly, Friedlander is billed low in the credits, even below the associate producer. And look for famous actor Lee J. Cobb making an early film appearance here in an uncredited part as a highway gang foreman in Chapter 4.

It's plenty clear from this film that the market for movie serials in 1934, at least as Universal defined it, was not just for 10 year olds. Perhaps they left kid-oriented fare to studios like Mascot (soon to become Republic). In any case, the plotting in this serial was clearly geared to adults. Despite the robot, the vanishing ray and all the death gadgets, this is essentially a Depression-era story for and about adults.

Some bizarre moments to watch for: When Stanfield tells Van Dorn he is going to visit the treacherous Barnett, the Professor says, "Here, take this death ray with you." It comes out sounding like "Don't forget your mittens."

Van Dorn refers to Stanfield and Gloria as "the young idiots."

As henchmen go, Dorgan (played by Richard Cramer) is a pretty decent guy. Something must be wrong here—he's almost likeable. In most serials, the villain usually criticizes his ineffectual henchmen for failing to vanquish the hero.

Hank Davis

Onslow Stevens and Ada Ince

Most henchmen put their inept tails between their legs and skulk off the set. Here, we get a whole different kind of confrontation. Dorgan is not intimidated by Barnett, his boss. After he's accused of bungling, Dorgan tells him, "All right, you can do your own bungling from now on. I'm through. Van Dorn turned a steel giant on us that neither bullets nor stonewalls can stop. And you sit here in a safe place and criticize!" Those words should be engraved on the walls of the Henchman's Union Hall.

The robot finally gets to strut his stuff in Chapter 11, which is called "The Juggernaut." For openers, the robot breaks through a wall and menaces a few folks. That's par for the course. What we don't expect are the absolutely surreal scenes of the robot pacing on the front porch of a rustic cabin or, better yet, walking through the woods. The latter may be one of the most unusual scenes you'll ever see in a serial and belongs up there with the best of Universal's horror images. The moment is absolutely eerie—you can actually hear the sound of the crickets chirping beyond the mechanical noises. When the robot comes upon a farmer and his horse-drawn cart, the horses react in fear. Plainly, they are not acting. The robot is out of control—pure physical energy without any guiding principles. That's what makes him so scary, to the farmer and horses alike. It's a scene every bit as memorable as the famous episode with Frankenstein's Monster and the little flower girl. Chapter 11 is simply superb: 20 of the most inspired minutes of serial moviemaking likely to be seen anywhere. It's too bad that the robot disappears for nearly 10 chapters, but when he finally reappears it was well worth the wait—much like the nearly seven decades we have been without this vintage serial.

Burn 'Em Up Barnes

If child-star Frankie Darro ever had a better role or approached his work with more enthusiasm than in this 1934 Mascot serial, I've yet to see it. And the truth is, it's no wonder. *Burn 'Em Up Barnes* is a real delight. It's full of slam-bang energy and adventurous performances, directing and camera work. We could throw a boxcar full of Ritalin at this hyperkinetic film and not calm it down. It's just hard not to appreciate this kind of primitive, breakneck moviemaking. Almost none of it is shot indoors on soundstages, and the location work is consistently attention grabbing.

The serial starts off like an extreme sports video, with shots of dirt bikes, speedboats and racing cars. The acrobatic motorcycle driving rivets your attention in the very first reel. Obviously, there's lots of rear-screen projector work here, but it creates the illusions of a photographer standing in the middle of a track and barely jumping out of the way in time as bikes streak by. Pretty heady stuff for 1934 no-budget filmmaking. A photographer named George is killed in Chapter 1 in a racing accident for which Burn 'Em Up Barnes—the King of the Dirt Tracks—feels responsible. Being a heck of a decent fellow, Barnes promises to look after George's younger bother, Bobby (Darro).

The rest of the plot is standard-issue B-movie scripting. Barnes meets a lovable lass named Marjorie (played by Lola—"Don't call me Lois"—Lane). Lola owns a garage and school bus company that just happens to be located smack

Frankie Darro, Al Bridge and a contested canister of film

dab on top of a giant oil deposit. Of course, none of the good guys know anything about this. But evil villain Drummond (Jason Robards, Sr.) certainly does and he spends most of his spare time plotting to get Lola and company off her land. If that means blowing up the occasional busload of school kids, well, hell, there's some serious money to be made here, so why not? Can you imagine how evil this guy would be with today's oil prices? To make matters worse, Lola's business is thriving now that Barnes (ably played by Jack Mulhall) has joined forces with her. Now the bad guys have to sabotage everything Barnes does as well, since any financial success he brings to the table makes it less likely Lola will sell out to the villains.

Barnes is not a white-collar kind of guy. Wherever he goes, action and adventure seem to follow. He works as a test pilot and a stuntman to support the bus company, and Drummond and his henchmen put him into continuous peril. In this sense, the plot is quite similar to the original Pearl White version of *Perils of Pauline*. No matter where our hero goes, these guys have reason to lie in wait with sabotage in their hearts. In an unusual bit of serial plotting, Barnes finds out that Drummond is the bad guy midway through Chapter 3. No mysterious masked villains to uncover for a dozen chapters here. When Darro shoots some incriminating footage of the bad guys at work—get a load of the 1934 equivalent of a camcorder. Technology has sure come a long way. This footage becomes a focus of everyone's attention and the characters essentially play field hockey with the canister of incriminating film for quite a few chapters. In a revealing moment, a couple of heavies are dispatched to follow Darro when he takes the film in for processing. We see them walk into Consolidated Film Industries, a real company where Mascot actually sent its film—including this one—for processing.

By Chapter 5, the DA has the film and it looks like the bad guys will be brought to justice. Can this be Mascot's first 6-Chapter serial? Not to worry. In fact, when we finally see the DA screen the film that Darro shot, it's basically a rerun of Chapter 2, including scenes of Darro, himself, taking the pictures. That's quite a trick! Not surprisingly, it's going to take the full 12 chapters to bring this adventure to a close. Mascot hedged its bets about sustaining an audience. Just in case any new viewers drifted in along the way, the basic plot about the bus company and the hidden oil deposit is stated prominently week after week. Nobody was going to remain clueless for very long.

Some nifty moments to watch for: Look closely at the car chase at the end of Chapter 2. At one point, Darro looks right into the camera and spoils the illusion. The street scenes in Chapter 6 are absolutely real. No back lot work here. There's been some speculation about where these exteriors were filmed. Leading contenders seem to be Van Nuys and Encino, although at one point you'll plainly see the Petaluma Grocery. In Chapter 8, Barnes becomes an actor and gets cast in an action thriller much like this one. We get to see on-location filming—a picture within a picture.

One of the less pleasant sides of watching these filmed relics of pop culture is reminding ourselves just how shabbily ethnic minorities were treated in the name of family entertainment. This time around, African Americans are spared and the Italians bear the brunt. It's a laugh a minute as Tony, the immigrant car mechanic, butchers the English language. When he draws a gun on the bad guys, he utters the words "Poosh 'em up," a variant of "Stick 'em up" and a not-so-subtle reference to the New York Yankees' star Tony Lazzeri, whose nickname was "Push 'Em Up Tony," usually corrupted to "Poosh 'em Uppa Tony." It's hard to imagine making similar fun of the Latino ballplayers who constitute close to 25 percent of major leaguers today. But in 1934, the ethnic laughs just kept a'comin'. "You betcha my life" says Tony, as he trips over an oil can and confirms the widely held view that most non-Wasps were both mentally and physically challenged. This might have been reduced to a 10-chapter serial were it not for weekly reminders of Tony's foreigner foibles.

Great musical scores in low-budget filmmaking were not to be found in 1934. This serial features 40 seconds of opening title music—most notably under the weekly catch-ups—that is not just corny; it is totally irrelevant to the speedy, action-laden motif of the serial. Sometimes they do get it right, though. In Chapter 3, there is appropriately rousing music under the cliffhanger. At the end of Chapter 11, there is some surprisingly tense string music at the final moments of the episode, leading to the cliffhanger. It's quite effective, but it makes you wonder where the music director was during the previous 20 reels.

Hank Davis

The Return of Chandu

No disrespect intended, but it's sort of hard to take this loopy old melodrama seriously. Even by the deliciously warped standards of movie serials, this one is nearly in a class by itself. To its credit, *The Return of Chandu* (Principal Pictures, 1934) has Bela Lugosi, and that makes up for a multitude of sins. More than that, the serial casts Bela in what is probably the closest he ever came to playing the hero. Needless to say, Bela was the villain *du jour* in a seemingly endless stream of films, whose quality became progressively more threadbare as the years went by.

But back to 1934. Here, Bela gets to shine in the role of Guardian of the Good. He plays Frank Chandler, alter ego of Chandu the Magician. Even though the young 'uns in the movie call him "Uncle Frank," it's clear from the start that this Uncle has another side to his identity. Chandler, we are told, was born in the Orient and has a whole array of magical powers. He performs tricks that defy rational explanation, can control people's wills and is not above turning himself invisible when the need arises.

The character of Chandu the Magician was no stranger to American popular culture. Chandu was already an established radio star prior to this 1934 serial. In fact, just two years earlier, *Chandu the Magician* had appeared on the silver

screen in an early big-budget MGM talkie. He was played by suave leading man Edmund Lowe. To confuse things slightly, Lugosi also appeared in that film, as Chandu's archrival, Roxor. Plainly, his appearance as Roxor, an evil scientist bent on world domination with the help of a ray gun, was a lot closer to the public's perception of Lugosi. In any case, two years later, the character of Chandu was back on the screen, this time played, not by Lowe, but by Lugosi. A tad confusing, to say the least.

As the serial opens, Chandu's niece, otherwise known as Princess Nadji, has been sent to live in California. Right from the start, she senses terrible danger. Her American cousin tries to cheer her up and turn her into a normal party animal with such classic lines as "This isn't

Egypt. I thought we left all that nonsense behind with the mummies." But Nadji is not convinced. There is a whole bunch of evildoers, otherwise known as the Sorcerers of Ubasti, who want to abduct Nadji to their evil little island, where they can sacrifice her and bring some ancient god back to life. Thankfully, Princess Nadji has Uncle Bela, a.k.a. Chandu, on her side.

Chapter 1 ends with Chandu facing his butler and mesmerizing him in order to gain information about the threat to Nadji. Before the butler can reveal anything of value, he is shot in the back with a blowgun through an open window. Curiously, when the butler falls to the floor, the wound seems to be in his chest. Per-

Bela Lugosi as the heroic Chandu.

haps Chandu should begin by working his magic on the continuity department.

Once Chandu saves Nadji from the first wave of bad guys in Chapter 4, the scene shifts to the mysterious island of Lemuria. Apparently, the lost Kingdom of Lemuria (not to be confused with the island) waits beneath the sea to rise up and take over the world with its black magic. Or something like that. The only thing stopping the evil natives is a blood sacrifice, which is where Princess Nadji comes in. It's going to be a heck of a challenge for Uncle Frank and, as the closing credits ask at the end of Chapter 4, "Will Chandu relax his vigilance?"

Vigilant or not, it's unclear whether Bela and Nadji are supposed to have a chaste relationship. Is he the well-meaning father figure protecting her virginal soul, or are his intentions not quite so spiritual? The All-American looking college kids (circa 1934) who surround them keep referring to him as Uncle Frank, but instead of a character from *Leave It To Beaver*, we get Bela Lugosi, looking all

Chandu (Bela Lugosi) is captured in Lemuria.

sinister and wearing a jeweled turban. Not your average Uncle Frank. Also, Bela seems to have a very non-American view of personal space; he leans into Nadji's face quite often and she always seems to be on the verge of a swoon.

Whenever Bela/Uncle Frank/Chandu gets stuck, he gets all pensive-looking and says, "Oh Yogi, my teacher." Next thing you know, this stocky little guy with a catcher's mitt and a New York Yankees uniform appears. But seriously, what happens is we hear a voice giving Bela some Oprah-like tips such as "Don't lose faith" or "Look harder." Seems like pretty lame stuff, but nobody said the journey to spirituality was easy.

Some of the dialogue in Chapter 7 is priceless. Shipwrecked on an island, Bela says to his nephew, "Look! Footprints! This island must be inhabited." To which the nephew replies, "I bet they're natives!" As opposed to what? Tourists from New Jersey? And Bela takes it further with "Those are the footprints of cat worshippers." Good work, Bela! What gave it away? Was it the instep? The arch? The natives are described in the title cards as "half-human savages." Wonder what the other half is. It's hard to tell by looking, since what they seem mostly like is a bunch of poorly paid extras in skimpy costumes.

A word about three of the actors supporting Bela. Maria Alba, a Spanish-born actress who often played exotics in about 20 films between 1928 and 1935, plays Nadji. Her film career was divided between American and Spanish productions. She died in 1999. Also appearing in a small role is Joseph Swickard, who would go on the following year to play Dr. Manyuse in *The Lost City*. And then there's Lucien Prival, appearing in the role of Vindhyan, the sorcerer priest. Prival also appeared as Dagna, another sorcerer-priest type in Republic's 1936 serial (their first) *Darkest Africa*. He was absolutely horrible in that role and, sad to say, he's even worse here. Prival seems to have graduated from the James Cagney tough-guy school of acting, and can't get it through his head that he's supposed to be playing an exotic jungle character, rather than some kind of New York street punk. Whether it's bad casting or bad acting or both, Prival's presence adds a jarring note to both serials.

All things considered, *The Return of Chandu* has a pretty impressive look for a cheaply made independent serial. There are lots of exotic locales and lavish sets. You may not be able to place some of the sets, but you'll have no trouble spotting the great wall and giant gate left over from *King Kong*. Next to recycling footage from earlier

Chandu rescues Nadji (Maria Alba)

films, there is no better way to cut costs than reusing the lavish sets from earlier big-budget films. *Chandu* also profits from some appropriately exotic title music composed by Abe Meyer. There is also an eerie eight-note sequence played on the tympani. It has a genuinely creepy effect, but ultimately suffers from overuse.

In the end, things work out OK on the island of Lemuria. Just when Chandu is really up against the wall, he is given the one-time, nontransferable right to invoke the Great Incantation. The words are no sooner out of his mouth when the whole expensive palatial set starts to crumble, killing the High Priest of Black Magic and all his "half-human" followers. The independent Principal studios hedged their bets by releasing *Chandu* not only as a 12-chapter serial, but also as two separate feature films. The first, bearing the same title as this serial, consisted of the first four chapters edited down (slightly) to feature length. The remaining eight chapters were condensed (obviously a heavier hand was used) into a second feature called *Chandu on Mystery Island*. If there had been plastic dolls and t-shirt rights to *Chandu*, you can bet Principal Pictures would have sold those too.

Hank Davis

1935
The Adventures of Frank Merriwell

Relatively few of the heroes of movie serials began life on the pages of comic books. It's true; they may have *looked* like comic book heroes by the time the serials got through with them. But in some cases, heroes of the cliffhangers came from sources quite removed from the comics. One of the least common sources were actual books with real covers and nothing but words on their pages. Frank Merriwell was one such case, and a very famous one at that, although his name has been all but forgotten. Merriwell was the college hero of a series of stories written by Gilbert S. Patton (under the pen name Burt L. Standish) in the early 1900s. Merriwell also appeared on the radio at two different times. There was a brief series of 15-minute dramas playing three times a week between March and June 1934 on NBC. The show wasn't much of a success, but it did better the second time around as a weekly self-contained 30-minute drama appearing (on NBC) between 1946 and 1949.

In many ways Frank Merriwell is the prototype for Jack Armstrong, the All American Boy. Remember that a college education was a pretty rare thing back then. Higher education was, to put it mildly, an elitist business. Back then, people without college degrees, which is to say nearly everyone, had some pretty clear attitudes about those who enjoyed such privilege. College girls, for example, were often viewed as spoiled debutantes, and the guys were seen as snobby, well-dressed fops, who sang college songs, said, "boola boola" or "zis boom bah" a lot, and had lots of free time on their hands.

Just about every one of these stereotypes is on display in *The Adventures of Frank Merriwell*. Frank, himself, is a case in point except for two important differences. 1: He is *not* a snob. The writers take great pains to show us how well he gets along with everybody, whether or not they're as rich and talented as he is. 2: No matter what you can say about him, Frank is one hell of an athlete. He's a star at everything. You name it—football, baseball, rowing, high jumping—Frank can do it all. And he certainly does it all in this 1935 serial from Universal. The opening titles identify Frank Merriwell as "Hero of a Thousand College Stories." All the guys want to be his pal; all the women want to be his girl. No wonder his biggest adversary in this serial is not a masked villain with a death ray, but a guy from his own class who is just sick of Frank's effortless success.

It's not Frank's fault that he's rich, talented and good-looking. He does everything he can to be a regular guy. He says "swell" and "fellows" a lot. He really tries to fit in and he's certainly got his hands full of trouble in this serial. When he's not scoring last minute touchdowns, pole vaulting to victory, hitting home runs and pitching shutout baseball, he's battling undersea monsters, fighting savage Indians and wrestling lions and tigers. Then there are the train

Classic Cliffhangers

Jean Rogers and Don Briggs with coach Jack Donovan

wrecks, runaway buses and washed out bridges. And don't forget the bad guys who are after his father's gold. Life is just one big challenge when you're rich and good-looking.

Without a doubt, this is an adventure-packed serial (advertised as the "super-serial of the year"). Director Cliff Smith never hangs around one location very long. We go from the college campus to a north woods logging camp, to a sailing ship, to the Mexican mountains. The serial may look old but it never looks cheap. Well, almost never. It's sort of hilarious to see Frank in his vintage diving suit attacked by some grainy stock footage of an octopus. Close-ups of Frank's fearful face in a diving mask are intercut with ancient looking inserts of an octopus in a tank. Technically, it's the low point of the serial.

There are some unintentional moments of hilarity. In Chapter 1, Frank stops to save a dog on his way to the big game (great vintage baseball footage, by the way). Right away we see that Frank's an OK guy—he chooses a puppy over a ball game. But then his reckless driving to get to the game on time nearly kills some innocent people on the road. Frank's response? He takes out his wallet and pays off the victims.

Somewhere around Chapter 10, Frank rescues his father from the clutches of a few bad guys. By now Frank and his college pals have ended up south of the border where they are dismayed to find that the people "speak Mexican." Frank's solution to the communication problem is to speak louder, and say things like, "Oh, you've *got* to understand." At this point, the serial abruptly turns into a Western complete with a posse of Mexicans soldiers riding to the rescue ("We are always berry happy to be of service to the Americans").

Hank Davis

The Merriwell family has a black servant named Jeff who is predictably fearful and superstitious. By Chapter 11, when you think most of the trouble is over, Jeff announces, "I feels trouble in mah bones." Of course, he's right. You just have to trust your houseboy. Part of the trouble comes when Frank and his college pals (all of whom look to be well into their 30s) visit the local circus. They sit in some wooden stands and watch (silent film) inserts of a circus. The circus clips are almost as grainy as the octopus in Chapter 8. Suddenly a freak storm hits town and the giant tent is torn to bits, leaving wild animals running amuck. Frank battles some lions from the earlier film in crudely edited inserts in which he plainly never appears. Somebody rolls around in the straw with jungle beasts, but when Frank gets up, he doesn't have a scratch on him. He straightens his wavy hair and the gang moves on to the next challenge.

Frank's chief rival Peters tries to frame him with bogus tales of gamblers (in a plot line lifted almost directly from Mascot's serial *The Galloping Ghost* with college football hero Red Grange). The problem is that no one in his right mind would believe that the rich, good-looking and righteous Frank would ever throw a game, much less for money. When Frank and his best friend tell the coach what's going on, they have no trouble convincing him that the gambler story is a ruse. Frank turns to his buddy and utters the immortal line, "That coach is really one white guy."

This serial features a surprising amount of actual footage of athletic events. In Episode 11, Frank's cozy little alma mater (Fardale College) plays their big game against "Tech." Newsreel footage inserts are used from a big game somewhere. There are at least 50,000 people in the stands. You can bet your life it wasn't filmed at Fardale. In fact, it's surprising that Universal had to invent a fictional college for their hero. Apparently Yale wanted nothing to do with Frank or this serial (or their price was too high) in 1935. When Frank Merriwell finally did appear in a comic book (very briefly) in the 1950s, it was called *Frank Merriwell At Yale*.

Despite all his athletic prowess and wavy hair, actor Don Briggs speaks in a rather high-pitched, melodramatic voice. There's not much macho in sight in this serial. Even the bad guys and their leader aren't very menacing. There's plenty of fighting, of course, but surprisingly Frank isn't very good at it. More often than not, he's knocked out. Whatever Frank lacks in fighting skill doesn't seem to bother the lovely Jean Rogers who plays his best girl, insofar as it's possible to tell that Frank has one. But, alas, the relationship didn't last. Several months later, Ms. Rogers graduated from Fardale and moved to the planet Mongo, where she snuggled up to Flash Gordon and tried her best to avoid the clutches of Ming the Merciless. But that's another story.

The Call of the Savage

This 1935 serial from Universal was based on a highly successful story appearing in *Argosy* magazine, originally called "Jan of the Jungle." That was probably a credible title back in the early 1930s, but today it takes a little getting used to. "Jan of the Jungle"? How about "Mel of the Market"? Or "Pete of the Pool Hall"? "Hal of the Highway" or "Bill of the Ball Park?" You don't want to get started on this; it can go on for a while. Fortunately, the nice folks at Universal named their serial *The Call of the Savage,* which keeps the meter intact but doesn't lend itself to such easy parody.

The film stars Noah Beery, Jr., who, along with his actor father, was no stranger to the world of movie serials. The direction by Louis Friedlander (a.k.a. Lew Landers) is surprisingly pedestrian. Just a year earlier, Landers had done a noteworthy job directing *The Vanishing Shadow* for Universal. There's nothing memorable about his touch here. The plot begins somewhat strangely: The Carnafellow Foundation (a clever amalgam of Carnegie and Rockefeller) announces a $500,000 award for the discovery of a cure for infantile paralysis (the word "polio" is never mentioned). To this end, the Foundation arranges for four doctors to go to Africa to conduct their research. But here's the catch: The award doesn't simply support their collective efforts; it's a prize for the individual who cures the disease. Isn't that dandy? You can just imagine the competition, treachery and god-knows what else this kind of arrangement is going to stir up among these four doctors.

The evil plotting begins within six minutes of the first chapter. It's hard to imagine what the Foundation directors were thinking. Were they trying to find a cure for polio or cre-

Battling each other for JUNGLE SUPREMACY! in the Heart of DARKEST AFRICA!

FIRST TIME on the SCREEN

PREMIER PICTURES presents

SAVAGE FURY

with
NOAH BEERY, Jr.
DOROTHY SHORT
From The Argosy Magazine Story
"JAN OF THE JUNGLE"
Directed by LOUIS FRIEDLANDER

ate a movie serial? Another oddity is that these doctors seem to be doing their experiments on lions, tigers, leopards and chimpanzees. Why? Since when does biomedical research depend upon jungle creatures as subjects? If nothing else, this gives the producers the excuse to insert stock footage of natives and wild animals. *Lots* of it. It's true that jungle movies typically depend on stock footage to flesh things out, but this serial takes that device to a whole new level. Universal had a full vault in 1935, including quite a bit of silent footage that also appears here, appropriately dubbed with sound.

Within minutes of the movie's start, Dr. Trevor finds a cure. Take a moment and think about that. This is supposedly 1920, some 35 years before Jonas Salk announced his cure for polio that we all know about. Perhaps Dr. Salk was slowed down by his reluctance to experiment on lions and tigers? Anyway, as soon as Trevor tells the good news to his wife (who looks like she's dressed for a formal debutante ball back in New York) he adds, "I have reason to believe someone is trying to get that formula from me." Gee, doc, what tipped you off? Was it the sullen looking guys lurking outside every door, or was it the half a million bucks that hangs over the discovery?

In order to protect his cure from these hovering evil forces, Trevor engraves half of the formula on to a metal wristband that he clamps on to his 3-year-old son, Jan. See where this is going? Jan heads off into the jungle with his pet chimp named Chicma. No sooner are the two of them off the set when all hell breaks loose. There are perils everywhere, including the evil Dr. Bracken played by Walter Miller. Animals are inexplicably breaking out of their cages all over the compound; they are tearing each other apart and have a pretty good go at the good doctor and his wife too. Soon the research station is engulfed in flames and natives are scurrying everywhere (more stock footage). Meanwhile, safely away in the jungle is the little boy who will grow up to be the title character (of the magazine story), with the formula to cure polio clamped mutely around his wrist. The remaining doctors, schemers all, assume the cure is lost and return to New York empty handed.

For the next 15 years or so, little Jan grows up, slipping safely among stock footage of marauding lions and tigers and monkeys and cheetahs and hyenas. Then in a rapid dissolve, we are looking at 18-year-old Jan, a.k.a. Noah Beery, Jr., still wearing his bracelet and swinging through the jungle in a loincloth, while stock footage of wild animals continues unabated around him. Now the plot takes a twist. A boat arrives containing the remaining doctors, who have been hearing strange reports about a white boy living in the jungle among stock footage of wild animals. Could this be young Jan, all grown up and still carrying the formula with him?

As the doctors disembark (looking no older than when we first met them), it is now the present day (1935). Not surprisingly, their greed surfaces immediately and the plotting begins anew. There's a formula to be recovered and money to be made. We learn that Dr. Trevor, Jan's father and rightful owner of the formula,

Noah Beery, Jr. helps his pal H.L. Woods conquer a fear of snakes.

is still alive. His memory is lost and he wanders aimlessly through the jungle, also dodging stock footage of dangerous animals. He and Jan are really cut from the same loincloth.

At some point Jan meets and becomes smitten with the lovely Mona, played by Dorothy Short. Mona is actually a bit of a pain in the neck. She screams at virtually everything that moves around her, and every one of her little jungle walks ends in some kind of disaster. She attracts hungry lions the way most people attract mosquitoes. She even manages to *back* over a ledge into a lake full of crocodiles. Maybe Jan is attracted to her klutziness. Actually, it's hard to know what's going on in Jan's head, if anything. The writers actually give us a "Me Jan, you Mona scene." The truth is, Jan doesn't appear any too bright. Admittedly, he's been out of circulation for 15 years, but some of his actions seem to slip beyond "wild" into "slow-witted." There's a classic moment when Mona falls asleep on the floor of a cave. Jan looks at her and utters the immortal line "Mona sleep! Ha ha ha!"

Dorothy Short deserves special mention. She made her career working in Westerns, serials and B-movies in the 1930s and 1940s, appearing in 35 films

Hank Davis

through 1953. Her claim to fame was starring in the cult classic, anti-marijuana film *Tell Your Children* (1938), which spent years as a road show staple before claiming an entirely new audience in the late 1960s under the title *Reefer Madness*. Short died in 1963 and never got to see a whole new generation of audiences howling at her mannered performance from under a thick veil of sweet-smelling smoke.

If anything, there are too many animals here, which seems an odd complaint to make about a jungle movie. But it's true. The animal shots seem haphazardly inserted from all kinds of poorly matched earlier sources, and often this grainy stock footage gets in the way of the plot. In Chapter 10, for example, things grind to a halt while we watch some footage of Zulus hunt and kill a lion. Actually, some of these scenes would never have passed muster with Disney. They are far too graphic and serve as a reminder that it really *is* a jungle out there.

When the lava starts flowing in Chapter 9, this adventure kicks into high gear. Forget Jan of the Jungle; it now looks a lot more like Jan of the French Foreign Legion. Once we're inside the Lost City of Mu, things look and sound like a *Flash Gordon* serial set in a magical science fiction empire. In fact, there is some very noticeable *Flash Gordon* music here a year before *Flash* was filmed. When you hear the sound of the ceiling of spears descending on to the heroes at the end of Chapter 10, you'll recognize it as the noise made by one of Flash's space ships as it darts across the universe. Ming the Merciless isn't here, but in his place we have John Davidson chewing the scenery as the evil Prince Samu.

Whether he's playing Jan of the Jungle or a sidekick of Tailspin Tommy (Universal, 1934-1935) or the father of television's Jim Rockford, Noah Beery, Jr., brought the same unassuming, sweet-natured charm to his roles. No wonder James Garner was devastated by Beery's death in 1994. It does seem a little odd to find what seems like Will Rogers or Huck Finn swinging from the trees in darkest Africa, but when they hired Beery to play the part, the producers must have known that was exactly what they were going to get.

The Lost City

Take a deep breath. This is it. This one takes the cake. *The Lost City* is by far the most outrageous, over-the-top, bizarre movie serial ever made. It's unlikely that a major studio or even a Poverty Row outfit like Mascot would have released something this extreme. Produced in 1935 by distributor Sherman Krellberg, *The Lost City* set new standards for bad scripting, bad acting and bad direction that may have been approached but were never collectively equaled over the next 20 years. And did we mention the racism? Again, this serial sets new lows in a way that makes Willie Best and Stepin Fetchit seem like Martin Luther King.

This is not to say that this serial isn't lovable in a perverse, high camp kind of way. In fact, it is. The acting is often laughable; this is another one of those silent movies that talk. The villain, played by William "Stage" Boyd—a nickname used to distinguish him from Hopalong Cassidy's alter ego—simply chews up the scenery in the role of evil scientist Zolok. Boyd had fallen a great distance since his Broadway stage days and died of acute alcoholism on March 20, just before this serial was released to theaters. There's no telling how inebriated he was during much of this performance. Claudia Dell, the perpetually endangered heroine,

brings all the mannerisms of the silent era to her role. She seems incapable of experiencing an emotion without screaming or wringing her hands. Trivia fans may note that Boyd and Dell had actually appeared together at least once before, in the 1932 independent production called *The Midnight Warning*. William (Billy) Bletcher, who plays the sympathetic hunchback/dwarf named Gorzo, provides an almost Shakespearian touch that is totally at odds with everything happening around him. It's a treat to hear him improvise "ooga booga" language with the natives. Bletcher is another interesting story. His credits—often for unbilled voiceovers—include more than 300 films in a career that ran from 1915 to 1971. One would never know it from watching him here, but Bletcher made a good living in the film industry, working in everything from Bugs Bunny car-

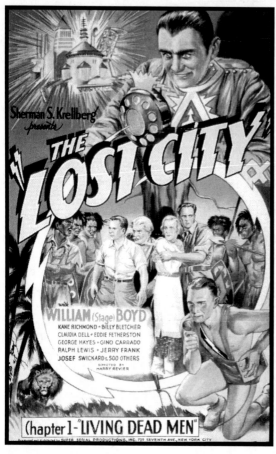

toons and *Our Gang* comedies to *The Wizard of Oz.*

The hero, played by serial veteran Kane Richmond, is appropriately wooden. It is the supporting actors, however, that command more attention. Look for Western movie sidekick "Gabby" Hayes billed here as "Geo F. Hayes" in the relatively unlovable role of Butterfield. He's every bit as greedy as Zolok but, in truth, he's the most believable actor in sight. Finally, look for strongman Jerry Frank appearing as Appollon. Actually, it's hard to miss him. He's quite a good example of what they used to call "beefcake." Frank has the best serial pedigree of any actor on the lot. The muscular actor/stuntman appeared (usually as a "thug" or "henchman") in at least 20 serials including *The Batman, Dick Tracy Returns* and *Flash Gordon's Trip to Mars.*

The plot reprises many familiar themes. It starts with the Earth being plagued by severe weather disturbances (provided by the usual silent movie and newsreel stock footage). The planet needs a good-looking swashbuckler to save it. Bruce Gordon (Richmond) pinpoints the disturbances as coming from darkest Africa and sets off to make things right. Just one year later, Flash Gordon would face the same crisis and pinpoint the planet Mongo as its source. But that's another story. So off goes Bruce (not to be confused with Flash) Gordon, along with his trusty sidekick Jerry in pursuit of a solution. When they get to Africa, they are directed to Magnetic Mountain, where they find arch villain Zolok at the core of the problem. He's kidnapped the good-hearted Dr. Manyus (Joseph Swickard) and his lovely daughter Natcha (Dell), and is using Manyus' inventions for evil rather than for the benefit of mankind.

Some notable moments to watch for: After passing the giant rubber spider in Chapter 8, the special electrical effects produced by Kenneth Strickfaden are admirable. In case this name is unfamiliar to you, think of Dr. Frankenstein's lab and those waves of electrical current zapping everywhere and arcing toward the sky. Even in the present lowly production, Strickfaden's work is, once again, impressive. In 1935 alone, Strickfaden contributed to *The Phantom Empire*, the classic *Bride of Frankenstein*, as well as this serial. A new biography of Strickfaden by Harry Goldman, *Dr. Frankenstein's Electrician* (McFarland) commemorates this forgotten craftsman.

One of Zolok's pet projects is taking the local natives and turning them into mindless giants. It's not so clear that these guys were ever great thinkers before they were transformed, but turning them into giants really adds insult to injury. The natives don't seem eager to participate in Zolok's plan. Sam Baker, who just happened to have the right physical qualities for the role, plays the main giant zombie. Baker had no difficulty memorizing his dialogue, which consists entirely of guttural grunts and shrieks. Baker's brief Hollywood career focused largely on jungle B-movies, as characters known as Gwana and Zungu. He also played the title role in the 1927 opus *The Missing Link*. Presumably, Zolok figures he can take over the world with an army of these mute zombies, which he goes about creating one at a time. It's sheer serial lunacy. This zombifying machine is, again, the work of Dr. Manyus, who regrets that Zolok is putting it to such inhumane use. It's a nice sentiment, but exactly what beneficial use did Manyus have in mind when he created it? Stretching bodies and destroying minds for the *good* of mankind?

Television is everywhere in this 1935 production, implying it was an appliance found in every home. Of course, 70 years ago, few people had a clue about how television worked and fears about someone using it to eavesdrop were rampant. Zolok monitors his entire kingdom ("a radius of a thousand miles") using television. No cameras (which were huge, clunky devices in 1935) are visible anywhere, but all you've got to do is try to have a furtive conversation in a cave and Zolok will zero right in on you. A paranoid's delight: Television sees you everywhere, all the time. One more invention is worth noting. Dr. Manyus has created an operation to turn black men into white. Instant white folks. You just march black Africans in and out come white men. Presumably, the NBA did not sponsor this research. "Dr. Manyus, you're a genius!" exclaims Grant Richmond. Dr. Manyus smiles with pride and replies, "Science can accomplish anything!" Again: Surgical genocide is just one more way he was hoping to benefit mankind before the evil Zolok forced him into servitude.

In Chapter 11, Dr. Manyus and his daughter have two of the funniest lines in the screenplay. The good doc says, "Zolok, spare us this horror," to which Natcha replies, "It's no use, father. He's so crooo-ell." Not since Good King Wenceslas gathered winter fu-el has a one syllable English word been so dragged out for effect. One of the most delightfully cheesy things about this serial is the (brief) closing music that accompanies each chapter. This production uses a written version of the Columbia Studios voiceover technique. We read something like "Did the lions get Natcha?" or "What will happen to Ben & Jerry? WILL THEY ESCAPE?" Meanwhile, we hear an orchestral crescendo, written to create or

"The LOST CITY"

sustain tension. It sounds like a tiny excerpt from an entire score but the 10-second closing is all we get. What makes it cheesy and memorable at the same time is the fact that the kettledrum—which plays a big role in this brief segment—is pitifully out of tune. His big note is a good half-tone flat. Did nobody hear the problem? You can tune kettledrums with a tiny device that looks just like an old-fashioned skate key. Maybe the joke about drummers being tone-deaf is really true. In any case, this same musical cue not only appears here but also is reused in *The Clutching Hand*, another independent serial from 1936.

Some time in the early 1960s, a TV channel in New York began to broadcast *The Lost City* as part of a series of vintage serials. Their intent may have been harmless entertainment but they never got past the first few episodes before the switchboard lit up with outraged protests. The 1960s was not a time to be sharing the racism in this serial under the heading of "nostalgia." The casual viewer might look at this serial and wonder why anyone in his right mind would bother writing or reading about it 70 years after its release. If you've read this far, you obviously don't need convincing that the extremes of popular culture are worth understanding. If you're a bit ashamed to have such unusual interests, take comfort in this: When producer Sherman Krellberg died in 1979, his widow offered her husband's files to the Library of Congress. They willingly accepted for their collection his correspondence and business records, a cool 11,000 items in all, detailing the dealings of a vintage entertainment schlockmeister. You can visit the collection yourself; it consumes nearly 20 linear feet of shelf space in our nation's capitol.

The Miracle Rider

He may once have been "The Idol of Every Boy in the World," but by 1935 Tom Mix was an aging cowboy star whose body had been surgically wired back together, who dyed his hair black, and who worried that his false teeth might interfere with his dialogue. He was in his mid-50s, the IRS was hounding him for back taxes and he had five ex-wives dunning him for alimony. In short, Tom Mix was not in his prime when he made *The Miracle Rider*. But he still commanded a hefty price ($10,000 per week for four weeks' work) and he could still draw audiences into theaters. Incredibly, this serial, which cost Mascot about $80,000 to make, produced revenues close to $1 million. Let's put that cool million into perspective. The initial chapter which runs over 40 minutes, cost theaters $15 to rent; the remaining chapters cost $5 each. The entire 15-chapter serial could be rented for $85 and Mascot got its product out there to over 12,000 theaters. Mix helped with the publicity, calling the serial "a rip-snortin' he-man chapter play which would thrill every kid in town."

What do we find when we turn off the publicity machine and look at this se-rial with 70 years' hindsight? There certainly is plenty of rip-snortin' action and most of the men are certifiably virile. As for thrilling every kid in town, let's just say that kids were probably easier to thrill 70-plus years ago. At 15 chapters, the serial is plainly too long. If you think of it as a movie, it runs over 5 hours! That's just too much for the basic plot. Beware 5-hour-long movies you can summarize in one sentence: Mix befriends the Ravenhead Indians, who are being run off their land by evildoers who want to mine a secret explosive on their land. How's that? We can fill in some details, of course. Mix is a Texas Ranger whose father was killed protecting the Indians. Mix has vowed to continue his dad's

Bob Kartman as Longboat

work. The Ravenhead tribe is basically decent, if a bit gullible and superstitious. Chief Blackwing (he was murdered, too) has a daughter named Ruth (Jean Gale) who looks like a cute white chick wearing an Indian costume. She's sort of flirty with Mix although, in true serial form, he remains oblivious until the final moments of the last chapter. Longboat (played by the ever-serviceable Bob Kortman) is the one bad Indian. He sells out his people and works in cahoots with the bad guys who have promised to make him Chief when they take over.

Charles Middleton plays the head villain, Zaroff. Middleton would go on next year to play the defining role of his career: Ming the Merciless in the original *Flash Gordon* serial. Middleton would actually return twice more in that role in 1938 and 1940. He's really a good actor, ideally suited to bad guys. It's fun to watch him work here. In some ways he is the only actor on the set who brings any depth to his part. He seems genuinely duplicitous and lacking in conscience. And then there's his voice. As soon as you hear it, you think "Ming! What's he doing here?"

The cast also includes Jason Robards, Sr. as one of Zaroff's henchmen. It's not a particularly noteworthy role or performance, but it's interesting to see the father of the more famous Robards, Jr., in action. One of the serial's strengths is the present day (1935) setting. That enables us see horses (lots of them) interacting with more modern forms of transportation: Horses chasing cars and oil trucks and motorcycles with sidecars are not everyday sights.

The serial is very pro-Indian, which may rest well with today's sentiments, but was something of a box-office oddity in 1935. It's plainly the white men (except for Mix) who are the troublemakers. In fact, in Chapter 1 ("The Vanishing Indian") we begin with a history lesson showing how notable men like Daniel Boone, Davey Crockett and Buffalo Bill attempted to combat the greed and callousness of white men around them. Time after time they'd face the "Let's kill 'em all" attitude towards Indians by suggesting, "There's plenty of land and buffalo here for all of us." These warnings would usually be ignored, leading to some sort of bloodshed (courtesy of stock footage from movies like *Last of the Mohicans* or *Fighting with Kit Carson*). It is in this spirit that Tom Morgan (Mix) becomes a Texas Ranger. The Indians make him an honorary Ravenhead and name him "The Miracle Rider." It's actually a pretty classy way to start a serial.

Enter Ming the Merciless, a.k.a. Zaroff. Zaroff's oil company is just a front for his real moneymaker, a rich vein of X-94, a super-explosive found in quantity under the Ravenhead reservation. Needless to say, he wants these noble savages to go live somewhere else so he can do his mining in peace. Zaroff has a little speech that he makes in just about every chapter of this serial (he's still repeating it as late as Chapter 13). It goes something like this: "I'll be the most powerful man in the world. Kings and Queens will be at my feet." To prove his point, Zaroff has some kind of TV screen on his office wall which flashes emails or teletype messages saying things like "Awaiting your next shipment of X-94. Will pay you $5 million on delivery." The messages, by the way, are always signed "Leon." An odd touch. Is Trotsky behind this intrigue?

Zaroff's strategy to get rid of the Indians is to make them believe that the legendary Firebird is after them. To tap into this scary bit of tribal lore, he has constructed a small remote control rocket that he launches periodically, causing them to flee in terror. "The land is cursed," they mutter in fear as they make plans to leave. Mix keeps trying to tell them that it's all a scam, but they have Longboat, one of their own, reinforcing their terror. The rocket subplot adds a very effective science fiction touch to this serial, much in the spirit of Gene Autry's *The Phantom Empire*, another Mascot production from 1935. In fact, genre bending is one of this serial's strongest points. Just when you think it's a Western, someone pulls up in a car or an oil truck. And just when you think it's cowboys and Indians, a rocket ship goes flying overhead.

Some moments to watch for: They missed a chance for a great take-out at the start of Chapter 3. Mix is parachuting out of the rocket with nowhere to land below. Along comes his horse at a gallop. Will he land right in the saddle? Unfortunately, they settle for a more prosaic outcome with Mix landing in a tree and then jumping onto the horse's back. The take-out in Chapter 5 involving wild horses and a burning wagon is really quite spectacular. On the other hand, some of the other take-outs are absolute cheats. Chapter 8 begins with Mix surviving a climb down a mountain on a rope that must have had kids hooting and hollering in protest. Some of the chapter titles are surprising for 1935: Chapter 5 is called "The Dragnet" (about 15 years before Jack Webb hit his stride); Chapter 8 is called "Guerrilla Warfare." The scenes with Mix and Ming matching wits are a highlight. Too bad they happen pretty late in the serial. Finally—check out those Indian blankets. Many have designs resembling swastikas, a decoration innocently embployed by Native Americans many years before it was used as a symbol of evil.

A last word about the girl and the horse. First the girl. Everything you need to know about how serials and serial heroes felt about women is on display in

Tom Mix uses his foot and fist on Tom London.

the final chapter. Mix has just learned that he's been appointed Director of Indian Affairs in Washington. He's about to leave, which distresses the leading lady no small amount. Incredibly, he notices this and invites her to come with him! Just when you're thinking, "Wow! This serial really *is* progressive," Mix drops the other shoe. He says "The Director of Indian Affairs needs a..." Wife, right? Wrong. Instead he says, "needs a secretary." Oh, boy! A desk job in the nation's capitol! What a romantic guy.

And now the horse, which is plainly a greater presence in Mix's emotional life: First of all, Tony, Jr. gets star billing, right under Mix's name in the credits, above the title. Throughout the film, Tony, Jr. has been portrayed as the intellectual equal of, say, Rin Tin Tin. In Chapter 2, some men are sitting around a table and there's a knock on the door. One of them gets up and opens it, only to find Mix's horse standing there with a "Come help my master" look on his face. Incredible, here's a horse who knocks rather than kicks down the door. At the start of Chapter 9, when Mix is temporarily blinded, he says to Tony, Jr., "You've got to be my eyes. Take me back to headquarters," and the horse immediately turns and heads down the trail. In the final chapter, Tony saves the day by honking the car horn and startling the thugs who are holding Mix at gunpoint. What a horse! Too bad this is Chapter 15. Otherwise you might come back next week in time to watch Tony tune the car engine, change the oil and rotate the tires.

The Phantom Empire

In a career that spanned half a century, Gene Autry proved that minimal talent was no impediment to success. Taking an unblinking look at his accomplishments, we can see a man not blessed with striking good looks, assertive virility or acting ability, who was hardly a great singer or musician. Yet he managed to remain a popular favorite throughout a string of B-movies and over 300 pedestrian recordings. It's true, "Rudolph the Red-Nosed Reindeer" made him a bundle and he invested well when his acting days were over, but you have to wonder what kind of karma carried this non-exceptional talent to the status of American icon.

Autry signed a contract with Nat Levine and Mascot Pictures relatively early in his career. The early days of Autry's film career are recounted in fascinating detail in Jon Tuska's book *The Vanishing Legion: A History of Mascot Pictures 1927-1935* (McFarland). Tuska describes Autry as "the blandest of screen presences." Studio owner Nat Levine called him "completely raw material." Like Tuska,

Levine does not mince words. "He knew nothing about acting, lacked poise, and was awkward. He wasn't much of a horseman either." Autry was sent to work with stuntman and second-unit director Yakima Canutt to develop some semblance of expertise with horses.

After two supporting roles, Autry was billed as "Radio's Singing Cowboy" and given the starring role in one of the great movie serials of all time, *The Phantom Empire*. For those of us who love serials, it is hard not to enjoy this one. From just about every adult critical point of view, it is an atrocious piece of juvenile filmmaking. But, of course, movie serials were never meant to be judged by critical adults. For what makes *Citizen Kane* great makes serials laughable. On the other hand, for sheer lunacy, innocence and zany charm, there are few serials that can top *The Phantom Empire*.

Produced in early 1935, this serial was really ahead of its time. At least it was ahead of landmark productions

Gene Autry confronts Stanley Blystone in the Kingdom of Murania.

like Universal's *Flash Gordon* (1936), which copied much of *Empire's* look and style. In fact, were it not for the popular and financial success of this serial, *Flash Gordon* might never have been made—at least, the lavish version we all know and love.

Consider the plot of *The Phantom Empire*. There is a rich radium deposit located just under Gene's Radio Ranch. Of course, he doesn't know about it. But the bad guys do and they want easy access to it. That won't happen as long as Gene and his pals are hanging around the ranch, drawing tourists and sitting on the front porch making music. If the bad guys can just eliminate the whole lot of these yokels and their daily radio broadcasts, they will be rich beyond measure. Gene, on the other hand, just wants to "aw shucks" his way through life, showing up for his daily 2 p.m. broadcasts so he won't lose his contract with the network. Every day, he comes barreling up just in time, parks Champion, grabs his axe and sings some Western swing ditty while his good natured, lobotomized-looking pals provide musical backup.

This would have been a fine, regulation issue serial if it had stopped right there. To its credit, *The Phantom Empire* goes way beyond. There's a whole other level of adventure lurking just out of sight. About 20,000 feet beneath their cowboy boots lay the underground kingdom of Murania. Queen Tika is pretty riled up by all the squabbling that's going above her head. She watches the surface people on her special TV screens and moans about life up there on the surface. What's wrong with these people? They always seem to be in a hurry. "Death, suffering, speed, accidents." She's deeply troubled by the culture up there and wants to keep the idiots on the surface out of her perfect underground city. With all the tourists at the Ranch and all this plotting over radium, it's getting harder and harder to keep two worlds apart. Note that Tika is a rarity among alien rulers: She is not bent on domination of the Earth. She has no plans to invade the surface. She is the Greta Garbo of the underground—she just vants to be left alone.

In addition to all this intrigue, there's a bunch of neighborhood kids calling themselves the Junior Thunder Riders. They hold secret meetings, shout, "To the Rescue!" a lot and go off wearing pails on their heads trying to save people (mostly Gene). You really need a scorecard here: Gene, the kids, the radium-thieving bad guys, the mysterious Thunder Riders from the underground kingdom of Murania, Queen Tika, an underground mutiny. On top of the thundering hoof beats and punch-ups, there is also a delightful cast of robots who live—if that's the right word for it—and work in Murania. The robots are more than worth the price of admission. They mark only the second time that robots appeared in a sound serial (*The Vanishing Shadow* was the first) and they easily win two coveted awards: (1) the funniest robots in any sci-fi movie, serial or otherwise, and (2) the cheapest looking robots to ever show their faces. Their great little faces, cute ears and funny little hats are a joy to behold. Best yet, the robots are obviously constructed of the thinnest "steel" you can imagine. You've probably seen heavier-gage sandwich wrap. In fairness to the producers, these robots appeared in multiples. All of those other Robot Superstars you can think of, like Gort or Robby, were solitary creatures that got the full attention and resources of the art department. In contrast, there are scads of these little guys and a minuscule budget to boot.

The producers of *The Phantom Empire* didn't leave much to chance. For kids in the audience, they provided kid actors, and tons of 'em. They are headlined by Frankie Darro, who was fast becoming a fixture on the Mascot back lot, and Betsy King Ross—the "world champion trick rider," as she is billed in the credits. Betsy is sho 'nuff cute, but she has a voice that recalls fingernails on a chalkboard. For fans of Gene Autry, the producers allowed the man to sing no fewer than seven different songs, including a couple of them more than once. For sci-fi fans, we had "The Scientific City of Murania," as it was introduced in Chapter 1. That included ray guns, turbo lifts, lots of electrical special effects (courtesy of Kenneth Strickfaden) and all kinds of scientific parlor tricks, like raising the dead. As Queen Tika proudly proclaims, "Nobody is dead in Murania unless we do not wish to revive them."

On top of this, *The Phantom Empire* offers just about every B Western cliché you could hope for, with lots of fancy riding and stunt work thrown in for good measure. And in case all of this action becomes too intense, there is Smiley Burnette doing his patented hillbilly stooge routine. The truth is, by serial standards, this is an absolute winner. If it succeeds in reducing the audience to uncritical innocence, it will provide a grand viewing experience. There are lots of stunning cliffhangers, great action sequences, some intentional and unintentional moments of hilarity, world-class stunt work and some state of the art sci-fi FX (although the state was 1935). Then there's the great final destruction of Murania, accomplished by printing a photo of the city on a glass plate and heating it, while the camera recorded the emulsion gradually melting away. Whoops—I just gave away the fact that Murania is destroyed. A secret 70-plus years in the making—callously blown in a throwaway sentence. While I'm at it, I might as well shock readers by saying that the bad guys are foiled, Gene gets to keep the ranch and everyone rides into the sunset, some of them with pails on their heads.

Some wonderful dialogue to listen for: Queen Tika (who seems to get all the good lines) pronounces Autry's name "Aw-Tray." It's odd that nobody (including Gene) made a point of correcting her. When Gene is revived from the dead, he wakes up (in a hilarious scene) talking gibberish. The Queen questions her chief surgeon and is told, "He speaks the language of the dead." Autry goes on blabbering in gibberish while the other actors try to speak their lines.

"But you told me I could question him," the Queen protests. The reply: "One may always question the dead. But one needn't expect an answer." Pretty heavy philosophical stuff for an audience of 10 year olds.

In Chapter 9, the two kids, Betsy and Frankie—who use their real first names in the serial—do quite a job of mouthing off to the Queen. It was a masterful piece of screenwriting. The kiddies in the balcony must have loved it. Kids actually telling off an adult, hell, a *royal* adult! Wowie!

The robots are involved in the serial's most hilarious moments. In Chapter 10, Gene's two hillbilly sidekicks climb into robot suits in order to make their getaway from Murania. They bounce around like a couple of drunken tin men. God help us, it's pretty funny stuff. So is the brief scene in Chapter 11 when the same two idiots pull the wrong switch and cause the robots working in the underground mines to start dancing with each other. But the unquestioned highlight of robot humor occurs in Chapter 7 when a robot slaps Gene in the rear end as he is getting out of an elevator. This extra in a tin suit making five bucks a day must have had the time of his life.

It is worth noting that Mascot chose to bill Autry as himself—there is no character name—at a time when he was anything but a national star. This was a brave move by studio boss Nat Levine. It was also a move that ultimately paid off more than either man could have guessed in 1935. *The Phantom Empire* went on to make a pile of money for Mascot, both as a serial and, five years later, as a 71-minute theatrical feature titled *Radio Ranch*. A feature version was re-released years later with the new name *Men With Steel Faces*. A more descriptive title might have been "Men With Very Cute Tin Faces."

Tailspin Tommy
in The Great Air Mystery

So successful was the first *Tailspin Tommy* serial (1934) that Universal set about producing a second version barely a year later. Both were based on Hal Forrest's popular newspaper cartoon strip but there were some noticeable differences between the two films. Universal was banking on the public's fascination with aviation and daredevil pilots so that they wouldn't notice or care about differences in casting. Gone was Maurice Murphy who had starred as Tailspin Tommy Tompkins just a year earlier, replaced here by Clark Williams. Also gone was Patricia Farr, who had starred as Betty Lou Barnes. This time we get to watch the ever-lovely Jean Rogers. Ms. Rogers was about to permanently endear herself to serial fans by playing Dale Arden in the first two *Flash Gordon* serials, but for now she's just an aviatrix. Even a new director took over the helm in the second serial, as Ray Taylor replaced Lew Landers.

Just about the only familiar face carried over from the first *Tailspin Tommy* serial was sidekick Noah Beery, Jr., who reprised his role as Skeeter Milligan. In some ways that's all that really mattered. It is Beery's ah-shucks, All-American boy, down-home charm that resonates most with audiences to this day. Curiously, neither of the actors cast by Universal in the title role manages to make much of an impression. Both are serviceable but essentially bland characters; they are easily interchangeable cogs in this wheel. It is Beery who anchors the proceedings.

Tailspin Tommy (Clark Williams) and Skeeter (Noah Beery, Jr.).

Hank Davis

Tommy deals with a crisis on the dirigible (with Delphine Drew and Jean Rogers).

There really isn't much here in the way of plot; in many ways the two serials are also interchangeable parts. This is essentially an aviation serial, and as long as those spiffy, fragile little bi-planes stay airborne, there isn't much to complain about. Exactly what gets them up there and whom they're chasing through the air at any given moment doesn't matter all that much. America was still on its honeymoon with aviation; flying still exuded excitement, danger and romance. *That* is what comic strips and movie serials like this or *Burn 'Em Up Barnes* are all about. Character development and plot come in a very distant second.

The basic story line has to do with some corrupt profiteers who try to steal the oil reserves of a mythical Caribbean or South American country. It doesn't matter a lick. There are good guys and bad guys, pretty girls and lots of very old airplanes. They shoot at each other, fly in and out of volcanoes, engage in aerial dogfights and do lots of loop-the-loops a thousand feet off the ground. There is also a very cool mysterious character known as The Eagle (a.k.a. El Condor). In fact, it is his character (and his wonderfully decorated plane) that prompts us to include this serial rather than the earlier *Tailspin Tommy*. This character appears in the very first episode, attracting everyone's attention before we know what to expect. Both the pilot and his plane are decorated to the hilt with the kind of detailed graphic art that has become associated with urban graffiti. We just automatically assume that he's going to be a villain with all that costuming but, surprise of surprises, he's on the side of the angels. This becomes abundantly clear by the second chapter. The adventure remains enjoyable even knowing that the mysterious Eagle character is played by the talented actor Pat O'Brien, who is probably best remembered as the title character in *Knute Rockne All American* (1940). Perhaps the oddest thing about the construction of this serial is that by Chapter 2 we've got three clearly established heroes—Tommy, Skeeter and the mysterious Eagle, but no clearly defined adversary. You almost wish a villain would commit himself so all these good guys could get to work.

It's impossible to discuss this serial without mentioning the very first cliffhanger. In fact, along with the presence of The Eagle, it is this sequence that helped sway the decision in favor of *Tailspin Tommy in the Great Air Mystery* over the earlier *Tailspin* serial. The cliffhanger involves a dirigible. While this may not have been a noteworthy choice in 1935, it certainly is today.

Back in 1935, before so-called "fixed wing" planes were a viable source of commercial aviation, dirigibles were serious business. Zeppelins were also occasionally used as a subject in motion pictures, as in the landmark 1929 film, *The Lost Zeppelin* (Alpha Video). Dirigibles were part of commercial aviation even before World War I and had evolved to the point of flying 50 miles per hour over thousands of miles. Their development was delayed by the war, but when Germany was allowed to rekindle its civilian aviation program, the Zeppelin Company took up where they had left off. The flagship of their fleet was called the *Graf Zeppelin* and by 1930 it had completed an around-the-world flight in just over 21 days. In fact, one of the sponsors of this circumnavigation was William Randolph Hearst (think *Citizen Kane*). This little bit of aviation history is worth noting because it is all but lost to most people today. Dirigibles have disappeared from public consciousness and, yet, here is one at the forefront of this 1935 serial. On one hand, we know so little about them as to be captivated by this part of the serial. On the other hand, most of us know exactly when and why zeppelins disappeared from public aviation. On May 6, 1937, the *Hindenburg* burned and crashed killing 36 people. Of course, when this serial was filmed there had been no horrific tragedies such as the *Hindenburg* explosion. That, too, gives this dirigible cliffhanger some poignancy.

Most of us remember the fate of the *Hindenburg* and can visualize black & white footage of the flaming wreckage, with Herbert Morrison's emotional narrative "Oh, the humanity!" on the soundtrack in our minds. But that was still two years in the future after this cliffhanger was written and filmed. In 1935 dirigibles were credible sources of carrying people and mail. It was those tiny little unstable airplanes that were considered perilous infernal devices.

I asked about a dozen people to tell me something about the *Hindenburg* (don't try this with anyone under 20). The composite version seems to run like this: The Germans were trying to establish a radical new form of aviation and on its maiden voyage the *Hindenburg* crashed and burned, thus removing this rather odd bit of technology from the "real" history of aviation (i.e., airplanes).

Wow, is that wrong. In fact, the *Graf Zeppelin* had already flown over a million miles of commercial flights moving people and mail before its successor, the *Hindenburg,* was even built. The *Hindenburg* was even bigger, could cruise faster (about 80 mph) and carry more passengers (as many as 72) than its predecessor. The ship was powered by four 1,200-horsepower Daimler-Benz motors. It made its inaugural flight in March 1936 and had already been to Lakehurst, New Jersey (where it eventually burned). The giant zeppelin carried 7 million cubic feet of lighter-than-air hydrogen, an immense payload of highly flammable gas. Plans had been made to replace the hydrogen with inert helium but Germany did not have access to the world's limited stores of this admittedly safer gas. The Germans were not publicly worried about this. There had been no fire-related accidents on previous flights. In fact, the designers so minimized the risk of fire that they installed a smoking room for passengers.

Back to the serial. The cliffhanger in Chapter 1 involves a dirigible in peril that Tommy, Skeeter and Betty Lou must survive. And so we are treated to some fairly intimate detail of a dirigible in flight. Under normal circumstances, watching a dirigible in flight is as exciting as watching paint dry. But these are far from normal circumstances. The dirigible here is being buffeted by a storm (someone calls it a "typhoon"). This is, to say the least, a disturbing sequence to watch. It's not even clear how well done or realistic these scenes are; the problem is that most of us have no way to judge. This is like looking at dinosaur footage and trying to gauge how "realistic" it is. Really, how would we know? What we certainly realize is that this ship is enormous. That in itself is somewhat shocking. The actual *Hindenburg* was over 800-feet long, more than the length of three Boeing 747s sitting end-to-end. It's like a floating whale up there compared to the gnat-sized bi-planes flown by Tommy and Skeeter. Anything that big is, of course, immensely vulnerable. It simply cannot maneuver easily. It's a giant sausage filled with flammable gas moving slowly through the air. That has never been more apparent than it is in this serial.

Of necessity, the cotton casing is lightweight material. It's not going to take much to puncture that giant sausage. While it may be true that there's not an army of kids running around up there with pointy sticks, there are two very pressing concerns: One is Tommy's plane, about to dock below, with all its metallic parts sticking out in every direction. What if one of those struts pokes a hole in the cloth casing? The other is the weather conditions that the scriptwriters have conveniently provided. Just how impervious to thunderstorms were these ships? The historical record is mixed. If we focus only on German zeppelins, there are no recorded weather-related incidents despite flying through some seriously inclement conditions. There's no telling if the storms were as extreme as the one in this movie, however. The bad weather here does two things. It produces a large number of lightning strikes (which appear to have been scratched directly on to the negative). It's not as if the weather gods are *aiming* for that giant sausage full of flammable gas, but one way or another it's just a matter of time before they hit

Tailspin Tommy waving to all his fans.

pay dirt. Worse yet, by far, are the high winds that buffet this essentially powerless casing full of gas. The way it gets tossed around up there is horrible.

This is where I am powerless to judge what is on the screen. I've got to assume that what we see is sheer fantasy. The ship seems to rotate on a 45-degree axis, as powerful winds push its nose up or down in the air. I have no idea if that is possible, but if it is, the effect on the passengers, much less the structural integrity of the ship (consisting of aluminum struts), must have been devastating. Imagine seeing an ocean liner tossed on a heavy sea by waves of such size that the ship literally rose and fell 45 degrees from horizontal. When the dirigible in this scene finally does split in half, it's quite disturbing. Because we have little understanding of how these ships are designed, there's no telling whether there's any hope of saving the passengers or crew. Subsequent scenes of the survivors clinging to the cloth-covered ribbed wreckage in ocean waters seem a bit tame given what we have just witnessed. It's almost amusing when Tommy flies by in his toy plane to rescue these people, and begins to drop aviation flares on the wreckage. Dropping flares onto 7 million cubic feet of escaping hydrogen! But of course neither Tommy nor the screenwriters have seen footage of the *Hindenburg* disaster; that kind of fire is still unimaginable.

Just how high-tech is the aviation here? When Tommy's plane is taking off after a bad guy, Skeeter just runs along beside it, jumps on to the wing and grabs one of the struts for support. It's no different from jumping on the running

Tommy and his gal pal, Betty Lou

board of a Model A Ford as it drives away. In Chapter 6, an explosive device is attached to Tommy's plane. When he looks down at the dashboard controls, the timer is carefully labeled "Time Bomb." Nothing like an organized saboteur. When Tommy nearly crashes his plane after someone cuts a crucial wing cable, he concludes, "It looks like somebody jimmied mah left flyin' wahr." That's it. That's all you have to know. You need them "flyin' wahrs" to make the thing work. On two occasions when Skeeter yells for his assistant to turn the propeller to start the engine, I'd swear he says "Contract" rather than "Contact." Was this some kind of in-joke about a labor dispute at Universal?

There's some great dialogue here from the same team that brought you the "flyin' wahr" line. Tommy asks a villain, "May we have a day or two to think it over?" The reply is, "Until tomorrow morning, yes." It's a truly great surreal line. "Sure, take a couple of days until tomorrow morning." Two characters discussing the mysterious masked flier: "He's a fiend, this El Condor," and the reply is "He's also a good shot." There's plenty of vintage sexism here ("Now listen, you girls, stay here! This is a job for men!"). Amusingly, lines like that just seem to provoke Jean Rogers into doing something outside the stereotype.

On the other hand, Rogers' character, Betty Lou, is also a pilot—a nice touch in an aviation serial—that allows the main couple to flirt harmlessly while 3,000 feet above the ground. The mythical country of Nazil (Nicaragua meets Brazil?) has everything you'd expect in a serial. There's an active volcano and lots of Polynesian-looking natives running around with spears and shields. There's an admirable lack of stock footage in this serial, especially for a Universal production. One of the more obvious exceptions occurs in Chapter 6 when there are inserts of a fiesta. Tommy and Skeeter and their girls are sitting at a table and pointing and suddenly there is a grainy screen full of happy Mexicans, dancers and guitarists partying away. Is there nothing that Universal doesn't have stashed in its vault? Lions, tigers, Indian attacks, gay caballeros?

There's a surprising moment in Chapter 9 when one of the bad guys falls out of The Eagle's plane without a parachute. Obviously, it's only a stuffed dummy, but the whole thing is pretty realistic. The camera stays on the body all the way down, from the initial shriek at falling out of the plane to the moment of contact with the ground. We even get to hear the final dull thud. It's one of the most vivid death scenes in a movie serial. In Chapter 10, after a steady diet of 1935 Fords, we finally get a dozen men on horseback. In Chapter 11, in addition to airplanes and horses, we add a sailing ship. Suddenly there's a tall outrigger being buzz-bombed by The Eagle while a 1930 speedboat zooms around. This actually allows for some pretty adventurous and unusual photography. It also makes for a very bizarre final cliffhanger. The speedboat containing our heroes is supposed to be out in the open sea in the middle of nowhere (off the coast of "Nazil"). As the speedboat prepares for a horrible collision, we see some stock footage of a buoy. Despite Universal's best efforts, there is something else in that shot that we're not supposed to see. It is either an ocean liner with about three smokestacks or the skyline of a big city with lots of tall buildings. Whatever it is, it sure doesn't belong in this shot of a doomed speedboat out on the sea.

Things get very busy and complicated in the final chapter. With about six minutes to go, it seems unimaginable that this plot will be wrapped up in any reasonable way. Worse yet, there's not an airplane in sight. There are plenty of savage natives and stock footage of war dances and jungle drums and even some speedboats. It seems a heck of a wrap up for an aviation serial. Suddenly, there are leopards on the loose! OK, who's to say there are no leopards in "Nazil"? For all we know, there could be killer unicorns. But it just seems a bit cheesy. What to do with a fleeing bad guy? Bring in a leopard to eat him. By the end of Chapter 12, the action resembles more of a cartoon than a chapter play, or perhaps somebody's idea of serial parody. In the final scene, our friends get an offer from "Paragon Pictures" to make a movie about their exploits. Isn't that clever?

The biggest problem with this serial is the nearly total absence of a villain. True, there are some bad people whose goals put them in conflict with our heroes, but these guys bring no overarching sense of menace. In fact, the closest thing we have to a mysterious figure (The Eagle) doesn't last long enough. After nearly killing Tommy accidentally in Chapter 10, The Eagle simply reveals his identity. Word spreads quickly in serial land so we spend the final two and a half chapters without any kind of mystery hovering over events. By Chapter 11, Tailspin Tommy and The Eagle are flying duo and poor Skeeter (Tommy's former co-pilot) is relegated to hanging around with Jean Rogers. Poor guy.

The titling of books and movies is often a bit of a con job, especially with an exploitable medium like serials. Consider *The Great Air Mystery*. There's no real "mystery" here. Just a marketable word and a couple of greedy oil guys trying to protect their investment. There's nothing remotely "great" in sight, but fortunately there is lots of "air." The serial does deliver what it promises. An airplane is onscreen more than 75 percent of the time—until the last chapter, anyway, when leopards and outriggers take over. It's always sobering to see just how profoundly times have changed. In 1935 when this serial was produced, the studio publicity machine barked out phrases like "Adventure! Thrills! Excitement!" Today what the serial manages to convey more than anything is a palpable sense of innocence.

The Rustlers of Red Dog

No one is ever going to argue that this is a great serial. But it does have enough really interesting backstories to make it worthy of our time.

The Rustlers of Red Dog is the first of four serials Johnny Mack Brown made for Universal. Brown is an interesting character. Remembered today as a cowboy actor, it is easy to forget that his screen career began at MGM playing "straight" roles opposite the likes of Greta Garbo and Joan Crawford. He didn't hit the saddle until he came to Mascot in 1933 and starred in *Fighting with Kit Carson*. Prior to his career as a screen actor, Brown was a college football star. Luckily for him (or perhaps *because* of him), the University of Alabama came to the Rose Bowl in 1926, where he became a well-publicized sensation for his last minute heroics on the field.

Nobody is going to confuse Johnny Mack Brown with a great actor, but he does seem well suited to being an aw-shucks Western leading man. In *Rustlers*, his character verges on being larger than life. There are many lines and circumstances to suggest that his character, Jack Wood, is a Platonic form of Good rather than a flesh and blood man. But then, that's why many people love classic Westerns: Good and Evil walked the earth and were clearly delineated. They certainly are here. Wood is a reluctant hero. He doesn't *want* the job of town marshal. He'd rather be living surrounded by peace and quiet, and misses few chances to tell you that. He admits having left a trail of dead men behind him, but he's also quick to say that they all shot at him first. He's not a man; he's an Ideal. He is bound by Principle, which is like wrestling with one hand tied behind your back. His Sainthood may shackle him, but he sure can shoot straight!

And the bad guys? They are unprincipled sociopaths. The two big guns are named Rocky and Snake. Snake is not a name you assign to a righteous, upstanding citizen. And Rocky? More often than not it's a name given to prizefighters and raccoons. These guys are pure Old West sleaze. They're as Bad as Johnny Mack Brown is Good. Early on we see them gunning down lovable old men. Heck, they'd shoot down innocent women and children, and probably kill your pet pooch for sport.

The first five minutes of the serial does a surprisingly good job of documenting the rough-hewn, life-is-cheap realities of the pioneer days. They reveal everything you need to know about the brutality and unfairness of claim jumpers during the Gold Rush. Note that it's not so much rustling that's going on; it's gold, not cattle, that seems to be their target. But *The Rustlers of Red Dog* is such a great title that who are we to quibble. It's like *Zombies of the Stratosphere*—a Republic serial from 1952. Who cares if there are no zombies in sight? How can you not admire the writer who dreamed up that title? Here, we see a procession of lovable-looking old prospectors, hard-working coots who finally strike gold, only to be shot down in cold blood by a callous gang of thugs who have come

Johnny Mack Brown and Joyce Compton

to Red Dog to prey on them. The whole town seems intimidated by these guys (who number about 15).

Johnny Mack Brown is joined by two pals in his quest for Peace, Law and Order. In fact, studio hacks billed them as the "Three Musketeers of the Old West." It's another variant of *Los Tres Amigos*. There's just something about good guys traveling in packs of three. If there were just two, tongues might wag, wondering about their sexual orientation. But with three, you just assume these guys are well-intentioned eunuchs doing the Lord's work. Walter Miller plays Deacon, a man obsessed with gambling. He never met a card game he didn't join. Miller brings a Robert Mitchum-look to the part, although he talks a lot like W.C. Fields. Ultimately, Miller is undone by a screenwriter who insists on turning every utterance by his character into some sort of card-game metaphor. He'll talk about "drawing to an inside straight" when a simple yes or no would suffice. When the Indians (literally) light a fire under him, he's still going on about full houses and stacked decks.

Raymond Hatton who, like Walter Miller, was a seasoned veteran of the big screen, plays Laramie, the third Musketeer. Laramie cares not for gambling; he'd rather spend his time with booze or women. He's hardly a stud muffin, but the local saloon floozies are drawn to him like honey. He's usually got one of them in one hand and a bottle in the other. At one point, Laramie has an interesting discussion with a horse, asking him why horses can't learn to live with humans the way dogs do. An odd moment, to be sure. When Laramie isn't whoring or

NAT LEVINE *presents*

RUSTLERS OF RED DOG

with **JOHNNY MACK BROWN**

The Three Musketeers of THE OLD WEST

DIRECTOR: *LOUIS FRIEDLANDER*
CAST: *JOHNNY MACK BROWN, JOYCE COMPTON, WALTER MILLER, RAYMOND HATTON, HARRY WOODS*

A UNIVERSAL PICTURES SERIAL in **12** CHAPTERS

boozing (or interrogating horses), he is playing the harmonica. In fact, he may do all three at the same time, although there is no onscreen evidence of this. We do see him reach for that harmonica a few times too often. It's a wonder Johnny Mack or Deacon haven't used his mouth organ for target practice. Can you imagine sitting around the campfire with this guy night after night listening to this tuneless blather? It's a wonder these guys continue to travel together. In fact, they really do seem to have very separate agendas. When he needs their help in a quest for Good, Brown usually has to drag Deacon away from a card game and Laramie away from a woman. And yet they go, time after time.

These 1930s Western serials by Universal have two consistent qualities, one good, one bad. The good is the surprisingly gritty appearance of the sets. The town here seems pretty realistic with its narrow streets, wood sidewalks, log buildings and tarpaper roofs. Even an indoor shot of Laramie and one of the saloon ladies looks real, with flies buzzing around the tabletop. It's a small touch, but it's very telling.

On the other hand, these early Universal Westerns have a serious flaw, and it's hard to ignore. They are absolutely padded with stock footage. Plainly, Universal had a wealth of previously shot Western scenes in its vault, most of them from silent movies. The dawn of the sound era rendered these films commercially useless, yet they had cost good money to produce and contained elements that might be recycled with a little ingenuity. This serial shows how such ingenuity looked in practice. The action barely moves ahead for five minutes without an insert from an earlier film. It seems as though perhaps the script had been written to accommodate all this early footage, or whether the script was completed and *then* the search began for appropriate inserts. Frank Thompson's book *Lost Films* suggests that the source for much of the inserted footage here, especially those detailed looks at Indian life and villages, may have been the silent film *The*

Flaming Frontier, a Custer's Last Stand-based production released by Universal in 1926, starring Hoot Gibson.

There's nothing wrong with the use of older footage in principle; it's the execution here that often presents problems. For one thing, the footage is not well matched. It is often grainy, old-looking and speeded up. For another, it requires some plot contrivances that stretch credulity to the limit. The whole thing is kind of like the *Ramar of the Jungle* series from TV's infancy. Ramar and his pals would approach the camera on their jungle set. Then they'd pull back a few potted ferns, point into the camera and say, "Look!" At that point we would be treated to some grainy stock footage of a herd of zebras. Ten minutes later, they'd part the same ferns and we'd see footage of a herd of elephants. Even as a 10 year old, you knew that the word "Look!" meant "Cue the stock footage" in Ramar-land.

And so it is here. There are simply too many grainy Indian attacks. In fact, hard as it is to imagine, there is simply too much noisy action in this serial. Sure, action is good, especially if pitching your wares to kiddies. But this often degenerates into chaos with guns being fired, Indians whooping it up, and characters from other movies falling to the ground. A scorecard is needed to keep track of what's going on. In fact, if everything you see in Chapter 1 had really been filmed for this serial, there would have been almost no budget for Chapters 2-12.

Speaking of Indians, it's almost refreshing to see some politically incorrect moments. Indians are not noble savages here; they are primitive, no-good brutes who threaten the white man's progress across the continent and Manifest Destiny. White men talk calmly while Indians, primitives that they are, always seem to shout. There is a moment in Chapter 2 that demands attention. An Indian shoots an arrow right into the doll a young girl is holding. At first it appears to have been her baby sister she's protecting from the wagon train attack. The scene is still pretty harrowing—even after realizing it was just a doll. These varmints are shooting right at five-year-old girls. Wow. When Indian villains were shown in later serials, it was usually the case that they weren't *real* Indians but, rather, bad white men who dressed up as Indians in order to hide their own evil motives. Not here. When Johnny Mack Brown, the noblest guy around, wants to help a wounded Indian, Laramie says to him, "You're just wasting your mercy, Partner." To which Brown replies, "Maybe so, but we've got to civilize these red devils some way."

To its credit, Universal cast several real Indians in this serial. One, Chief Thunder Cloud, had become a regular on the B-movie Western front. Another deserves special mention. Playing a barely credited bit part in Chapters 6 and 11 is an Indian named Jim Thorpe. His name might not mean much these days, but Thorpe was anything but anonymous back at the time this serial was made. Born in Prague, Indian Territory (now Oklahoma), Thorpe was a medal winner in the 1912 Olympics. He later played pro football (halfback for the Canton Bulldogs, 1915-20; 1926; Cleveland Indians, 1921; New York Giants, 1925; Chicago Car-

Johnny Mack Brown

dinals, 1928). He was also an outfielder for the New York Giants, Cincinnati Reds and Boston Braves (1913-1919). But in a series of events that may have reflected racist attitudes of the times, Thorpe was stripped of his Olympic medals after it was revealed that he had previously been paid for athletic performances. Things went from bad to worse and Thorpe ended up living an alcoholic hand-to-mouth existence that included menial jobs and frequently uncredited roles in Westerns. In 1935 alone, he appeared in 17 films, 15 of them without billing. In 1951, 17 years after this serial appeared, the gritty details of Thorpe's life were brought to the public in the film *Jim Thorpe, All American* starring Burt Lancaster. Jim Thorpe died two years later on March 28, 1953. His face has since appeared twice on U.S. commemorative postage stamps, in 1984 and again in 1998, and he is a Charter member of the Pro Football Hall of Fame. Thorpe was inducted into the U.S. Olympic Hall of Fame as a Charter Member in 1983 and the Olympic medals that were stripped from him were returned to his family in 1992.

Director Lewis Friedlander (Lew Landers) does a competent job with what he has to work with here, which is a jumbled repetitive story line infused with way too much stock footage. What is memorable about Friedlander is his busy work schedule. An unsung hero of early serials, the man directed four titles for Universal in 1934 alone. In addition to *Rustlers*, he also directed *The Red Rider, Tailspin Tommy* and *The Vanishing Shadow*.

The music in this serial is a hodgepodge, ranging from horrendous (typical for the era) to surprisingly stirring. The opening title theme borders on hilarious, played by a Depression-era band that manages to sound more like a German bratwurst ensemble than anything about the Old West. The closing title music is no better, coming across like a high school marching band at a football game.

However, about nine minutes into Chapter 8 there is some very authentic sounding and moody string band music that suits the moment surprisingly well. It's hard to believe that the same music supervisor who selected the inanity under the titles would have stumbled upon these sounds.

The dialogue (except for Walter Miller's gambling metaphors) is generally serviceable. Folks talk the same as most other serials ot the era . One character actually says, "Head for the hills!" Guns are called "shooting irons." You'll hear plenty of "pronto" and "vamoose" and an occasional "plum loco." One bizarre moment to watch for in Chapter 7: Our hero

Jim Thorpe at the 1912 Olympics

and Ms. Lee are getting cozy in a covered wagon after he has saved her life (yet again).

There is a particularly impressive cliffhanger in Chapter 10. Johnny Mack Brown is shot as he drives a stagecoach. The coach flips over on him (an obvious dummy) as it rolls down an embankment. This is the real thing; no miniatures were used. If we believed for one moment that the black-clad dummy really were Johnny Mack, he'd be done for. Nobody survives this kind of physical abuse. Amazingly, at the start of Chapter 11, our hero dusts himself off and walks away.

Joyce Compton, who looks more like a silent movie heroine than an Old West toughie, plays Brown's love interest, Mary Lee. She is a bit of a screamer, which seems out of kilter with the part. It isn't until Chapter 8 that we get anything resembling "love stuff." Actually, it's nothing more than a few longish glances and the fact that Brown has stopped calling her "Miss Lee" and has moved on to "Mary." Wowie! By Chapter 10, Laramie observes, "That girl's got ideas. She's gonna' break up our partnership." To which Deacon wisely replies, "Yup. The cards are stacked against us. Too many hearts." At the end, Johnny Mack Brown actually touches the girl. As he embraces her, he looks beamingly at Deacon and Laramie and says, "My partners!" Sigh. What a guy! He'll probably take them on the honeymoon too. But that's another serial.

1936
Darkest Africa

Whether you love it or hate it, this serial—the first of 66 issued by Republic Studios—is a landmark event. Arising from the ashes of Mascot Pictures early in 1936, Republic began its life with a fairly safe venture. The jungle was usually a lucrative place for serial and B-moviemakers. Indeed, one of the final moneymakers released by Mascot Pictures in 1934 was called *The Lost Jungle*. It featured real-life animal trainer Clyde Beatty displaying his pugnacious ways with both animal and human foes.

In *Darkest Africa*, Beatty struts his stuff in even more impressive fashion. Beatty and his animal act were no strangers to popular entertainment. There is no question that the man knew how to please a crowd. The real question is whether he was equipped to play a swashbuckling, romantic lead. Beatty certainly didn't fit the conventional image of leading man. He was neither large nor particularly good-looking. The truth is, Clyde was a wiry little guy with big ears and curly hair. His sleeves are always rolled up and he seems ready to throw a punch at the slightest provocation. Needless to say, this serial does its best to provoke him.

Beatty plays an animal trainer named Clyde Beatty. Talk about perfect casting! In the first episode, Beatty meets a jungle boy named Baru. Played by 11-year-old Manuel King, Baru has got to be one of the strangest looking kids ever to stand in front of a camera. In his favor, King had a wild animal act of his own and could be counted on to stand side by side with Beatty when the four-footed ones attacked. Baru convinces Clyde to join him on an incredible mission to rescue his sister Valerie, who is being held against her will as the goddess of a lost city called Joba in darkest Africa. It's hard to imagine that Baru and Valerie (played by the beautiful Elaine Shepard) could have climbed out of the same gene pool, but Beatty, who looks like he hasn't seen a woman in years, eagerly accepts the assignment. The two of them are joined by Bonga, a loyal gorilla played by Ray "Crash" Corrigan who would go on to star—without his gorilla suit—in Republic's second serial, *The Undersea Kingdom*.

Once on their way to the lost city of Joba, Beatty and his sidekicks encounter an array of crooks, hostile natives, lions, tigers and a wonderful tribe of winged Bat Men. These characters, which fly and swoop all over Joba, are the true highlight of the serial. More on them later. If Bat Men are the highlight, then the absolute low point has got to be Dagna, the jungle ruler. It's not clear whether the damage was done by the scriptwriters, the casting director or actor Lucien Prival, but this character misfires at every level. Dagna is laughably miscast. It's clear they needed somebody with majesty: somebody like Charles Middleton, who played Ming in the *Flash Gordon* serials. What they got was a guy from a

George Raft movie: a petty, shifty-eyed, North American criminal, circa 1936. It's not just that he's bad actor. It's that Prival exudes no dignity or poise whatsoever. He's a petty thug who talks tough in a 1930s B-movie way—hardly the ruler of a mysterious Kingdom. Forget the silly costume—you keep expecting Edward G. Robinson or James Cagney to walk in and slap him silly.

Even by serial standards, *Darkest Africa* is clearly juvenile entertainment. Much of it is like a silent movie, with Baru and Bonga running around, pointing and overacting. The dialogue, when it occurs at all, is stilted and minimal. The credits at the start of every chapter include some entertaining misinformation. They suggest that an actual gorilla, rather than Ray Corrigan, plays Bonga. They also list Tiger Men and Bat Men as if specimens from these exotic species were hired just for the serial. The Tiger Men that capture Beatty in Chapter 2 sport lots of different hairstyles. Some wear very 1960s-looking afros about a foot high. Others wear normal North American haircuts for the mid-1930s. Still others have shaved heads. Apparently, the casting call wasn't very specific. The title cards that appear after each cliffhanger are pretty primitive looking—they are really not far removed from the intertitles used in silent films.

No fewer than three of the chapters end with the same cliffhanger. Each time, Clyde grabs a rope and starts to swing somewhere. Then somebody—a palace guard or a revolting slave—sees him and cuts the rope, forcing Clyde to plummet to his doom. The fistfight at the end of Chapter 4 shows you how far Republic came in just a couple of years. Even non brawling fans, *per se*, might appreciate the beautifully choreographed fights performed by Republic's ace team of stuntmen

Beatty (armed with stick) vs. a Bat Man.

during their golden age. In contrast, watch Beatty and the two bozos he battles at the end of Chapter 4. It's amateur night in darkest Africa. The hidden city of Joba was a lovely miniature set crafted by the Republic artisans. Obviously, the Studio appreciated its own handy work. The city of Joba turns up intact nearly 20 years later in the Republic's latter-day serial *Radar Men From the Moon.*

Without doubt, the flying Bat Men are the highlight of this serial. On paper, this effect should not have worked so well. In fact, it sounds ridiculous. But on film, where it counts, the effect comes to life. Carved balsa wood figures—they look like Roman gladiators with outstretched arms—glide down invisible wires. Their wings never move, but the effect is magic, even chilling. The scene with a Bat Man flying right over a panicked native is a standout. Perhaps the best part is the tracking shot of the bat's shadow as its soars low over the ground, distorted by bushes and rocks. It's not clear whether the Bat Men are supposed to be normal guys in winged costumes or some kind of bat/man hybrid species. All we know is that they look awkward on the ground and graceful in the air. Republic used the same kind of flying effect to great advantage five years later in *The Adventures of Captain Marvel* (see Volume II of *Classic Cliffhangers*).

It's revealing to see that blacks are portrayed as superstitious, ignorant second-class citizens, even in their own land. They all call Beatty "Mr. Clyde," no matter where they meet him. Admittedly, this is 1936 and we'd expect no less if the serial were set in Mississippi. But you think that somebody would cut these black actors a little slack when they're talking to a white guy in the middle of the

African jungle. Even 11-year-old Baru calls Beatty by his first name.

Ray Turner plays a character named "Hambone." Turner provides the racist comic relief for the serial's impressionable young audience. Hambone tries to sell some natives a mousetrap, but it goes off on the chief's finger. Turner was definitely a graduate of the Stepin Fetchit School of Racial Dignity. He's got the eye-rolling, slow-witted shtick down pat. On a hot day he says, "Mah feets feel like I'm must have crossed Asia, Africa, the Panama Canal and Texas." Amazing. At least we are spared hearing "Feets, do yo' stuff."

In his personalized history of serial making at Republic, director William Witney remembers Beatty and this serial very fondly. Beatty's animal act, according to Witney,

was the real thing. With all due respect to Mr. Witney and his delightful book, the results do not bear witness to such talent. Most of Beatty's animal encounters in this film seem staged and lackluster. Sources suggest that many of the fight scenes between Clyde or the kid and the "ferocious jungle animals " were actually filmed in Jungle Land, a tourist park located near Brownsville, Texas. The "wild animal" inserts featuring Beatty and his tigers are often grainy and out of focus. It seems painfully obvious that some of these scenes use tame animals with which Clyde had more than a casual working relationship. In several scenes, Beatty literally has to throw the animals from left to right in order to simulate an energetic adversary, rather than the playful or lethargic beast he is facing. It's like watching Bela Lugosi and the giant rubber octopus in *Bride of the Monster*. You can almost see Ed Wood standing off-camera, imploring Bela to throw the limp contraption around to make it look fearsome.

In chapter 14, Clyde picks up a rifle and shoots at a lion point blank. Fortunately (for the lion) the gun is empty, but it seems strangely wrong to see Beatty shoot an animal. It's one thing to poke chairs or snap a whip at them. It's quite another to blast away at them with a high-powered rifle. The scene suggests the unpleasant possibility that the man doesn't respect the very animals that keep him in silk shirts and fancy cars.

In the final moment, Baru comes out in shirt and pants with his hair combed. Even without the loincloth and unkempt hair, he's still a weird-looking kid. Clyde proposes to Valerie by asking Baru if he'd like to have him as a brother-in-law. What a romantic guy, proposing marriage to the younger brother. The kid, of course, answers with the all-purpose 1930s reply "Swell."

Flash Gordon

It is hard to overestimate the importance of the first *Flash Gordon* serial or its impact on audiences in 1936. The original *Flash* makes just about everyone's list of Top Ten serials and it's not uncommon to find it sitting at the head of the class.

Unlike most serials, the appeal of *Flash Gordon* went beyond Saturday matinee audiences. This was essentially a full scale, lavishly produced science fiction epic, chopped into 13 installments to keep folks coming back week after week. Its success was so great it virtually guaranteed work for stars Buster Crabbe, Jean Rogers, Charles Middleton and Frank Shannon, as sequels were produced by Universal in 1938 and 1940. Based on Alex Raymond's comic strip, the movie serial made popular culture icons out of Flash, his leading lady Dale Arden, their brainy colleague Dr. Zarkov and archenemy Ming the Merciless.

The original *Flash Gordon* comic strip appeared in 1934. It survived the departure of Raymond in 1944, and was still kicking around as the 21st century dawned. There were Flash Gordon books, a radio show in the 1930s and '40s and a television series in 1953-4. Then there's the cinematic industry spawned by this serial. First, the original chapters were surgically altered and released as feature films, variously titled *Rocket Ship, Spaceship to the Unknown, Space Soldiers* and *Atomic Rocketship*. These crudely edited features were still in theatrical release well into the 1960s. In 1972 there was a X-rated feature called, appropriately enough, *Flesh Gordon*. Then in 1980 producer Dino DeLaurentiis gave Flash the big-budget treatment, hiring Queen to create the musical score and a post-*Exorcist* Max Von Sydow to play the role of Ming the Merciless.

The plot of this serial (as well as Raymond's original comic strip) was loosely borrowed from Phillip Wylie's novel *When Worlds Collide* (which itself became a major film in 1951). The story is simple: Flash "gives up his polo game" and takes off with Dale Arden and Dr. Zarkov in an experimental spaceship bound for a mysterious planet that is on a collision course with the Earth. There they meet Ming the Merciless, who is controlling the path of the planet in his attempt to dominate the Universe. Ming puts Zarkov to work in his lab ("Give him everything he needs except his freedom"), and Ming and Flash become mortal enemies. For 13 chapters they fight but never kill each other. Everyone is always around for the start of next week's episode.

In the wake of all this conflict we meet some memorable characters and a few really nifty creatures. Some stellar stunt work by uncredited masters like Ray Corrigan, Jerry Frank, Eddie Parker and Tom Steele appears. There are hawk-men, shark-men, and lion-men. On the less human front, Flash takes on the famous fire dragon/lobster-man, an orangopoid (a guy in a gorilla suit with a horn on his head), a sacred tigron, a couple of lizards with rubber stuff glued on their backs and an octosac—a creature who makes his home in grainy underwater

Jean Rogers, Frank Shannon and Buster Crabbe

stock footage. Along the way, Flash hooks up with good guys Thun and Prince Barin, and battles with the boisterous King Vultan, who easily wins the award for worst actor and best laugher. If Vultan's "ha ha has" changed to "ho ho hos," he'd be an interstellar Santa Claus.

With 70-plus years separating us from this serial, several things are apparent that may not have been so obvious to earlier audiences. First and foremost, it is hard not to see that Flash is, for all intents and purposes, a eunuch. A beautiful guy, sure, but totally lacking in sexual awareness. He neither sends nor receives sexual messages. Men value his friendship and physical prowess and women long for him, but he is above it all, clueless while afloat in a sea of lust. Princess Aura (Ming's daughter) all but tears his costume off, but Flash is unmoved. His interest in Dale is totally chaste. (They do kiss in the last 3 seconds of the final episode, but by then we have his number.) Flash is clearly more concerned with rescuing her than ravishing her. In fact, things are so bad that Flash doesn't even seem to notice when Dale is replaced by another actress—Carol Hughes—in the final *Flash Gordon* serial (1940). He just goes on calling her "Dale" and never says anything like "Hey, you're not Jean Rogers!" Meanwhile, Ming pants after Dale ("Your eyes! Your hair! Your skin!"); Aura can barely control herself around Flash; Prince Barin loves Aura and can't bear to watch her swooning over Flash; King Vultan also has it bad for Dale ("My little dove"). Even middle-aged Dr. Zarkov runs around in a pair of shorts that would work at a Club Med mixer.

Hank Davis

Zarkov (Frank Shannon), Prince Barin (Richard Alexander), Aura (Priscilla Lawson) and Flash

Through all these swirling hormones, Flash remains totally focused on his job: saving the Earth and defeating Ming's evil empire. Maybe he'll celebrate with Dale when they get back home, but as befits the times, it will be under the covers with the lights out, following a proper church wedding.

Second, Ming's character reveals just how suspiciously Asians were viewed in the 1930s. This serial was made five years *before* the Japanese attack on Pearl Harbor, but fear of "the Yellow Peril" was alive and well. Consider—Flash journeys to outer space and meets an evil character bent on world domination, who just happens to be an Asian guy. Nobody comes out and says it, but Ming's palace is filled with dragons, he wears a kimono–like robe, his face is recogniz-ably Oriental and he bears the name of a Chinese dynasty. Just your average outer space villain.

The serial has a very upscale look and sound, but odds are Universal would not have built sets this lavish or commissioned music this grand for a mere serial. Fortunately, they were able to use props, sets and previously scored soundtracks from some of their recently completed horror classics. The great god Tao comes from 1932's *The Mummy*, and many of the elaborate sets and music are lifted directly from *The Bride of Frankenstein* (1935), which was barely in the can when shooting of *Flash* began. Film historians will tell you about similarities between sets constructed for *Flash* and Fritz Lang's classic film *Metropolis*, shot 10 years earlier in 1926. That alone reminds us what an achievement this serial

Buster Crabbe as Flash in a studio publicity shot

was. Remember that 10 years earlier—when Lang was filming his epic—puts us squarely into the silent film era. Talkies were still in their relative infancy when *Flash Gordon* hit the big screen. This is a pretty impressive journey for a toddler. The music, too, is not quite as original as later generations have been led to believe. Yes, it was recycled endlessly and later identified as having been borrowed from this serial. But the truth is those memorable themes came from classical composers like Richard Wagner, and previous Universal films, including *The Invisible Man* (1933), *Destination Unknown* (1933), *Bombay Mail* (1934), *The Black Cat* (1934) and *The Werewolf of London* (1935). That's a lot of recycling.

Looking back, it is hard to imagine a time when those little smoking spaceships on wires represented state of the art FX. They, along with much of *Flash Gordon,* have been satirized countless times by comedians and film students but, in truth, the serial is beyond satire. Perhaps that is why the original *Flash Gordon* remains so lovable today. Before the advent of DVD and video, 16 mm prints of this serial circulated among collectors and often fetched prices that truly seemed to come from outer space. Now, copies are widely available on video and DVD, assuring that a new generation will experience peril from the planet Mongo and watch the good guys rush off in spaceships to save planet Earth.

Hank Davis

The Undersea Kingdom

"It has everything you want," screamed the theatrical trailers in the summer of 1936. "Mechanical men! A disintegrator ray! Rocket submarines! Earthquakes! And in all takes place in a city beneath the sea!" The trailer went on to boast that this was "Republic's most exciting serial," a claim that might have been more impressive if the studio had released more than one previous serial. Only *Darkest Africa*, shipped to theaters three months earlier by the fledgling Republic Studios, stood as competition.

Despite all the hype, *The Undersea Kingdom* is regarded today as an enjoyable, if somewhat bizarre serial. The plot follows a familiar tradition: The Earth is been plagued by natural disasters. Earthquakes are occurring all over the planet. Civilization is helpless to stop the mass destruction. Only one man can save the planet. Fortunately, he's good looking and is available for serial work. He takes off for an exotic location in order to confront the madman who is creating all these problems back on Earth.

Now, where have we heard that story before? If you answered *Flash Gordon*, score 10 points. If you also answered *The Lost City*, score another 10 points and give yourself a bonus for knowing about a more obscure serial. And don't think this plot line died out with *Flash Gordon*. Good-looking heroes saving the Earth remained a staple of serial moviemaking right to the bitter end. The interesting thing is that *Flash, Lost City* and *Undersea Kingdom* were produced within months of each other in late 1935 for release the next year. And you can throw Gene Autry's *The Phantom Empire* (released earlier in 1935) into the mix as well. The similarity is more than passing, whether the action took place on the planet Mongo, the underground kingdom of Murania, an obscure part of darkest Africa or the undersea world of Atlantis. Only the names have been changed to protect the producers.

This serial begins with stock footage of graduation ceremonies at the Annapolis Naval Academy. The military brass concludes that Crash "will make a grand naval officer." Just in case there are any doubters, we see scenes of Crash winning at shotput and high jumping, after which he stars at the Army-Navy game (actual footage from the Polo Grounds in New York is used). For visual dessert, Crash also shows us he's a championship wrestler and then manages to save a kid. All of this takes place during the first five minutes of the serial. What, no Nobel Prize?

Except for hair color, it's really easy to confuse Crash Corrigan with Buster Crabbe. In fact, every time somebody calls him, you have to wonder if they say, "Crash" or "Flash." In any case, when it's time to start the action, Crash/Flash pays a visit to Professor Norton. The old guy (played by C. Montague Shaw) has a lab full of scientific props. All of them are detecting unusual earthquake activity that Crash announces is being "caused by some human agency at the bottom of

Classic Cliffhangers

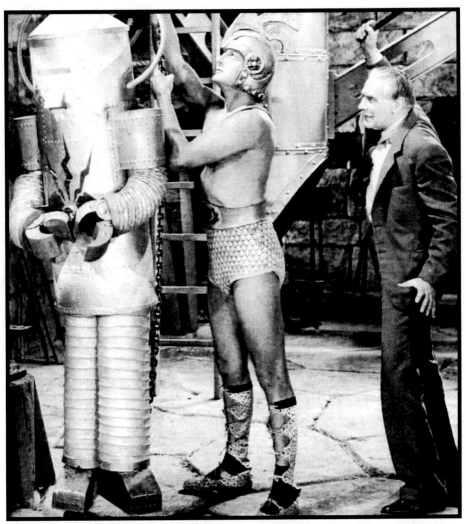

Montague Shaw prepares to knock Crash Corrigan cold.

the ocean." That means it's time for an expedition. Crash and company (including the professor's kid Billy and Diana, a "go-getting newspaper girl") hop into an experimental submarine and head south. When they arrive, they find Unga Khan, the "mad tyrant of Atlantis," played by veteran serial actor Monte Blue. Khan is suitably crazed and hell-bent on destroying "the upper world." Like most serial villains of this genre, Khan has a TV (called a "Reflecto") in his office (remember, this is 1936). It allows him to watch film clips of life on Earth. Every time he blasts off one of his ray guns, we get to see a few seconds of stock disaster footage. Khan also has a small army of standard Republic robots—a cross between an android and a hot water heater. They're great in this serial, and just as fun in *Mysterious Dr. Satan*, *Zombies of the Stratosphere*, and a host of other Republic cliffhangers.

Hank Davis

Lon Chaney, Jr. has Crash tied to the Juggernaut like a hood ornament.

It is probably an illusion but, compared to most serials, *The Undersea Kingdom* often looks lavish. There are lots of extras wearing costumes and as many as 20 horseback riders on screen at once. And nobody can accuse screenwriters John Rathmell and Tracy Knight of being unimaginative. Any time there are riders on horseback, Roman chariots and robots in the same scene—well somebody is earning his money. There are a lot of electrical special effects on display as well. They're fun to watch, but by no means as impressive as the ones created by Kenneth Strickfaden in Universal's *Frankenstein* series or *The Lost City* serial. Surprisingly, this serial's use of miniature props is substandard. Within five years Republic would set the industry standard for miniature special effects. However, in this 1936 cliffhanger, they hadn't yet hit their stride. Scenes involving a toy submarine are pretty poor. The frequently used undersea shots of the submarine are no better than Universal's famous rocket ships in the Flash Gordon serials. All that's missing here are the visible wires. The same scene of a descending submarine is repeated about 10 times in Chapter 1. Instead of smoke coming out of Flash's rocket, we get bubbles coming out of Crash's sub.

Considering that this takes place in Atlantis, there's not a drop of water in sight other than a tiny lagoon somewhere. There's lots of talk about "the upper world" but no indication that this is the lower one. The houses are all made of stucco and the rooms are decorated with Persian carpets. This is a pretty unique vision of Atlantis. One of the great recurrent themes here is a totally incongruous armored car that goes whipping thru the landscape (in speeded-up footage), weaving around horses and chariots. It looks suspiciously like the jungle rover in Universal's 1937 serial *Tim Tyler's Luck*. The vehicle, called "The Juggernaut," makes a noise like an air raid siren whenever it travels. In one of the best cliff-hangers, Crash Corrigan is attached to the front of the Juggernaut like a hood ornament and Lon Chaney, Jr. threatens to ram it through the gates of the city. "Go ahead and ram," growls Crash, and Lon obliges him.

In most Republic serials, the good guys are searching for some kind of high tech device that will stop an attacking robot in its tracks. One of the reasons robots (called "Volkites" in this serial) seem so menacing is the fact they just keep advancing in their unstoppable, soul-less way. Here, Crash seems to have figured out how to stop them. Faced with a marauding robot, Crash simply throws a chair at it. The robot falls over like a floor lamp. So much for high-tech solutions.

Lee Van Atta, who plays Junior in the original *Dick Tracy* serial (1937), appears here as Billy, Professor Norton's son. Billy isn't as much of a geek as most serial kids, and actually holds his own in a couple of surprising scenes where he bosses some adults around with a gun. Lon Chaney, Jr., heads the list of secondary players in a fairly undistinguished role as one of the chief bad guys. Lon shouts just about every one of his lines. It was not likely a role he or his fans cherished. Smiley Burnett, who also appeared as a slow-witted sidekick in *The Phantom Empire* and the idiot Mike McGurk in *Dick Tracy*, appears here in much the same capacity. It's not really Burnette's fault in the same way that it wasn't Stepin Fetchit's. Both guys were making a buck in some very unenlightened times. Burnette was just doing what he was told, which was to play the dumb hillbilly. Did he realize this was in no way a step up from the fearful, superstitious Negro, another staple character of 1930s moviemaking? Just in case the audience isn't sufficiently primed to howl at his ineptitude, the soundtrack provides barnyard music to create just the right atmosphere for our gleeful disdain.

In Chapter 12 the Earth is saved by some stock footage of Navy battleships. Crash and Diana, who haven't kissed, much less said a dozen words to each other during the entire serial, are off to get a marriage license at the end. Republic must have had big plans for Corrigan (born Ray Bernard), allowing him to star here under his own name. Corrigan went on to appear in two more Republic serials (*The Painted Stallion* and *The Vigilantes Are Coming*) before disappearing into the role for which he became most famous — a gorilla. Corrigan was the proud owner of a custom designed gorilla suit that he proudly wore, usually unbilled, in B-movies for years to come.

Robinson Crusoe of Clipper Island

Here is Republic's fourth serial, filmed during the summer of 1936. Given the grand itinerary that lay ahead (*Dick Tracy* was Republic's very next serial), this one is something of a disappointment. It is simply not among the studio's best work.

Much of the blame lies with the casting of the leading man. Ray Mala was undoubtedly an *interesting* person and a hard worker (more on his career later). But he was not the kind of presence around which you can create a movie serial. In fact, the failure of his character tells us something about successful movie serials and the people who play in them. But first, let's cover the basics. The story concerns the Pacific Dirigible Company and its attempt to offer regular service between San Francisco and Australia. In order to accomplish this, they need a refueling station and Clipper Island, whatever or wherever that is, seems to lie halfway along the route. So far, so good. The trouble is, an international espionage ring is dead set on sabotaging their efforts. Most of their shenanigans take place on Clipper Island, aided by the corrupt Porotu who is in league with the bad guys. Porotu hopes to become ruler of the island, taking the job away from the lovely Princess Melani (pronounced Mee–LAN–ee). Into all this intrigue enters our hero, Mala, apparently a Polynesian, but now working for the U.S. Intelligence Department. For 14 chapters Mala battles the bad guys and their leader, the mysterious "H.K." In true serial style, H.K. is actually one of the central characters, working anonymously to bring down the Dirigible Company for reasons that are never entirely clear. H.K. doesn't wear a mask or fancy disguise. In fact, he's shown sitting around a table with a bunch of confederates. The trick is that he's photographed across the table with a desk lamp blocking his face. This is a lot less hokey than wearing a giant scorpion costume or skull mask, but it's also a lot less fun.

The casting credits look pretty funny onscreen. The top-billed actors are Mala, Rex and Buck. Mala uses his real name, but at least he's a human. Rex and Buck are a horse and a dog, respectively. Actually, the fourth-billed character is Mamo Clark. We thus come very close to a serial featuring Mala, Rex, Buck and Mamo. Ms. Clark, while no great actress from the evidence at hand, did star opposite Clark Gable in *Mutiny on the Bounty* (1935). Buck also worked with Gable in *Call of the Wild* (1935). However, a search of the Internet Movie Data Base produced no evidence that Rex or Mala had ever worked with Clark Gable.

Mala's two pals, a hillbilly named Hank (William Newell) and an English novelist named Tupper (John Ward), provide the barely necessary comic relief. Neither alone is particularly funny; it is their odd couple routine that gets milked for yuks. Tupper's obviously fake British accent becomes quite grating early on. Somehow, however, it seems less offensive to laugh at a pretentious Brit ("tut, tut, eh, what?") than at a fearful, superstitious Negro or a funny sounding Chinese.

The only other actor of note is John Piccori, appearing here as the scheming Porotu. About half of his lines are spoken in some kind of Polynesian gibberish, but since the natives seem to understand him, who are we to say that Piccori was faking it? Serial fans will of course recognize the actor for the work he turned in for Republic just two months later—as the evil surgeon Moloch in *Dick Tracy*.

Which gets us back to the leading man and the fact that Ray Mala just wasn't cut out for this kind of role. Mostly, it's his voice. Whatever the opposite of *gravitas* is, Ray Mala has it. His voice is thin and his delivery is sing-songy, almost childlike. Part of this is no doubt cultural. Mala (born Ray Wise) was an Alaskan native of Inuit ancestry. Back in 1906, the year of his birth, he was known simply as an Eskimo. Mala appeared in three films before this. The first two were widely heralded documentaries called *Igloo* (1932) and *Eskimo* (1933). The very innocent and childlike charm he brought to these roles works against him here. Mala continued to play (often unbilled) parts as Indians, Eskimos or unnamed exotics for the balance of his career, which consisted of two-dozen films. Of note to serial fans, Mala appeared in *Hawk of the Wilderness* and *The Great Adventures of Wild Bill Hickock* (both 1938) in which he played the supporting roles to which he was more ideally suited. Mala actually appeared in the third *Flash Gordon* serial in 1940 in an uncredited part that is easily missed unless carefully scrutinizing Chapters 7-9. There is Ray Mala in all his exotic glory, appearing as Prince of the Rock People. The actor died of a heart attack in 1952, shortly before his 46th birthday.

Agent Ray Mala with Princess Melani (Mamo Clark)

Film editor (yet to become director) William Witney recalls the filming of this serial in his autobiography. His recollections of working with both the human and animal actors illuminate much of what we see on the screen. For example, it is interesting to learn that stuntman Loren Riebe performed the dazzling 200-foot dive that appears under the titles of each episode, and Buck the St. Bernard actually had a double (a pooch named Cappy). The exteriors were filmed on the Santa Cruz Islands, about 20 miles off the coast of Santa Barbara. Although many of the exterior shots reveal breathtaking natural beauty, there are still far too many process shots (rear screen projection) filmed back on the mainland under cost cutting time schedules.

A few moments to watch and listen for: Buck, the St. Bernard star, is a real drooler. You don't usually see huge strings of gob hanging from the serial hero's face—dog or not. One of the serial's sillier conceits is pretending that a bunch of guys beating on drums are conveying specific information. Other than general messages like "Danger!" or "Dinner is served" it is unlikely that drums can express entire thoughts like "Princess Melani is dressed in a yellow sarong and is going to die tonight at 10:30 Pacific Standard Time." The movie actually provides subtitles when the drummers are working. Then, again, this is a serial in which actors talk ooga-booga Polynesian and speak entire sentences to dogs and horses.

Some great dialogue between Mala and Princess Melani: After Tupper has forgetfully left her crown on a rock while he stops to tie his shoe, the crownless Princess says, "My people will never accept me as their Princess." To which Mala replies, "Don't take it too seriously." That's it. An actual quote. There's a funny sequence in Chapter 9 reminding us what the science of code breaking used to look like before there were computers. When Mala is closing in on H.K.'s headquarters he asks for "every available man" to shut down the biggest spy ring in North America. Five guys show up.

Among the many cultural disputes between hillbilly Hank and British Tupper is a predictable conflict over music. Hank manages to zero in on some surprisingly engaging Western swing and boogie, which triggers a whole wave of aristocratic protests from Tupper. Speaking of music, there is plenty of it in this serial. It is nearly continuous and quite appropriate to the mood. Kudos to musical supervisor Harry Grey for a score well ahead of its time; only four years earlier, serial soundtracks were often musical wastelands.

The cliffhangers here are a mixed bag: The flaming boat in Chapter 1 is pretty impressive, especially the scene involving Rex the horse. In the very next chapter, however, Mala and Buck are attacked by some of the least convincing and grainy stock footage of a shark that ever saw a projector. It's really baffling why filmmakers or producers who made a living from these effects didn't make an effort to keep their stock in any better shape than this. There's even an obvious break in the film that has been spliced.

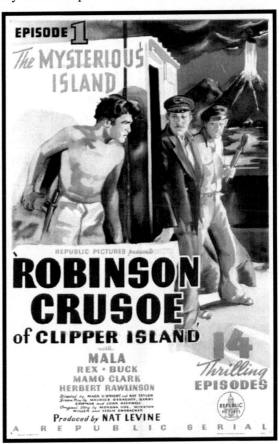

The cliffhanger for Chapter 7 is a real cheat. First, Princess Melani is shown slipping off a rock ledge after she has plainly succeeded in jumping to safety. Then we see her and Mala fall to their doom. At the start of Chapter 8, the whole sequence seems to have been transformed into something that never happened. Republic rarely practiced this kind of dishonorable slight of hand in later years. Indeed, no studio could have and retained credibility with its audience. On the other hand, the cliffhanger plane crash at the end of Chapter 10 is quite well done and the takeout is within the credible range.

A filmmaking issue: In Chapter 4 there is the to-be-expected scene of Buck and Rex

Mala delivers a right to the jaw.

helping Mala when the bad guys attack him. That's fine. But it's not fine when the entire sequence is repeated in Chapter 7. This is not one of those flashbacks or "retrospect" episodes that knowingly recycles previous footage. We actually have that for 6 minutes in Chapter 14. But this is different; it's just a recycled sequence that the editors or screenwriters assumed the kids would have forgotten from barely three episodes earlier. You think that's bad or cynical? The same animal footage appears yet again in Chapter 9. Somebody must have been crazy about those scenes of Rex stomping a bad guy or Buck leaping into the camera.

Referring to Mala, one of the henchmen says in Chapter 4, "It's ridiculous that one man should cause all this trouble." That is probably the most generic line of dialogue in this entire serial. It could probably be transplanted verbatim into half the serials ever filmed. The identity of H.K., the head bad guy, is narrowed down to either Jackson or Canfield in the last four chapters. Both are insiders operating above the law, who have avoided detection to this point. We won't tell which of the two is finally unmasked by Mala, but here's a clue you might consider: In *The Devil Horse*, a 1932 serial also produced by Nat Levine, the head villain is named Canfield. Coincidence? Maybe. You'll have to stick around until four minutes before the end of the final chapter to find out.

We can tell you this. In the end, the animals (both of them) save the day: Rex with his hooves and Buck with his drooly mouth and teeth. In fact, Rex is responsible for even more than that: In Chapter 12, when Mala is talking to Princess Melani (from a very respectful distance), Rex uses his head to knock them together until they're embracing. Mala actually thanks the knowing horse. Earlier in the film, Mala tells Princess Melani, "If you work with me, the United States government will help you!" He delivers the line with such innocence and enthusiasm; it is a sobering reminder of the days when those words actually meant something in the world. What would Mala or Princess Melani think of the world today when American kids traveling abroad often put Canadian stickers on their bags to avoid being hassled or worse?

Ace Drummond

There are moments in this 1936 serial from Universal that show why movie cliffhangers continue to fascinate audiences today, almost three quarters of century after they were made. The 13 chapters of *Ace Drummond* contain a generous glimpse of priceless cultural innocence and inspired lunacy. Consider this from Chapter 1: Passengers are seated aboard an old-style prop plane, flying somewhere over Asia. One of the passengers is fiddling with the controls on his radio. There are no private headsets; each passenger has his very own radio, mounted on the wall above his seat. The passenger says " I'd give a million dollars to hear a good jazz band right now." The stewardess walks by and says, "Try 740." He turns the dial and a band begins to play clear as a bell (although it's hardly anyone's definition of jazz). The music continues for a few bars and then some guy in the back row starts to sing, as if he were appearing in a nightclub. Magically, he knows the arrangement perfectly, has all the lyrics down pat and sings in the right key like he had been rehearsing with the band for weeks. It's a scene right out of *Airplane*, and every bit as hilarious. Only this is for real; this is the very stuff that all the *Airplane* movies were making fun of 50 years later.

The song is called "Give Me a Ship and a Song." After sitting through 13 episodes of this serial, the lyrics and the arrangement will be imprinted on audiences' memories. The song appears in at least half of the chapters in this serial. Whenever the action slows down for a moment, count on this hilarious piece of 1930s musical fluff crackling through on the soundtrack. It's one thing to have a hero sing a song in nearly every chapter. Gene Autry managed the trick in *The*

Peggy (Jean Rogers) and Ace Dummond (John King)

Dr. Trainor (Montague Shaw) and his daughter Peggy meet with The Grand Lama (Guy Bates Post), Kai-Chek (Chester Gan) and The Dragon (Arthur Loft).

Phantom Empire. The big difference is that Gene managed to sing a different song nearly every week. Here, our hero keeps coming back to the same hokey material, episode after episode.

The name of this repetitive singer is Ace Drummond, otherwise known as "G-Man of the Air." He just happens to be the star of this serial as well as a whole lot of comic strips before it. Drummond was created by World War 1 flying ace Captain Eddie Rickenbacker. Both the serial and the comic strips were inspired by actual events in the life of this very popular wartime hero. Drummond's character is known as "America's beloved ace of aces" and "the inspiration of youthful airmen the world over." John King, an actor who had previously appeared in a supporting role in Universal's *The Adventures of Frank Merriwell*, takes on the lead here and carries it off in credible fashion. Other than being saddled with multiple performances of a very lame song, he acquits himself quite nicely. He's everything a movie serial hero should be: athletic, kind to animals and children, respectful of his sidekicks and romantically unresponsive to the woman by his side. That woman happens to be the lovely Jean Rogers. She's an old hand at having guys ignore her.

Like other serials of the era, the emphasis in *Ace Drummond* is on airplanes. There's lots of fancy flying and some nifty air battles on display here. There also seems to be surprisingly little use of model planes to produce these effects. These days, it's hard to imagine an audience so enamored with the novelty of watching an airplane, but it's worth remembering that barely seven years had passed between the making of this serial and Lindberg's flight across the Atlantic.

Chapters 1 and 2 of *Ace Drummond* both end with airplane crashes. In serials produced 10 years later, when the cliffhanger involved a plane crash or explosion, the take-out next week usually showed the hero bailing out of the plane just before the crash. The approach in *Ace Drummond* is noticeably different. The crash takes place exactly as you saw it last week—with the hero still inside the plane. However, he somehow manages to walk away from the fiery crash or capsized wreckage without a scratch. On one hand, the take-out seems less of a cheat because you don't have those phony "jump out just in time" scenes that were always missing from last week's episode. On the other hand, it's more than a tad surprising to see anyone walking away from the burned out shell of a plane that's been compressed to the size of a dog crate.

The villain is a character named The Dragon. He is opposed to the development of an international airline, which would be a major step toward world peace. It's never quite clear why Mongolia would be an essential part of this plan, but the Dragon plainly does not want flights from all over the world landing at his local airport. He's got a pretty scary arsenal of bombs and electrical devices to bring down all the flying machines that penetrate his air space.

The Dragon uses a novel gimmick. Once again it's a disembodied voice, this time appearing through what looks like an electric fan. Actually, the device is called a prayer wheel, but to anyone not of supposedly Mongolian descent it's going to look a lot like an old G.E table model fan. The whole thing is actually kind of creepy. These devices sit motionless in a room until The Dragon decides he has something to say. Then the blades on the nearest prayer wheel/fan start to turn. Some kind of evil pronouncement can't be far behind. They all end with the words, "The Dragon Commands." It's outrageous stuff, but not out of line for your typical serial villain. When Ace finally discovers the secret of the talking fans, he decides to test his theory by sending a message through. Take three guesses what he uses as his test message. Yup—we get to hear his favorite song again—coming through a prayer wheel.

This serial features a regulation issue spunky kid. Played by Jackie Morrow, Billy is full of great ideas and spends most of his time lounging around in a suit and tie. Why didn't anyone let kids be kids in the 1930s? Either they look like street urchins and hang around in lovable gangs like the Bowery Boys or the Dead End Kids, or they're dressed like they're ready to apply to Harvard Business School. Fops or delinquents, those are the two choices for movie kids. At one point Billy jumps behind the wheel of a car and chases a bad guy down a treacherous mountain road. The kid can't be more than 12 years old but he drives like he grew up on the Indy 500. Apparently the rules for driving in Mongolia are a bit looser than back in the States.

Since this is the 1930s, there's plenty of racism to go around. When Ace sees some written material, he refers to the "queer looking Oriental language." Not to the locals, Ace, old boy. When he finds a prisoner in an underground cage in the Hall of Dead Kings, his first words are, "Why, he's a white man!" It's clear that

The mysterious talking prayer wheel

patriotic heroes don't worry too much when non-whites are locked in underground cages

For some reason, episode 12 (which normally would be the final chapter) disintegrates into a Keystone Cops routine, requiring one more chapter to wrap everything up and reveal the identity of the Dragon. Ford Beebe-directed *Ace Drummond*. Serial fans typically associate Beebe with the famous *Flash Gordon* serials issued by Universal. In truth, Beebe only directed the last two. He had no part in the first *Flash Gordon* cliffhanger. (Frederick Stephani handled that job.) After his work on *Ace Drummond*, Beebe went on to direct *Jungle Jim*, Universal's last serial of 1936. Interestingly, when the camera scans a page of comic strips at the start of each episode of *Ace Drummond*, the strip that appears right above *Drummond* is *Jungle Jim*. Obviously, Universal was not above advertising their business relationship with King Features and doing a little free advertising.

A couple of actors better known to later audiences are on display here. Lon Chaney, Jr. appears—as he often did in serials—as a bad guy. He's called Ivan—an evil name even 20 years before the Cold War. This is one of about a half dozen serial roles Chaney played before graduating into starring roles in Universal horror films of the 1940s. Noah Beery, Jr.—again a folksy sidekick—is the other familiar face, although his greatest fame came over 40 years later when he played Rocky, James Garner's father, in *The Rockford Files*. Beery is a very young man in this serial. He plays Jerry, Ace's best pal. Jerry is decent, unsophisticated and trustworthy to the core. He may not be the brightest light in the firmament, but he's the guy to turn to when the chips are down. It's hard not to notice that these are exactly the same qualities Beery brought to the role of Rocky nearly a half century later. Jerry refers to biplanes as "ships." We see them as ancient, flimsy relics of a bygone era in aviation. But in Jerry's farm-boy world-view, they are awe-inspiring *ships*. It's a passing moment in the serial, but it says a lot about Beery's character and the time period.

Jungle Jim

Now *here's* a huge slice of American popular culture. Back in the early 1930s the comic strip adventures of *Tarzan* (drawn by Harold Foster) were too successful not to inspire imitation. And so Alex Raymond introduced *Jungle Jim* for the King Features Syndicate on January 7, 1934. Raymond is most famous today for having created the comic strip *Flash Gordon*, which was itself a reaction to the success of *Buck Rogers*. The truth is, Raymond's two characters, *Flash* and *Jim,* appeared as a split entry, with *Jungle Jim* residing at the top half of the page. Both were hugely successful.

Like his fictional pal Flash Gordon, Jungle Jim was not content to remain on the newspaper pages. The jungle hero moved first to radio in November 1935 (starring Matt Crowley and, later, Gerald Mohr), and then made the move to the big screen in this Universal serial ("12 pulse-pounding chapters") from 1936. After confining himself to radioland and the comics for over a decade, *Jungle Jim* returned to Hollywood in 1948 and appeared in 16 B-movies for producer Sam Katzman at Columbia Pictures. Finally, the character made the inevitable move to television and appeared as the star of a weekly TV show in 1955-56 after the movie series dried up. Both the TV show and Columbia features starred Olympic medal-winner Johnny Weissmuller, known to most viewers for his earlier portrayals of Tarzan (1932-1948).

Critics have cynically described *Jungle Jim* as "Tarzan with clothes" but this doesn't do justice to the character. It is certainly true that Mr. Weissmuller was getting a bit long in the tooth to run around the jungle nearly naked, but it is also true that the idea of a great adventurer walking through the jungle in a cool safari suit, taking on smugglers and wild animals while saving beautiful lady scientists was pretty engaging stuff.

There is some suggestion that Weissmuller was offered the role of *Jungle Jim* in this serial but declined due to a conflicting obligation. Since that conflicting obligation was a string of Tarzan appearances for MGM, it's easy to imagine why the role went elsewhere. And so Grant Withers got to strut his stuff as the dashing safari guy. Withers is just fine in the role; he's good looking, robust and actually shows some emotional range.

The serial itself is a fine piece of work: It looks much more expensive than it was. There are lots of lavish sets, obviously left over from other movies. Scenes of the stone-walled catacombs lit by torches are quite atmospheric. There are also plenty of extras running around, many of them actual, authentic African-American actors. It seems obvious that finding Africans inhabiting the jungles of the dark continent would be a routine matter, but not in Hollywood. Tinsletown seemed to be under the impression that African jungles had large Polynesian populations. That is not the case here. What is a little bizarre is the confusion of African natives and American Indians. Movies of this period often view the world in simplistic terms: There are white folks (cowboys, Jungle Jim–types) and there are "primitives" (Indians or natives). The latter, apparently, all make the same noises when they attack. It's a sort of high-pitched "yip" or whooping sound. Here, that sound seems to occur whenever the natives run in groups, usually during a battle. It happens even when the actors are obviously close-mouthed. Those "yips" are coming from somewhere, probably the sound track of an old Western in the Universal vault. Even the tribal war chants and jungle drums sound like Indian music dubbed on to silent African native footage.

Here's the basic plot: Jungle Jim takes off with his pal Malay Mike (Raymond Hatton) to rescue young Joan Redmond (Betty Jane Rhodes) and let her know that she is an heiress to a large fortune. Bear in mind that this woman is happily entrenched as a jungle goddess with power over the local lions and natives. Just why she would want to leave is unclear. The only danger she faces is a competing heir who wants her dead so he can inherit the family fortune. He, let's call him Uncle Bruce, hires a couple of cutthroats called Slade (Al Bridge) and LaBat (Paul Sutton). A word about LaBat: He is a real "Lucky Pierre from Trois Riviere" character, complete with de French Canadian haccent and de checkered lumber-jack shirt, eh? His name was probably an in-joke from the writers since Labatt is a best-selling Canadian beer. (For the record, not all Canadians speak French and John Labatt, founder of the brewery, was an Irish immigrant.) Whatever his roots, the LaBat character is wonderfully played by Paul Sutton who has a great voice and went on to use it to full advantage playing Sgt. Preston of the Yukon on the radio from the mid-1940s to 1954.

Anyway, from here the serial could be called "Dueling Safaris." Jim and Mike try to reach Joan and clue her into both her potential and her peril, while the evil Uncle, Slade and LaBat try to capture and/or kill her. Throw in the usual contingent of animals and native tribes and *voilà*— 12 exciting chapters. Apparently the writers thought that might not be enough, and so we also have two additional characters to stir things up. The Cobra (Henry Brandon) is a ne'er-do-well who has the local natives under his control because he has convinced Joan that he is her father. Brandon, who sports boyish good looks and a youthful voice, was 25 when he made this serial. He barely could pass for Joan's older brother, much less her father. There's some serious miscasting at work here, although Henry Brandon would come into his own three years later playing the title role in *Drums of Fu Manchu*.

Grant Withers and Betty Jane Rhodes

The Cobra has a (presumably older) sister called Shanghai Lil, played by Evelyn Brent. Brent was 38 years old and brings some serious authority to the role; in fact, she seems almost over-qualified. Four years later Brent appeared in her best serial role in *Holt of the Secret Service*. She amassed over 120 film credits dating from 1915. There's something about the word "Shanghai" hanging over this serial. Not only is it the name of Brent's character, but the actress also appeared in a film called *Daughter of Shanghai* made the same year as *Jungle Jim*. For that matter, Paul Sutton (LaBat) appeared in a film called *Shadows Over Shanghai* made the following year. Although strictly a heavy here, Shanghai Lil played a much more salient role in the comic strip life of *Jungle Jim*. In that world, Jim reforms Lil and goes on to become her boyfriend/companion. There's not a glimpse of that going on here.

Some other observations: The shipwreck scenes in the first five minutes of the serial are very effective. Seeing the crated animals on the ship's deck during a storm, is also pretty impressive stuff. There's a scene of a tiger walking into the below-deck quarters of the mother and daughter that's quite visually stunning. In general, the tone of this serial is pretty mature. Obviously, it's going to appeal to kids because of all the animals, but the production is really treated like a reasonably adult drama rather than as pure fluff for the young 'uns.

One thing we've got to comment on. When the title character makes his entrance about seven minutes into Chapter 1, he does so amidst one of the worst, most contrived and hilariously dated pop songs imaginable. It's called "I'm Taking the Jungle Trail." Critics may decry what's happened to pop or rock music to-

JUNGLE JIM

..with GRANT WITHERS
BETTY JANE RHODES

day, and I don't blame them. But they should listen to this cheesy piece of contrivance before talking about "the good old days." Worse yet, an instrumental version surfaces as the title theme, so we get to hear it every week. The song turns up all over, such as in Chapter 3 when Jim breaks into song (*this* song, God help us) while sitting around the campfire. Just where is the orchestra and full string section supposed to be hiding?

It's hard not to compare the plot of this serial to a similar story line in *Hawk of the Wilderness* (1938). That serial, too, begins with an ill-fated voyage to a far-off land, a shipwreck, a message in a bottle, the death of a parent, the abandonment of a child in the care of an ethnic minority bodyguard and the eventual emergence of that child some 20 years later as the star in a movie serial. In both cases, the message in the bottle gets found and an expedition to locate them becomes the starting point for Chapter 1. That's a pretty hefty set of similarities, although the time to call in the lawyers was 70 years ago.

When *Jungle Jim* is initially approached to lead the expedition, he utters the great line, "Sorry fellas. The Smithsonian has already booked me to hunt gorillas." Hey Jim: A simple "No thanks" would do. He pawns his customers off on an old pal named Red Hallahan. Since the serial is called *Jungle Jim,* not "Red Hallahan," we just know this ain't gonna work out. Soon Red is murdered and Jim forgoes the gorillas to go rescue Miss Joan. Each episode begins with a glimpse of the Sunday funny papers with *Jungle Jim* prominently displayed above the fold. If you look at the strip below the fold, you'll spot *Ace Drummond,* another Universal serial directed by Ford Beebe and Cliff Smith licensed from King Features, released months earlier.

It's always easy to criticize Universal for their excessive use of stock footage. They probably had the largest collection of it available anywhere, so it was inevitable that some of it would make its way into a B-unit production. True to form, it does. It may even be recognized from some other films. For example, the circus animal footage also appears in *The Adventures of Frank Merriwell* (1935), but the truth is that the use of stock footage is pretty restrained here. This is not to say there's not a ton of it. We still get the usual "Look, Bwana!" which means cue the grainy shots of birds, zebras, hippos, giraffes and elephants—you name it—and it's fleeing on old film stock. And if I see that same fuzzy-looking howler monkey one more time, I'm going to climb that tree myself and throw him into the lagoon. But there is also a surprising amount of new animal footage, filmed specifically for this serial. Some of it, like the monkey throwing rocks at a leopard in Chapter 3, is pretty impressive. Also notable is the apparent ease of actress Betty Jane Rhodes with the large cats she is supposed to rule. When a tiger discovers Joan in a cave (she hates tigers and has no control over them), she simply calls "Simmmmmbaaa" and every lion in the neighborhood drops everything and comes to her rescue.

In Chapter 1, Jim gets into a fight with a lion. It happens very suddenly, but it's worth watching for. They both land a punch (literally a punch) while the white goddess Joan stands by, cheering on her lion buddy. Plainly, she hasn't yet fallen for Jim; it's only Chapter 1. When Jim fights a crocodile in the water in Chapter 4, the battle is carelessly matched to previous footage. Not only is it grainy, but also the man in the older footage is left-handed, and Jim holds the knife with his right hand. Malay Mike is about all the comic relief this serial needs. Fortunately, Raymond Hatton, who was a professional comic sidekick, is quite restrained in the role. In one of the serial's dumber sequences, Mike goes out hunting for dinner and manages to run into both a bunny rabbit and a skunk, two animals not normally associated with darkest Africa.

To its credit, this serial is nowhere as racist as it might have been. Joan's servant/guardian Kolu (Al Duvall) is treated well, but not up to the standard of white folks. When he refers to Joan, he calls her Missy Joan. Not even saving her life buys him any status. Kolu is instrumental in a pretty nifty take-out in Chapter 7 involving 10 marksmen who have lined up and let their bows and arrows fly at point blank range. When the volcano erupts in Chapter 7 the ancient stock footage really begins to roll. Keep waiting, the dinosaurs will soon appear. Bits and pieces of musical cues from classic Universal films can be heard throughout. With their memorable soundtracks still warm in the can, *Flash Gordon* (1936) and *The Bride of Frankenstein* (1935) get recycled here, starting around Chapter 8 and continuing to the end.

Speaking of the end, I am pleased to report that lions in Chapter 11 finally eat Uncle Bruce, who started this whole mess by hiring Slade and LaBat. I normally don't like to spill the beans like that, but like that wasn't going to happen. This is one guy who wasn't sailing back to America. At the very end, Jim and Joan officially become a couple. They hold hands. Withers was 34 when he made this serial and could have passed for 40. Betty Jane Rhodes was all of 16. Honestly,

Jungle Jim, Joan Redmond (The Lion Goddess), Betty Jane Rhodes and Malay Mike (Raymond Hatton) in 1936's _Jungle Jim_.

16 years old. I understand there are different rules in the jungle, but 16? Little Missy Joan, indeed. Actually, Betty Jane went on to a pretty illustrious career as a sometime actress and fulltime singer. She appeared on the radio with Bing Crosby and had a prolific recording career for Decca and RCA Victor in the 1940s. That's her version of "Buttons and Bows," you might remember. Grant Withers' story does not end so well. He appeared in over 200 films but had a sustained drinking problem that never got fixed. In 1959 he took his own life, leaving a note apologizing to all those people he had disappointed.

Jungle Jim finally met his match—a decline in public interest in the mid 1950s. The comic strip disappeared in 1954, the same year as the radio show. The movies finally dried up in 1955; in fact, in the last three features the name Jungle Jim did not even appear. Johnny Weissmuller was simply playing himself in his by-then familiar role. The television version was _Jungle Jim_'s last gasp and by mid-1956 it, too, was gone. It's hard to imagine that Johnny Weissmuller wasn't at least a bit relieved to hang up his safari suit.

1937
Radio Patrol

Remember the good old days when every neighborhood had a good-natured and reliable cop who walked the beat? When he wasn't busy chasing away bad guys, he helped little old ladies across the street. All the kids looked up to him and knew him by name. And his name was usually Pat or Mike. His last name was probably Dugan or O'Rourke. He was an Irish cop—a fixture of American life and fiction more than a half century ago. "Top of the mornin' to you, Mrs. Murphy. And how are you this fine day?" "Grand, just grand, Mike. And how's the Mrs.?"

There is no "Mrs." here, although Officer Pat is kind of sweet on Molly, a pretty young thing whose father has been imprisoned for crimes he didn't commit. In 12 episodes of *Radio Patrol*, a 1937 Universal serial, our hero gets the bad guy, befriends the kid, wins the girl, and clears her father's name. For Officer Pat O'Hara (Grant Withers), all of this is like a walk through the spring heather.

According to the blurb on the VCI tape box, this serial is "truly a relic of the '30s." No truer words were ever spoken, at least not in video packaging. The

original marketing by Universal was far less restrained. *Radio Patrol* featured "breathtaking drama" and "perilous pitfalls." It was "a spectacle of spies, speed and spunk." Trust me: That's not the way it's going to look today. Each episode begins with a *very* 1930s-looking kid, sitting alone on a couch reading a *Radio Patrol* comic book. The camera zooms in on his spellbound face, and we see the title of this week's episode (Chapter 3—"Flaming Death"). The events leading to last week's cliffhanger are revealed in a series of comic panels. And if that isn't enough, we then see the events as the usual pre-cliffhanger footage is rerun.

Like so many serials of the era, *Radio Patrol* began life as a comic strip. The original strip appeared in Boston in 1933, a time and place when Irish cops were found on just

Grant Withers battles Max Hoffman, Jr.

about every street corner. The big deal in both the comic and the serial was the invention of two-way radio in police cars. As the serial makes clear in the very first episode, criminals were having a field day before radio communication between cop and station house came along. The result is we get to hear a lot of "Calling Car 11, Calling Car 11. Bank robbery in progress. That is all. That is all." There is an unmistakable sense that the invention of radio transmission is going to stop crime in its tracks. May as well stick around for an era when the invention of cell phones will bring world peace.

Predictably, we also get to hear a lot of squealing tires and see plenty of car chases. They're surprisingly good, given the clunky equipment everyone had to drive. It makes you wonder why bad guys in vintage serials made such a fuss over ray guns and robots. A criminal with a decent Corvette could have written his own ticket in 1937. The music behind many of the action sequences will sound familiar to serial fans. It's borrowed from the first *Flash Gordon* soundtrack, which shouldn't surprise anyone given that Universal produced both serials and director Ford Beebe went from here to working on the second *Flash*. Thus, the music has gone from accompanying little space ships on wires to propelling speeding roadsters down "gun-riddled streets"—to quote the original theatrical trailer.

The bad guys in this serial are Egyptian. The chief villain wears a fez—a somewhat novel costume in movie serials. Bad Guy Headquarters is located in what looks like an Egyptian marketplace from 100 years ago. Scenes cut back and forth between "Metropolis" (read New York) and what could easily stand in for 19th century Cairo. Nothing is said about this mismatch, as if the Bronx were

10 minutes from the Sahara. About halfway through the serial, someone finally comments on the fact that the bad guys have their headquarters in "the Egyptian district." Say what?? Since when do American cities like Boston and New York feature Egyptian districts? "Why, you could forget you were in the United States," observes Officer Pat, and it's hard to argue with him.

The head villain is called Mr. Tejada. Most of the time, he is appropriately described as an Egyptian. He even keeps a prisoner locked in a sarcophagus. For some reason, later in the serial, Tejada is suddenly referred to as an Iranian. Iran? Egypt? In 1937, who knew the difference? Whatever he is, Tejada looks uncannily like a scaled down version of horror star Christopher Lee. There are lots of facial close-ups of his glaring hypnotic eyes. The shots are a vivid reminder of Karloff in *The Mummy* (1932) and Bela Lugosi in almost everything he ever did. Tejada is sinister rather than physically threatening. When he finally pulls a gun in Chapter 11, all he does it hit people with it. It never occurs to him to fire it at anyone. At one point, Tejada receives a radio message saying, "Master, Mr. Franklin has *retoined*." A priceless moment: Egypt meets Brooklyn.

The regulation issue spunky kid in this serial (and in the comic strip) is named Pinky. When kindly old man Adams, Pinky's dad, is offered a million dollars for his formula for "flexible steel," he says, "Why now I can get Pinky all those things I promised him." That must be one hell of a bike he's been promising the kid. Early on, Pinky accompanies a cop in a car chase. When the cop jumps out of the vehicle to pursue the thug on foot, he says to his 12-year-old sidekick, "Here, you take the wheel." Needless to say, Pinky speeds away as ordered. A 12 year old in a car chase with a thug. No wonder kids loved serials. Later on, when a cop crashes his car while trying to follow the bad guys, Pinky jumps out of the back seat and tells his dog to "follow that car!" Without missing a beat, the dog takes off and we get a shot of him running down Broadway, barking at an old roadster. Amazing. I mean, what's the dog supposed to do if he catches up with the car? Cuff the villains and lead them off to jail?

Compared to the comic strip, the *Radio Patrol* serial is actually quite restrained in the amount of ethnic blarney it offers. Nevertheless, it's hard to mistake the fact that everyone in sight is Irish. Even the dog is named "Irish"—which seems a bit odd since he's played by a German shepherd. There's plenty of comic relief provided by Officer Pat's sidekick, the equally Irish Sam. Unfortunately, Sam is dumb. Showing us how stupid (actually uneducated) Sam becomes a running joke. "Hey, Pat, these crossword puzzles are real educational. I just found out there ain't no 'h' in 'sugar'." Were there really such times?

By 1946 *Radio Patrol* had run its course in the Sunday papers. It limped along for four more years as a daily strip before giving in to the times with which it was profoundly out of touch. This ancient looking serial offers a glimpse of a world we are unlikely to see again. This was a time when all cops were Irish, police dogs spoke English, and seeing telephones in cars was worthy of our Saturday afternoons.

Hank Davis

Dick Tracy

This is a landmark serial for many reasons. If nothing else, it helped confirm Republic's reputation as a force to be reckoned with in the world of movie serials. These guys were for real–not just another fly-by-night indie whose output could be confined to the fringes of states rights distribution. It was just the fifth Republic serial and it served notice on the industry: Both economically and stylistically, Republic was here to stay.

Dick Tracy also made it clear that turning comic strip heroes into living characters on the silver screen was a bankable practice. *Tracy* began life as a comic strip in the *Detroit Mirror* in 1931 and within six short years had become a national phenomenon. Many comics-to-film efforts would follow this serial, but not many had come before it. The huge success of *Dick Tracy* did not go unnoticed. The serial also put its star on the map and at the same time vastly limited his horizons. Ralph Byrd's career continued until his untimely death in 1952, but he never really shed the image of the square-jawed detective. Even Tracy's creator Chester Gould took notice. His cartoon character grew to look more and more like Byrd over the years. It was a case of art imitating life.

Filmed at the end of 1936, the serial was a big production by Republic's standards. At a price tag of nearly $127,000, *Dick Tracy* was by far their costliest production to date. William Witney, credited as one of the film's editors, recalls journeying to San Francisco to shoot many of the exteriors that appear under the titles and as process plates throughout the 15 chapters. Fortunately for all, the Bay Bridge between Oakland and San Francisco was just opening and Witney and his crew was on hand to shoot historic footage of the structure's first hours. "We photographed the empty bridge. I don't think it has ever been empty

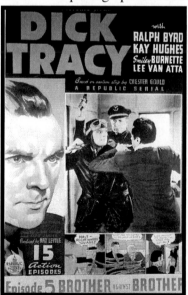

since. Our camera car led the parade and all of the dignitaries over the bridge. All of the footage was used in the serial." As serial fans know, those historic shots figure prominently in *Tracy's* opening chapter. Yes, they're intercut with some obvious miniatures, but the real stuff isn't dusty stock footage. It was shot directly for use in this serial.

The first seven minutes of Chapter 1 is a passable slice of *film noir*. It serves to illustrate the fear triggered by The Lame One, boss of the dreaded Spider Ring. He brings several of the local criminals together on a train for the sole purpose of intimidating them, and does a fine job. "The man's not human!" exclaims one of them as The Lame One's shuffling gait is heard outside their club car.

We next meet the ever-smiling Tracy, along with his brother Gordon (soon major plot device), secretary Gwen (soon window dressing), assistant Steve Lockwood (soon bland sidekick) and incompetent resident idiot Mike McGurk (played at full throttle by Smiley Burnette.) Golly gee, it sure is fun to laugh at uncoordinated and slow-witted characters, who happen to speak with a Southern accent. Perhaps this kind of rube humor is an acquired taste, but it's hard to see how it differs from the racist yuks directed at Stepin Fetchit and his cohorts. Might as well put it on the table right away; the single biggest flaw in this serial is Smiley Burnette. A little of his shtick might have been a passing reminder of quaint earlier times. But Burnette is a major player here; there's barely a chapter in which his character doesn't get some serious screen time. It doesn't wear well and ultimately dates this serial even more bluntly than all those bi-planes flying overhead. When he isn't tripping over his own feet, Mike is busy telling tall tales to impress the local kids, who easily see through his posturing. What is never explained in this ill-advised rush to lowbrow comedy is just what earthly reason Dick Tracy would have for associating with such a demented liability.

Another notable character is introduced in Chapter 1. Tracy visits an orphanage and is compelled to rescue one of the kids . He mutters something about needing to protect the kid because he's been seen by one of the Spider's Gang. Nonsense. Everyone knows it's just a chance to work a kid into the weekly doings so youthful audiences everywhere will have one of their own to identify with. And so "Junior" (Lee Van Atta) comes home with Tracy, more or less in the care of Mike McGurk, whose mental age he most closely approximates. Junior is an OK character. He's a smart, resourceful kid who holds his own in the adult adventures and even contributes an idea or two. (He also drives a truck in Chapter 1!)

Van Atta was 15 (he looks younger) when he made *Dick Tracy*. He had appeared in Republic's *The Undersea Kingdom* the previous year, and would go on making movies until 1939, at which time his film credits end and are replaced by some very impressive and genuinely perilous WWII heroics. Van Atta flew combat missions as an INS correspondent with the Fifth Air Force in order to send detailed reports back home. He died in 2002 at age 80.

Chapter 1 just brims with ideas. It deals with the Murder at the Puppet Show caper, which Tracy solves in less than 15 minutes. It also features the abduction of Gordon

Dick Ellis, Jock Henebry and war correspondent Lee Van Atta pose in front of their plane, *Seabiscuit*. Van Atta flew the mission with Ellis Nov. 2, 1943 and typed the story on the way home.

Hank Davis

Ralph Byrd, all tied up, with a solution in sight.

Tracy, which becomes a backstory for the entire 15 Chapters. It also established the presence of one of the most memorable devices in serial history: the Flying Wing, a clever and not unrealistic aircraft used by the Spider Gang. Finally, it establishes the first of many of the Lame One's plots to steal or extort huge sums of money from the city (presumably San Francisco). In this case, the Gang boards the Wing and flies over the (actually) new Bay Bridge, emitting sonic bursts that will shake the structure to its foundations. Tracy helpfully explains the principle to audiences by reciting the "Caruso's voice could break a wine glass" analogy. Nothing like entertaining the kids while educating them.

Also introduced in Chapter 1 is the character of Moloch, wonderfully played by character actor John Piccori. Moloch is the embodiment of evil, idly stroking his black cat while describing the "simple little operation" he will perform on Gordon Tracy in order to turn him into a tool of the Lame One. One of the odd points of this serial is the extent to which Gordon goes from captive, to trainee, to gang leader. By the end of the first chapter, Gordon Tracy, his mind altered beyond recognition, is leading the Spider Gang's weekly excursions. Gordon becomes genuinely creepy, with glassy eyes, a zombie voice, heavily made-up eyebrows and a white streak in his hair, probably inspired by Elsa Lanchester in *The Bride of Frankenstein* (1935). He has graduated from questionable convert to head honcho. It makes you wonder what this gang did for leadership before they kidnapped him. Such is the change in Gordon that two different actors were employed: one pre-surgery (Richard Beach) and another post- (Carleton Young).

Perhaps one of the odder qualities found in the *Dick Tracy* serial is the number of separate plot lines introduced week after week. The underlying themes (the captivity of Gordon Tracy; the Spider Gang's campaign of evil) remain constant, but there is a rotating door on weekly story lines. In this sense *Tracy* resembles older fare like *The Perils of Pauline* (1914) more than it does modern serials. In the oddly titled Chapter 3 ("The Fur Pirates"), the Spider's men pursue valuable

Classic Cliffhangers

Ralph Byrd, Lee Van Atta (Junior) and a couple of dummies face terror in the cockpit.

animal pelts on board a ship. Chapter 3 ends with the wonderful "Crushed to death between two ocean liners" cliffhanger. Next week the plot involves a dirigible and a necklace. In Chapter 6, it's a secret formula for Nickolanium, whatever that is. In Chapter 7, there's a secret gold mine that the Spider Gang wants to control. To do that, they have to outsmart a colorful and lovable old galoot named Death Valley Johnny. He's about to sell his claim to some New York jewelers when Gordon Tracy, impersonating a lawyer, steals the map and shoots Johnny at point blank range. Good thing he lives or I (and every 12 year old in the audience) would have stopped caring about whether or not Dick reclaims his lost kid brother. Chapter 7, by the way, has a pretty funny *CSI*-type scene involving state-of-the-art forensic equipment. This includes a Bunsen burner and a pair of tweezers.

After Death Valley Johnny, there is a caper involving a high-speed plane that goes 700 mph. Then there's the million dollars in gold missing from an ocean liner called the *Atlantis*. Next comes the kidnapping of a government engraver and a plot for counterfeit money. It just goes on and on in a way more associated with a weekly TV series than a movie serial.

A few other items of note: The (obviously miniature) shots of the Wing flying low over the ground or landing in the old power plant remain a delight. Indeed, there's something endearing about the Wing, despite all the visible wires. The fistfight scenes are not quite as elegantly staged here as they would become in subsequent Republic serials. The fire scenes, on the other hand, involving a deft combination of controlled fires on the set and stock footage, are very persuasive. The music, under the supervision of Harry Grey, also deserves special mention. The title theme music is instantly memorable even if it is laughably dated. It is pointedly fragmentary–alternating between the rousing sound of a Movietone newsreel and some lush, corny romance — sort of semi-classics rubbing shoulders with a third-rate dance band. As memorable as the music remains, the title track

Hank Davis

REPUBLIC PICTURES presents

DICK TRACY

with
RALPH BYRD
KAY HUGHES
Smiley BURNETTE
LEE VAN ATTA

Based on cartoon strip by CHESTER GOULD
A REPUBLIC SERIAL

Produced by NAT LEVINE

15 Action EPISODES

Episode 7 The GHOST TOWN MYSTERY

seems pasted together with little concern for abrupt mood swings. Actress Kay Hughes (Gwen), who was all of 23 years old during this filming, is blessed with a rather squeaky voice that 1937 sound recording equipment does nothing to flatter. She's working the same sonic range as Junior, and he's a pre-pubescent boy. Finally, two more bumpkins named Oscar and Elmer appear for a couple of minutes in Chapter 5. Did Producer Nat Levine really think he hadn't dumbed down the script enough? Even Ralph Byrd, who is forced to interact with these halfwits during their mercifully brief cameo, looks pained. Oscar and Elmer (who receive screen credit on all 15 chapters!) make Smiley Burnette look like a Nobel laureate.

Burnette's one funny moment comes at the end of the final chapter when he almost shoots himself in the foot. It's a sight gag that lasts for barely more than a second and involves no dialogue. A few more like that and his effect would have been subtle and positive rather than the wretched excess on display here. Plainly Burnette is and was beyond caring about such criticism. He died in 1967 at age 56, a veteran of over 200 film appearances and best known as Gene Autry's sidekick, Frog Milhouse. Burnette also wrote over 300 songs, a considerable legacy. The man was definitely attuned to his audience, even if his roles did not reflect what is most admirable about American culture. But they were lucrative.

Ralph Byrd died suddenly in 1952 at age 43. He had recently completed filming 39 episodes for the 1950-51 TV season of *Dick Tracy*. Whether he liked it or not–and undoubtedly he experienced both feelings–Byrd was locked into the Tracy role. To this day he remains the best-known screen version of *Dick Tracy*. The competition consisting of Warren Beatty and Morgan Conway doesn't pose much threat. Along with four Republic serials (there were three sequels to this 1937 entry), Byrd also appeared in two *Tracy* movies in 1947 and worked till his death on the early *Tracy* TV show. Ralph Byrd made other films, almost all of them cheap and poorly remembered. Whatever their limited qualities, such fare often revealed that as an actor Ralph Byrd was capable of far more than he could show playing the square-jawed detective. Sad or frustrating as that may have been for Byrd, he presented serial fans with an undeniable legacy. Ralph Byrd *is* Dick Tracy. Not many serial heroes appeared in sequels. *Flash Gordon* won the silver medal for making three appearances. But *Dick Tracy* won the gold: He and his alter ego, Ralph Byrd, appeared four times in serials with their names in lights. That's a record that will stand.

Secret Agent X-9

Often this 1937 serial from Universal is confused with another Universal serial also called *Secret Agent X-9*. The latter effort was released in 1945 and is largely notable for its star, Lloyd Bridges. While entertaining in a campy wartime way, the 1945 effort is nowhere as lovable and exciting as this earlier entry.

The character of G-Man Secret Agent X-9 was created by famous detective novelist Dashiell Hammett and first appeared in a 1934 comic strip that was slated to compete with *Dick Tracy*. A barely known artist named Alex Raymond, who had recently begun work on another strip called *Flash Gordon*, drew it. In one form or another, *Secret Agent X-9* supported a radio show, two movie serials and a comic strip that was still around in the 1960s. Given the massive changes in American society from the pre-WWII era to Viet Nam, that's a marvelous amount of staying power for a small piece of popular culture.

It's a bit puzzling to analyze why this 1937 serial is as enjoyable as it is. On paper, there's little that stands out. The plot is standard serial fare; in fact, it may even be a bit thin by those standards. The crown jewels of Belgravia (a lovely fictional East European name) are stolen by an ace international jewel thief named Brenda. Once they get to New York, the jewels get lost and there's a continuing shuffle to claim them between the G-Men and a band of thugs. And that's about all that goes on for 12 chapters. About the only source of tension is discovering the identity of Brenda. In usual serial form, we spend most of the 12 chapters wondering which of the characters we know has a double life as a man of many faces.

The acting is just fine, with no really front-line performer to carry the day. There are familiar faces in supporting roles here, to be sure, but none of them reveal anything resembling star quality. Notable among them is Lon Chaney, Jr. as one of the thugs. This is one of his bit parts before rising to prominence not only in serials (his appearance in 1942's *Overland Mail* gave him 10 times the screen time and feature billing), but also as Universal's enduring Wolf Man character. With the wisdom of hindsight, it is easy to see Lon Chaney here and know he is capable of much more. The same can be said for German-born actor Henry

Scott Kolk and David Oliver get the drop on some thugs, including a soon-to-be-famous Lon Chaney, Jr. (fourth from right).

Brandon who plays the role of Blackstone, head of the New York gang of thugs and second in command to Brenda (or *is* he Brenda?). Brandon, who was only 25 when he made this film, is an imposing, Errol Flynn kind of guy who carries himself like he knows it. Brandon acted in other 1930s serials including *Buck Rogers* and *Jungle Jim,* but went on to the serial highpoint of his career in the title role of Republic's 1940 *Drums of Fu Manchu*. He in over 100 films through the 1980s including the brillaint *The Searchers*, Brandon died in 1990.

Also notable is Jean Rogers, Universal's reigning serial queen at the time. She went from work on *Adventures of Frank Merriwell, Ace Drummond* and *Tailspin Tommy In The Great Air Mystery* to starring in the first two *Flash Gordon* serials (the roles for which she is loved by serial fans to this day). The year after this film, Rogers was gone from cliffhangers. She continued to appear in features until 1951 when she retired altogether. David Oliver handles the comic relief stint as the childlike, not-too-bright cabdriver named Pidge. As characters of this ilk go, he is far less offensive than many.

And this brings us to the leading man, the title character, played by Scott Kolk. Scott *who,* you might ask? Indeed. Scott Kolk appeared in films for less than 10 years. This starring role and an appearance in the 1930 classic *All Quiet On The Western Front* were probably the highlights of his brief career. Kolk retired from films the year after this serial was made. Born in 1905, Kolk seems an odd choice for the role. He is similar to Dick Purcell, another curious choice, when he starred in the 1944 serial *Captain America*. Both of these actors were competent, if undistinguished. They exude a likeable middle-aged charm that stops well short of dashing. They smile a lot, are probably kind to children and small animals, but they don't seem in any way larger than life. The comic book version of *Secret Agent X-9* certainly was both dashing and larger-than-life, as were most characters from the pen of Dashiell Hammett. Kolk's character is likeable, but seems conspicuously scaled down to human dimensions. This is not a plea to turn him into Superman, but there seems a lot of room between the flying man of steel and a guy with an office in the Federal Building who sometimes goes out on cases.

A couple of critical notes—there is a funny continuity error in Chapter 11. The Baron is shown escaping in a car with the steering wheel plainly on the right side. A moment later the negative is flip-flopped and the wheel and driver are back on the left. Universal has inserted several images from earlier films as a cost-saving measure. One is a near car-train wreck, and the other, curiously, is a street scene featuring a newsboy (would this really have been so expensive to reshoot?). Both stand out like sore thumbs simply because the inserted images are of relatively poor quality. It's like going from an Ansel Adams photo to something your Aunt Sally shot with a Kodak Brownie camera. Watch for a scene in Chapter 3 featuring what should be a country bumpkin farmer. There must have been some hayseed character actors waiting for work on the Universal back lot, but this guy wasn't one of them. The accent and demeanor aren't even close. He repeats his rural line twice to set the mood ("City slicker, eh? Well I'll learn you."), but the whole thing is laughably off the mark.

One jarring note that won't escape serial fans is the repeated use of musical cues from *Flash Gordon*. The choice might have been reasonable in 1937, but now that these themes and interludes have become irrevocably associated with the three *Flash Gordon* serials, their use here almost seems like piracy.

Perhaps one reason I found this serial so consistently watchable is the quality of the image available from VCI. I have rarely seen a cleaner print. Serial historian Fred Shay is the source of this material and fans and collectors should be indebted to him for providing it. The DVD box simply states, "Digitally remastered from 35 mm fine grain source." That barely conveys it. The scenes are beautifully lit, the grain is tight and the contrast is high. It's like looking at a series of sharp 1930s photographs come to life. This film couldn't have looked any better even at the premier over 70 years ago. In a perfect world, film quality and image quality would be considered two different things and that critical response can keep them separate. In reality, that isn't always the case. Image clarity brings an immediacy that affects the film's appeal. Just as muddy, third-generation copies of older films can put us off, we can be entranced by watching a mint first-generation source. In this case, I felt a bit like a time traveler finding a portal back to 1937. I felt closer to the setting, the actors and the creaky old plot. The effect was to bring new life to this piece of cinematic history.

SOS Coast Guard

Fons of director William Witney, then *SOS Coast Guard*, a Republic serial from 1937, will find special meaning in this offering. Not only is it the first cliffhanger that Witney took primary responsibility for directing (he had contributed to *The Painted Stallion* earlier in the year), but also it was during this shoot that Witney meet his future wife, Maxine Doyle. Although Doyle, who starred in *SOS Coastguard,* was a competent serial actress, it was Witney who went on to become, arguably, the best director in the history of movie serials.

Some 70 years after its release, *Coastguard* remains energetic and entertaining. The plot is fairly standard issue: Mad scientist Bela Lugosi (did he *ever* play the boy next door?) decides to sell his deadly disintegrating gas to a foreign power. Our government has got to stop him, so they send Lieutenant Terry King, played by the ever-smiling Ralph Byrd, fresh from his stint as Dick Tracy. All the other required serial ingredients are here, including a spunky girl reporter (Doyle) and a strapping and mean henchman (Richard Alexander).

The serial offers 12 episodes of what Republic did best. As we all know, that doesn't mean lengthy conversations. One of Republic's unsung strengths was their ability to generate catchy names—both for their serials as well as for the people and things that populate them. *SOS Coastguard* is no exception. Bela's character is named "Boroff," an obvious contraction of *Bor*is and Karl*off*. A

name that might have slightly irritated Lugosi, as the studio-fed publicity machine hinted at a feud between the two horror stars. Lugosi's henchman is named "Thorg," which sounds like something from a Neanderthal family reunion. Finally, the mysterious secret element needed to make Boroff's disintegrating gas is called "zanzoid." What a great name! You just know it's up to no good, whatever it is.

Richard Alexander does a fine job conveying the physical power of Thorg. His character spends at least half his screen time stomping around in a loincloth or submerged in cold water. Unfortunately, Alexander, best known for the role of Prince Barin in *Flash Gordon*, is *too* good an actor. Thorg emerges as one of the most sympathetic characters in the entire serial. Even when he's supposed to look menacing, there is a sense that a really nice guy is inside that hulking exterior, who is waiting to break free of all this Evil and tell Bela to play nice. When Bela coldly shoots Thorg in the back in

Bela giving orders at the microphone.

the final chapter, it's a good bet that more than a few kids in the audience were pretty upset.

A couple of other actors deserve special mention. John Piccori must have thought he was part of the Ralph Byrd traveling road show. Several months earlier he had appeared with Byrd in Republic's first *Dick Tracy* serial, playing Moloch, the evil hunchback scientist. Seeing him here in the role of Rackerby, it's hard not to imagine him stroking a black cat while planning our hero's demise. Lee Ford handles the mandatory comic relief bit in the role of Snapper McGee. Snapper is one of the most physically and behaviorally geeky guys in serial history. He is a direct precursor to Don Knotts, and it is difficult to imagine Ford playing any other role. Indeed, Lee Ford came back to play Mike McGurk in *Dick Tracy Returns* (1938) and *Dick Tracy's G-Men* (1939). In both, he brought the same half-witted bumpkin charm that Smiley Burnette had provided in the first Tracy serial. Characters like McGee, McGurk and Happy Hapgood in *Flash Gordon's Trip To Mars* remind us how fortunate we are that the need for yuks at the expense of the village idiot has all but disappeared.

Director William Witney reveals many amusing stories about the filming of *SOS Coast Guard* in his autobiography. None is funnier than Bela Lugosi's "mental block" which kept him from reciting a particular line of dialogue correctly. In a critical scene, Bela was supposed to utter the warning, "Quick, out the back door!" Try as he might, Bela could not get past saying "Qvik, out ze back yad!" The special effects are a mixed bag in this serial. There's a car crash at the end of Chapter 8 that just defies logic. It's simply too good to have been done with miniatures, although the alternatives seem unthinkable, given Republic's budget.

Hank Davis

On the other hand, there are a lot of very obvious rear-screen projection scenes involving ocean waves and a few too many toy boats on Republic's tiny pond.

There's quite a difference between seeing old cars and old boats. Obviously they're both 70 years old, but to most viewers today, the cars—especially those shown in rear screen projection street scenes, look ancient whereas the boats—well, they just look like boats. Something else to date the car scenes is how much dust is kicked up during the frequent chases. You'd almost think there were no paved roads in southern California in 1937.

The most important special effect—the disintegrating gas—was one Republic knew they could bring in under budget.

Bela and Thorg (Richard Alexander) in posed publicity shot.

The technique involved allowing film to literally melt while being projected. The effect, which is nearly psychedelic, had been used to perfection in Mascot's 1935 serial, *The Phantom Empire*. There it had been used to convey the destruction of the underground city of Murania. It was a good trick to have in the director's bag. Rocks could appear to melt, as could buildings or people. It was just what the doctor ordered in *SOS Coast Guard,* which Republic managed to bring in for a grand total of $128,530. The melting film trick managed to convey the menace of a secret weapon, and since nobody really knows how things look when they disintegrate, the images produced by melting film stock were as good as any (and cheaper than most).

The final chapter does as good a job of any serial finale of tying up all the loose ends. The bad guys are killed off, the good guys are victorious and the U.S. is saved with all flags flying. Knowing that in real life the director got the leading lady and spent the next 35 years happily married to her is the icing on the cake.

Tim Tyler's Luck

There is no better way to pack a movie theater with kids on Saturday afternoon than to give them one of their own to cheer for. Superheroes are fine and dandy, but to see *yourself* up there—or at least someone your age—battling bad guys, tigers and robots. Well, it didn't get any better than that.

Tim Tyler—not to be confused with B-movie star Tom Tyler—is part of the grand tradition of spunky American kids that reached its zenith in *Jack Armstrong—The All American Boy*. To his credit, Tim Tyler came first, appearing as a daily cartoon strip in August 1928. Three years later, a barely pubescent Mr. Tyler had made it to the Sunday papers, a major step up for one so young. In the comic, Tim shares most of his adventures with his pal Spud. By 1932, the two had relocated to darkest Africa, where there was no shortage of bad guys. A black panther named Fang, whom he saves and befriends, also joined comic book hero Tim Tyler on many adventures.

The popularity of *Tim Tyler's Luck* did not escape Universal Studios, who signed a deal with King Features in 1937 to produce a 12-Chapter serial. Veteran director Ford Beebe was brought in for the project. Beebe was still an unknown to most serial fans. Beginning the next year, his work on the second and third *Flash Gordon* serials would change that forever. The title role was given to young Frankie Thomas (barely 16 when shooting began). Thomas had only two film credits in his résumé but was a photogenic and spunky little tyke. He would continue to play the youth card throughout most of his career, appearing in four *Nancy Drew* films in the late 1930s, followed by some *Dead End Kids* titles. He earned a recurring role as Cliff Barbour in the 1949 TV series *One Man's Family*, but didn't hit his stride until the following year when he was cast as the title character of *Tom Corbett, Space Cadet*. To this day, it is the Corbett role that

Tim (Frankie Thomas) and Lora Lacey (Frances Robinson)

Thomas is remembered for. No doubt, fans of early TV space operas see Tim Tyler as a historical curio or glimpse of their interplanetary man when he was just a lad of 16.

The serial is a delightful slice of innocence from a long-gone era. It is essentially a Western set in the jungle. Even the "jungle" is quite erratic, looking one minute like darkest Africa and the next like Bronson Canyon, the setting for innumerable B Westerns. The natives are everything you'd expect in a 1937 serial: They are extremely dumb and speak some form of "ooga-booga" language. Tim, on the other hand, is quite conversant with English and is also able to communicate with his panther and chimpanzee, as well as passing elephants. He gives them all detailed instructions in English, which they obey to the letter.

The serial also features 21-year-old Frances Robinson in the role of Lora Lacey. As written, she's just a bit too old for Tim and a bit too young for anybody else. She's there to clear the name of her brother, who has been framed for a crime committed by Spider Webb, a wonderfully named bad guy. Robinson appeared in about 50 B-movies during the 1930s and '40s before making a career of TV work in the 1950s, with repeat appearances on *The Jack Benny Program*, *The Donna Reed Show*, as well as *Kraft Theatre* and *Four-Star Playhouse*. She died in 1971 with an impressive list of credits that began just two years before this appearance. The aforementioned Spider Webb was played by veteran movie bad guy Norman Willis. Willis is one of those fringe contributors whom movie historians love to discover years after the fact. Here's your cue, fellas. Willis appeared in over 100 films from 1934 to 1965. Most of his roles were either uncredited or listed as "henchman" or "gang member." You knew the face, but probably missed the name. Willis appeared (uncredited, of course) in the classic *Mighty Joe Young*,listed as "Man with mustache at bar." Norman Willis died in 1988 at the age of 85. Undoubtedly, he had stories to tell.

One more character in *Tim Tyler's Luck* is worthy of note. Earl Douglas plays a bad guy-turned-good named Lazar (Lazarre in some sources). Lazar provides whatever comic relief is needed after the chimp scampers away. He is a clone of Lucky Pierre from *Trois Riviere*. The character is delightfully childlike, loyal and incompetent. His English, too, leaves something to be desired ("Lazar he no go here, eh?"). Even the chimp has trouble understanding him. Born Luigi Yaconelli, Earl Douglas probably spoke as much French as the chimp. Between 1935 and 1941, he appeared in over 30 films, barely rising above the level of "unbilled henchman." He did appear in at least seven serials, however, including such memorable fare as *Flash Gordon's Trip to Mars* (1938).

Some inspired moments of serial lunacy include six guys in gorilla suits, jumping up and down and making what are easily the dumbest gorilla noises ever recorded. There is also an armored car, "invented" by Tim's father (a professor, no less). The sight of this heavily armored clunky vehicle driving through the jungle is worth the price of admission. The car is the single most expensive prop in sight and looks suspiciously like the vehicle used by Republic in their 1936 Crash Corrigan serial *The Undersea Kingdom*. If spending that much on a prop, it's always a good idea to rent it out to another studio.

Perhaps the funniest motif running through the serial is Tim Tyler's obsession with water. Whenever he encounters a tragedy, he grabs for his canteen. You can bet that when he finds a fallen comrade, whether it's a panther, a gunned down friend or his own father, he will immediately say, "We've got to get you some water!" When a great white hunter is shot and thrown over a cliff, Tim kneels by his broken body saying, "If only I could have gotten you some water." Apparently streams in this region of darkest Africa have marvelous healing powers known only to prepubescent boys.

Although this thick slice of nostalgia marked the only cinematic appearance of *Tim Tyler's Luck*, the comic strip carried on until 1972. That's a stark reminder of just how deeply this kind of juvenile adventure appealed to kids across more than 40 years of cultural change. The best version of *Tim Tyler's Luck* is available from VCI on a freshly minted DVD. The package includes, among other extras, a 2005 interview with Frankie Thomas. It's always a bit sobering to see our childhood heroes turn into senior citizens before our eyes. In his adult life, Thomas became an expert bridge player and instructor and wrote mystery novels (*Sherlock Holmes and the Masquerade Murders*). He died in May 2006 at the age of 85.

1938
The Fighting Devil Dogs

The Fighting Devil Dogs was the third Republic serial directed by the ace team of William Witney and John English. Released in May 1938, the results are a vintage example of very low-budget serial moviemaking. The central character is a villain known as "The Lightning," who plans to take over the world using a futuristic and rather scary-looking electrical weapon. His adversaries are a couple of Marines played by Lee Powell and Herman Brix, both of whom had appeared in Republic's *The Lone Ranger* serial just three months earlier. Powell refers to The Lightning as "a fiend who can menace the entire world with his diabolical machine." This is everything anyone needs to know about the plot.

The serial gets off to a good start, courtesy of some well-used newsreel footage of Marines landing in China. Within minutes of the start of Chapter 1, we learn what kind of guys our two heroes are: They save a woman and her baby from an air raid, at great personal risk to themselves. On top of such sterling qualities, both of these guys really look swell in their Marine uniforms.

Soon the action moves to "Linchuria," where our heroes have their first encounter with The Lightning and his mysterious weapon. The Marines find a house full of dead people, recently killed with nary a mark on them. It's creepy business, to say the least. Even the flies in the room are dead. Brix observes, "It smells kind of funny in here, like the odor in a power house." Good call, Herman. Electricity is indeed the culprit. It's being carried on a highly charged aerial torpedo which sounds like an air raid siren as it travels through the sky. By the end of the first chapter, we've seen its effects on a house and a boat—every living creature is killed. The Lightning also has a gun that shoots electric rays (wiggly lines etched on the negative). Either way, this is not a guy to mess with, and a frightening experience to find one of his little lightning symbols left behind as a calling card in your neighborhood.

During these early days at Republic, it seems to appear that the studio was just one big happy repertory company. Not only do we have Powell and Brix from *The Lone Ranger*, but a couple of prime holdovers from last season's *Dick Tracy* serial are also on display. One is actor John Piccori—memorable as Moloch, the demented cat-stroking villain in *Tracy*. Here, Piccori is no less menacing. Gone is the cat, but ever-present is the demented gleam in his eye, and the silent movie–like posturing. The other leftover from the *Tracy* serial is a prop, and a most memorable one at that. The Wing makes its return flight in *Flying Devil Dogs*, appearing in some new footage, as well as some liberally recycled scenes from the previous year's work.

The two Marine heroes are highly motivated to capture The Lightning. Not only is he a menace to our country, but he has actually killed some of their pals,

Aboard the Flying Wing, The Lightning confronts Eleanor Stewart as John Piccori (right) looks on.

along with Powell's father. The fight has become personal. The good guys work slavishly to neutralize the aerial torpedoes, but the arch villain seems to anticipate their every move. Is he among them? Have his henchmen infiltrated the good guys' inner circle? Don't answer that. The question is strictly rhetorical. Of course, he has. This is a *serial,* after all. The bad guys always walk unnoticed among the good guys. It's a reliable way of reminding us that they're not actually smarter; they win because they cheat.

If The Lightning has one weakness, it's on the soundtrack. The poor guy talks in an agitated nasal voice that sounds eerily like Don Adams in the 1960s television show *Get Smart.* If only The Lightning had come along 10 years earlier, he could have worked in the silent movie era without revealing his vocal deficiencies. But even if he sounds awful, The Lightning looks just grand. He's wearing one of the sharpest masks you're going to find in the annals of serial costumes. The black cape is nothing special, but that headgear looks like—do we dare say it—the prototype for Darth Vader.

With reused footage of the Wing, as well as *lots* of stock footage (war scenes, steel mills, tropical islanders, underwater scenes) and rear screen projection work, this looks like it was a pretty cheap serial to make. Actually, directors Witney and English brought the whole thing in on a budget under $95,000—a minuscule amount even by serial standards. In comparison, *The Lone Ranger* cost over

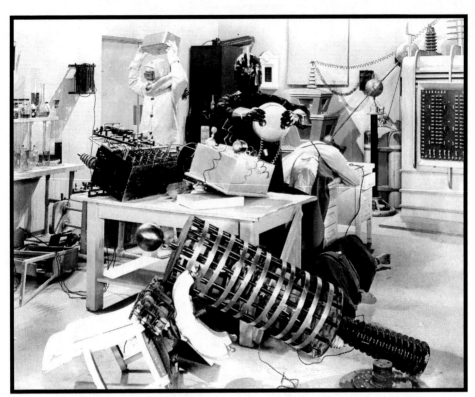

The Lightning trashes a lab before it can disable his thunderbolt weapon.

$160,000. We get an early example of cost cutting in Chapter 7 when we hear the dreaded line: "Gentlemen, I think we should review this case." In other words, cue the previous episodes so we can recycle about 10-minutes worth of film. In Chapter 8, the "two ships moving together and crushing the hero's speedboat" cliffhanger sequence is lifted intact from the previous year's *Dick Tracy* serial. Perhaps, not surprisingly, director William Witney was no great fan of *The Fighting Devil Dogs*. Discussing the project in his autobiography, Witney recalls, "It had definitely been a real quick cheater and Jack (director John English) and I were ashamed that we couldn't help make it any better. Everything had gone well. The leads were easy to work with, but even with our best efforts, we couldn't make it smell any better."

There's an odd plot touch in Chapter 9: The Lightning kidnaps the heroine in order to force her father to return a special piece of navigating equipment. He complies and it looks like The Lightning is ready to make good on his promise to release the girl. But she can't leave well enough alone and reaches out and unmasks him (saying "You!!!"). Of course, that means waving goodbye to any chance that The Lightning will follow through on his promise.

It isn't until Chapter 11 that someone finally observes that just maybe one of the inner circle can't be trusted. Apparently none of our heroes watch movie serials. Ever since Chapter 2, this has been painfully clear to even the dimmest

Powell and Herman Brix are attacked by three of The Lighting's men. Note the insignias on specially designed protective suits.

eight year olds in the audience. Once the possibility of a double agent working among us has been raised, the producers have another excuse to recycle yet more footage as we summarize all three of the suspects for the big resolution in next week's final episode. We won't reveal the identity of The Lightning, but rest assured, it is highly unlikely a guess correctly is forthcoming, unless guessing the least likely candidate. The last chapter is a lot of fun, crammed full of action and mental gymnastics. The highlight is a clever gimmick used to unmask The Lightning. That much we *can* reveal. All the suspects are seated in a room and told that the girl can identify The Lightning. The curtains are drawn back and the girl stands there, ready to talk. As she starts to make her fateful statement, one of the suspects pulls out a lightning ray gun and shoots her. In retrospect, it seems an odd thing to do, since the villain blows his cover in the very act of silencing the girl. But, alas! It was only a mirror image of the girl and she remains unscathed amidst a sea of broken glass.

The Lightning no longer has his secret identity. He flees in a business suit without his Darth Vader mask and takes off in the Wing. We know he's not going to get far, but he does bark out one immortal line of dialogue to what's left of his henchmen: "Get your dynamos going!"

Words to live by in these troubled times.

Hank Davis

The Spider's Web

Think of it like this, the success of a pulp or comic book hero inevitably leads to clones or copycat characters. First there was Superman and then shazam! there was Captain Marvel. Although they are no longer as famous today, the same thing happened in the case of The Shadow, a massively popular star of books and radio in the 1930s. The Shadow yielded a virtual clone named The Spider. Both characters were caped crimefighters, who enjoyed distinguished alter egos. And if that reminds you of Batman as well, you're plainly on the right track.

Even though the Spider was less popular than his inspiration, the Shadow, it was the Spider who first came to life as a movie serial hero in 1938, when Columbia Pictures released their screen adaptation. It was only the fifth serial produced by the studio. Surprisingly, the Shadow had to wait until 1940 for Columbia to bring him to serialized life on the big screen. And which of these caped crime fighters in disguise got the better deal? The verdict seems pretty clear nearly 70 years later. Despite its weaker source material, *The Spider's Web* is the better serial. Mind you, they're both good — which is saying something for two Columbia serials. But remember, they're both *early* Columbia serials — at least early enough to keep producer Sam Katzman out of the equation.

Since this is the first Columbia serial we've discussed, this is probably a good time to make some general comments about them. First we find that Columbia serials are a slightly different breed. They went about their cliffhanging business in ways that were noticeably different. These will be discussed in the individual serials. For now, it's best to be aware that critics tend to be polarized by these films. Some enjoy them; others absolutely disdain them. Columbia got into the serial business relatively late (1937) and stayed around until the genre barely had a pulse (1956). Just about everyone agrees that the best serials from Columbia were the early ones. Things got pretty bad by the late 1940s, and by 1950 they had pretty much hit rock bottom.

For now, let's take these serials one at a time. *The Spider's Web* is our first and it is more than just good. It's up there with the best issued by any studio. There's some great stunt work and the hyperkinetic pacing is up to the best of Republic's output. Appearing in his first of four serials, Warren Hull digs his teeth into a very meaty role. His demeanor is always jovial, cheery, lighthearted and even flippant. He shows no anxiety, no matter how bleak things look. Hull plays a man of many faces: suave criminologist Richard Wentworth (not to be confused with Lamont Cranston); former safe cracker Blinky McQuade and, of course, the Spider, himself. Most of the time it is actually stuntman Eddie Parker who appears in the cape. But when the Spider is sitting still and talking, that's Hull under the cape.

DIABOLICAL DESTRUCTION UNLEASHED BY AN UNKNOWN FIEND!

THE SPIDER'S WEB

Based upon "The Spider" Magazine Stories

WARREN HULL
IRIS MEREDITH
RICHARD FISKE

Directed by RAY TAYLOR and JAMES W. HORNE

A COLUMBIA CHAPTER PLAY

Hull's sidekick is a Sikh servant named Ram Singh, (Kenneth Duncan). True to the pulp version of *The Spider*, Hull often calls Singh "Warrior" when he talks to him. Singh calls Hull "Sahib" or "Mahster." Warren Hull was in danger of getting spoiled. He went from this production to his next Columbia serial, *Mandrake the Magician*, in which he again had an exotic manservant (called Lothar) bowing and scraping to him for 12 chapters.

Although Wentworth is well respected by the cops, they are not too fond of the Spider, whom they regard as just another criminal. Only the members of Wentworth's household know that he is in reality the Spider. Secrets just can't be kept from your cleaning lady, can they? In fact, the cops and the criminals are both after the Spider. Nobody suspects that Wentworth, Blinky McQuade and the Spider are the same guy. Hull has this canned speech that he seems fond of delivering: "The law is too handicapped with red tape. To save human lives, the Spider must operate outside the law." Ram Singh really is a faithful servant. He listens to this self-serving tripe over and over again. Hull must think the man is

The Spider (Warren Hull) with Iris Meredith, Richard Fiske and Ken Duncan

an idiot. He delivers the same lines, verbatim, episode after episode. And every time, Ram Singh, the great warrior, sits and listens attentively to the same jive. He never says, "Jeez, Sahib, how many times you gonna tell me that?"

The villain of the serial is called The Octopus. His mission is to sabotage the nation's transportation system. The Octopus limps into his boardroom (much like The Lame One in Republic's *Dick Tracy* serial) and addresses his henchmen, who sit around a conference table while he preaches to them about his goals and their ineptitude. He's got a lot to preach about—mainly on the topic of ineptitude. These guys are beyond redemption. And, of course, this is where director James Horne digs in. Horne cut his teeth on Laurel & Hardy comedies, and just loves to turn the bad guys into fodder for comedy. Serial fans either love or hate this about Horne's direction. The truth is, some of his shtick is very funny, but it undeniably comes at the price of tension and credibility. These bad guys are lovable 1930s thugs. Their voices are raspy and they say things like "I can get *woid* to him" or "That's a swell lookin' *goil*." In the middle of a gunfight, one of the thugs holds up a small wooden folding chair as a shield as if it could ward off bullets. It's a fleeting moment, but it tells you everything you need to know about James Horne's approach to serial bad guys.

The henchmen are actually interchangeable pieces. The Spider shoots them like he were swatting flies. Even The Octopus plugs his less successful assistants,

The dreaded Octopus, complete with artificial right hand

no matter how they beg for mercy. And, like houseflies, there seems to be an inexhaustible supply of thugs—one no brighter or more effective than the last. Both Wentworth and the Spider shoot these guys as fast as they see them, often with two guns blazing at once. The dead thugs just get crated off and new ones emerge. The effect is almost surreal. They might as well be coming back to life.

Here's some vintage serial lunacy to watch for: The Octopus commands, "Take him to the vibration room" as he prepares to dispatch one of his victims. The guy is made hyper sensitive to sound so they can finish him off by throwing a firecracker into his hospital room! What a way to die! Wouldn't it have been just a little easier to shoot him?

Wentworth uses television to spy on the Octopus (The reception is "clear as crystal"), and also pulls out a videophone in the final chapter. It is nearly 70 years later and we're still not using them as casually as Wentworth does in this 1938 serial. In Chapter 10, the Octopus' men shoot down an airplane with a ray gun mounted in a very modern-looking car trailer. Both the ray gun and the car look cheesy, but the trailer is a knockout. This really is a very 1930s movie. Everybody smokes. Everyone wears hats, even indoors. Everyone starts his sentences with "Say!" Everything is "swell."

On the critical front, there are some pretty awful take-outs in this serial. An elevator hurtling to earth turns out to have a safety brake. How fortunate. Later,

Hank Davis

Wentworth's plane is shown totally aflame, falling to earth like a stone. We're set to see our hero parachuting to safety next week in typical serial fashion, but no! The hero uses "high speed" to put out the flames. Huh? Next we see the plane flying gracefully along with no damage—not even a trace of soot. Worse yet, he drops about 10 bombs and destroys the ray gun that shot him down. Bombs? Just where did they come from in this little two-seater?

Like Universal, Columbia Pictures tended to use inserts with real traffic and fire engines. While probably looking credible in 1938, this newsreel footage was probably 10-15 years old. That means it's smack dab in the silent movie era. Viewing today, we can adapt to the look of 1938, but this stock footage seems ancient, as if the serial had suddenly gone through a time warp. The Columbia style of serial uses something called double cliffhangers. Arguably, they destroy whatever tension might have drawn audiences the following week. For example, we've just witnessed the Spider's plane plummeting to earth. Rather than leave us to ponder the plight we've just seen, a voiceover (read by radio man Knox Manning) tells us in essence, "Oh, that's no problem folks. He's back next week, where he'll encounter a *real* cliffhanger." We then watch the Spider shot at by an army of thugs. And then the immortal words are spoken, "Will He Survive?" Jeez, I'm only 12 years old and now I have *two* cliffhangers to worry about!

In Chapter 5, Hull breaks out his "old magic act" to entertain the folks. It's a nice homey moment and it must have impressed someone at Columbia Pictures. Hull was back in the magic business six months later, in the title role of *Mandrake the Magician*. And, if that weren't enough, he got to do his Spider act one more time in 1941 when Columbia released its much-awaited serial, *The Spider Returns*.

Hawk of the Wilderness

This may not be the best serial issued by Republic during its Golden Age, but it sure as hell is the prettiest to look at. Shot almost entirely on location and largely outdoors, the settings are just breathtaking and wonderfully photographed to boot. In his autobiography, director William Witney recalls traveling to Mammoth Lakes in the southern High Sierras in California. The location is full of big skies, towering pines and imposing (7,500 ft) elevations. Who says black and white film can't do justice to natural beauty?

The story line, while simple enough to film as a 12-episode serial, is more complex than many. There is a backstory for those who like them (undoubtedly, most 12 year olds in the audience didn't), but it's there all the same. The reason for this added complexity is quite simple: The film is adapted from a book (of the same name) by William L. Chester. A book! An actual collection of paper with printed words on them surrounded by two hard covers. Not an everyday occurrence for a movie serial! You can bet the nice folks at Republic were going to trumpet all that class for everything it was worth. Every single chapter begins

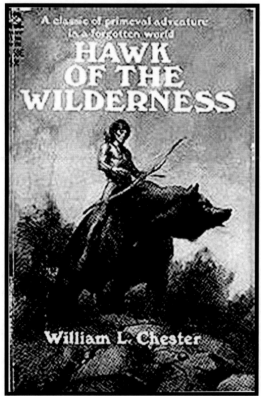

with a picture of the book and a reminder that the movie was based on it. The entire audience was protected from parental accusations of "wasting their time watching junk." Not today, Mom. It was based on a *book*!

The book may have had a dramatic title that the studio was not about to change, but the real name of this serial should have been "Tarzan vs. the Indians." Nothing would have suited it better. Of course, that would have meant negotiation with the Edgar Rice Burroughs estate and even more expense. But to understand this serial, keep the alternate *Tarzan* title in mind and it will all make sense. Here's a quick summary of what happens. Back in 1913, a dashing explorer named Lincoln Rand, along with his wife and young son

Herman Brix and the duly smitten Jill Martin

and their Indian companion, Mokuyi, have taken a ship to discover a lost island
north of the Arctic Circle. It is Rand's belief that a mysterious lost tribe of Indians
lives there (amidst great treasure, of course), and it is these Indians from whom
all other Indians have descended. So all the Sioux and Pawnee roaming around
Saturday matinees for the last century are the direct descendants of the folks on
this island waaaaay up North. Got that?

Before he can confirm his theory, a great storm overtakes the expedition and
all is lost—except for Mokuyi and the infant son. Right before their ship breaks
up, Lincoln Rand writes a message to his pal Dr. Munro, telling him that he has
found the island but has to abandon ship in the storm. The message gets sealed
in a bottle and tossed into the sea.

So who finds this message in a bottle 25 years later? No-good pirate/thief/mur-
derer Solerno (William Royle) and his band of thugs, who are running from the
Coast Guard. The message intrigues Solerno with its reference to great treasure.
Posing as an innocent sailor, he dutifully carries it to Dr. Munro (Tom Chatterton).
We have now fast-forwarded to the present time (1938). The old man is thrilled
to learn that his long-lost friend might still be alive and mounts an expedition to
the island, using Solerno and his band as a crew. As soon as they arrive, Solerno
shows his true colors, turning on Dr. Munro and demanding the treasure. But that's
not all. See how much plot you get when you option a real-live book?

Hank Davis

Not only does the Munro party have to do battle with their pirate crew, but they've also got an island full of Indians who mean them no good. These guys are either fearful that the white explorers have caused their local volcano to start acting up, or they are just permanently pissed off at some intuitive sense that their descendants have been doing poorly at the hands of the white folks back in North America, wherever that is. Remember, they've never been south of the Arctic Circle. Either way, they are on the warpath.

Their leader (Monte Blue) is the wonderfully named Yellow Weasel. He is mean and brutal and cowardlym and I have looked through hundreds of movie credits and never found a better name for an Indian villain. Yellow Weasel. Just think of it. Yellow *anything* would be bad enough. "You're yellow!" "I am not!" We all know what it means, and this guy is *it*. But to add on "weasel!" How much better does it get? There is probably no mammal, except for the rat, which gets worse press. Weasels could start their own Anti-defamation League. And here we have it all: Yellow Weasel.

When the survivor party lands on the island in a little dinghy, they are wearing suits, ties and hats. Did they think they were going to the opera? It makes you wonder if Columbus wore a three-piece suit. Their own mutinous crew and the local Indians under the leadership of Yellow Weasel set upon Munro's party. How are they to survive? Well, it turns out that when Lincoln Rand's ship sank, his faithful Indian companion Mokuyi grabbed the infant and swam to shore. That infant has grown up to be Hawk of the Wilderness—a.k.a. Kioga—a.k.a. Herman Brix. A few other a.k.a.s also apply. Herman Brix will soon be a.k.a. Bruce Bennett, for, as WWII approached, no one wanted to broadcast his German ancestry. The final a.k.a. is for Brix's character. They may call him Kioga here (I think he's referred to once as Hawk just to justify the title), but his real name should be Tarzan. He sure looks like Tarzan and spends half the movie swinging

Ray Mala and Herman Brix

from tree to tree with some portable vines he keeps around his waist. In fact, three years earlier, guess who had starred in a serial called *The New Adventures of Tarzan*? Yup. None other than Herman Brix, who has a real Buster Crabbe look (part Tarzan, part Flash Gordon) in this serial. Brix comes across as a likeable guy, with long blond hair, physically graceful and extremely honorable.

So now we have the Munro expedition party, the Indians, the mutinous pirates and the Kioga & Mokuyi team. A few other complications occur before we set these folks loose on each other. Tarzan/Kioga has a pet pooch named Tawnee. An Australian shepherd named Tuffy plays with him. He's a pretty winning little dog and when he gets shot in the leg (on camera, no less) in Chapter 2, the audience must have gotten real silent in a hurry. Fortunately, Brix rubs some magic poultice on his leg and all is cured, but Brix vows vengeance on the shooter and we love him for it. The expedition party also contains a smart lady named Beth Munro (Jill Martin)—the daughter of Dr. Munro, of course. She brings her boyfriend, Allan Kendle (George Eldridge), whose character flaws become obvious as soon as his feet touch the island. He's certainly not thrilled about the attraction that's forming between Beth and Kioga. He goes so far as to refer to Mokuyi and another Indian named Kias as "two dirty Indians." For good measure he calls Brix an "imitation white man."

Hank Davis

There is one more member of the Munro party that we might as well mention, because it is impossible to talk about this serial or react critically to it without including him. Fred "Snowflake" Toones plays the servant, George. Toones may have been a really sweet guy. It is known that director Witney took a liking to him and tried to find work for him as often as possible. Let's just bite the bullet and say that this is one job that Toones should not have taken or, even worse, that Toones should never have been offered. In an all-too competitive field, Toones' appearance here is the single most demeaning portrayal of a black man I can remember seeing. It is not just the material as written. Toones gets his teeth into it and does the subhuman humble shuffle to an extent rarely captured on film. To begin with, why in the world would anyone want to take a barely skilled, slowwitted servant on an expedition to uncharted waters? He simply has no place here except for us to laugh at him. His appearance in the credits is telling: At the end of a list of over 20 actors we see the two credits they've saved for last: Snowflake and Tuffy. Negro and dog. Subhuman all the way. At least Snowflake came first, although that may have been alphabetical.

Some will argue that this kind of ethnic comic relief should be taken with a grain of salt. It is a product of its times and a world that has (thankfully) changed for the better. There is truth in that; however, even by the standards of his day, Snowflake overdoes it. At first it seems he is there only for the Indians to comment on his black skin. But it gets worse. Some of Snowflake's scenes are accompanied by bassoon music, which has the unmistakable effect of telegraphing his dimwitted antics. When two thugs trick and overpower Toones, it hardly seems fair. Thankfully, some marauding Indians even the score rather quickly. In Chapter 7, Snowflake listens to Dr. Munro's overblown scientific account of why underground steam pressure had caused renewed volcanic activity. He listens wide-eyed, then says "YASS-uh, Boss. That sho am figured it out." Was this truly the state of race relations in the U.S. in 1938?

One more character is worth special note: Ray Mala plays Kias, an Indian from the hostile tribe who befriends Brix. Apparently they were childhood pals or something. Anyway, Mala puts his life and reputation on the line for Brix and ultimately pays the price in the final episode. Mala is fine in this role; in fact, one could say ideally suited to the part. Although he is second-billed, his character is pretty marginal. He's just another Indian, albeit a loyal one. He says his lines and hits his marks. He overpowers nobody and steals no scenes. This is worth pointing out because, two years earlier to the day, Mala had starred in Republic's *Robinson Crusoe of Clipper Island*, a role he was ill equipped to play. The important thing to note is *here* is a part Mala was perfect for. The man could have made a credible career out of work of this nature and you'd never see a disparaging word.

It's obvious the confidence Republic had in its use of miniatures in this serial. All of the ship-at-sea scenes, including those on a stormy sea, are courtesy of the miniatures department. There is some rear-screen projection work that is easily noticeable: characters sitting in a rowboat or on deck and film of the ocean projected (at much lower resolution) behind them. But the use of a toy ship on a toy sea has an inherent flaw that no amount of expertise was going to cure. Imagine a one-foot model of a clipper ship sitting in a five-foot tank of water. Technicians can stir up the water, get the ship to rock precariously, and photograph it in fast motion to smooth out the effect when it's projected back at normal speed (which will appear slow). Add some good lighting and background effects to that and it's all just dandy. Except for one thing. The waves are too big. On a real ocean, the normal ripples and breakers will be much smaller in comparison to the ship. On a toy ocean, the effect is out of proportion. People watching such scenes have an intuitive sense that something is wrong, but they rarely know what it is. The ship looks OK; the water seems real, yet the two don't quite match up. Since we're on a little sidebar here, it's easy to realize that the same thing happens when toy buildings burn for the camera. The flames are too big in proportion to the structure. No matter how well constructed that toy warehouse or colonial mansion is, once filmmakers torch it and watch it burn, it just doesn't look quite real in a movie. The Republic miniature department, perhaps the best in the industry, could not change the laws of physics.

A couple of moments to watch for in *Hawk of the Wilderness*: There's some *Joe vs. the Volcano* stuff going on in Chapter 8, but it's more "Beth vs. the Volcano." A duck (a migrating mallard from Tennessee) almost gets to save the good guys after their ship is destroyed. He's not quite as personable as the Aflac duck, but definitely a step in the right direction. There's a terrible cheat ending in Chapter 9 involving Brix's character being speared to the ground. We see and (worse yet) hear it, but in Chapter 10 we learn that it never happened. Look for the interesting burial ground scenes in Chapter 11 that involve some very creative props. In the same chapter, there is a demon monster (actually Yellow Weasel in

Herman Brix competes at the 1928 Olympics

a suit) roaming around a cave. Even knowing it's a fake; the effect is still pretty creepy. More of this would have been very welcome.

After Mala dies to save Brix from the demon's spear, Brix vows that the death will be avenged. Since this is the final chapter, he's got about 12 minutes to work. But never fear: Herman Brix, a.k.a. Bruce Bennett, a.k.a. Hawk of the Wilderness, a.k.a. Ki-oga, a.k.a. Tarzan, throws the evil Yellow Weasel off a cliff. There's a lot of loyalty on display during the final chapter and it's endearing to watch: Mala to Brix, Brix to Tuffy, etc. In the end, the thugs and the Indians turn on each other, leaving the good guys to flee in an airplane they conveniently find sitting in a clearing. In an unexpected and progressive touch, Beth is the only one who can fly the plane.

As the small plane flies low over Alaska, we see some aerial shots of waving Eskimos. The last line goes to Fred Toones: "I sho is glad we's back home again. YASS-uh." Why Toones would view the frozen north as "back home" or cause for celebration is anybody's guess. But I sho is glad he's happy. YASS-uh!

Dick Tracy Returns

Barely a year after the release of their highly successful *Dick Tracy* serial, Republic issued *Dick Tracy Returns* in September 1938. The results, while by no means as spectacular as the original, packed enough punch to keep audiences clambering for the next weekly installment for nearly four months.

If looking for evidence that sequels are usually inferior to the originals, this is probably a fair case to examine. But bear in mind that the original *Dick Tracy* serial is one of the best ever produced. It's unlikely that anyone expected to duplicate the thrills of the original. It's not every day that a futuristic airplane like the Wing soars over the Bay Bridge, intent on hurtling it into the waters below. And so audiences settled into *Dick Tracy Returns,* probably happy to see some familiar characters go through their weekly paces. Interestingly, just about all of the characters except Tracy were played by different actors this time around.

Like the first *Dick Tracy* serial, the plot of the sequel features a number of separate stories —almost one a week. Usually, a crisis is introduced within the first three minutes, and off we go. The villain—the evil Pa Stark —is the

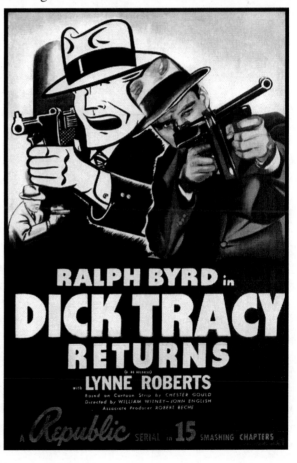

centerpiece of all this plotting. Wonderfully played by veteran actor Charles Middleton, Stark is a perfect foil for Tracy. He is more than ruthless and embittered enough to harass Tracy and his G-Men for 15 installments. In true serial form, Pa Stark is always trying to take control of some kind of device, whether it's a secret lens, a guided missile control or an experimental plane. Pa Stark has five sons at the start of the serial, but by the time Chapter 8 rolls around, he's been reduced to three. There's only one son left as the final chapter unfolds. Usually, serial henchmen are as anonymous and numerous as field mice. In this case, they are in short supply. One by one, Tracy and his help-

Ralph Byrd (in cockpit) and Dick Herbert

ers reduce Pa Stark's family until there's nothing left but the old man himself. Needless to say, watching his sons die week after week does little to improve Pa's mood, which leads him to hatch even juicier schemes to take over the world and do away with our hero.

Just like Chester Gould's comic book character, the screen version of *Dick Tracy* is entirely two-dimensional. One of Pa Stark's henchman sums up Tracy by saying, "That G-Man is a pretty tough monkey." Actor Ralph Byrd plays Tracy in a likable, ever-smiling manner and is never too busy to explain something to Junior, played this time by Jerry Tucker. Tracy's "All criminals are rats" speech in the first chapter tells us everything we need to know about his character. Tracy lives in a black and white world; there is no middle ground.

Fans of ace stuntman David Sharpe will take pleasure in seeing their man given star billing in this serial. Sharpe's name appears at the head of the secondary list of players—quite an accomplishment for a usually invisible stuntman. Sharpe plays Ron Merton, Dick Tracy's young protégé. The youthful Sharpe plays Merton in son-like style to Tracy's paternal figure. It's not difficult to see these guys in a father-son relationship, although, in reality, barely two years separated the actors. Both men were in their 20s when this serial was made.

Unfortunately, any hope that Sharpe's acting will be on display in a major way is dashed when his character is killed off in Chapter 1. Actually, the death of Sharpe in the first chapter must have been heavy going for some of the serial's more impressionable viewers. He is shot at point blank range just as he is reaching out for help. Not a pretty sight. It's not enough that his character is shot just as the serial gets going. Sharpe actually ends up on life support. What an irony: the most physical guy in the entire cast is confined to an iron lung! It's almost a relief when Pa Stark sneaks in and pulls the plug. Mike McGurk and Junior are both back in this sequel for comic relief. Both are annoying relics from nearly three quarters of a century ago. Junior was an easy way to get an audience-age kid right up on the screen. Mike McGurk is another matter—a reminder that laughing at the slow-witted was great sport in the 1930s. This time out, it's Lee Ford who gets to do the demented hillbilly routine. Though still annoying as hell, Ford is a step up from Smiley Burnette in the original.

Junior walks like a penguin. He spends most of the serial hanging around in what looks like a chauffeur's uniform. Junior looks like Johnny in those old "Call for Philip Morris" ads. He's obviously there to entice the kiddies back every Saturday, but his irrepressible spunkiness is a real pain in the neck. Most of the time it just gets him in trouble, which means Dick has to bail him out at considerable peril. Nevertheless, Dick Tracy is every kid's idea of a real dad. "You lay one hand on that kid," Tracy tells a bad guy, "and all the bullets in the world won't keep me from tearing you apart." It's kind of nice to know that there are grown ups like Tracy out there to protect you—even if you're an orphan like Junior.

Women in the audience (if there were any) were no doubt pleased to note that Tracy's assistant Gwen, played by Lynne Roberts this time (Kay Hughes was unavailable), actually shows evidence of brain activity. Gwen is entrusted with triangulating the location of incoming signals and does her job to perfection. In fact, the enlightened Tracy is actually heard to utter, "The day of women special agents is just around the corner." Way to go, Dickie, boy! One small step for a woman... The truth is, Gwen absolutely saves Tracy's bacon in chapter 14. It's one of the few times our hero follows his gonads and gets in trouble. At the start of the chapter, a pretty young thing comes into Tracy's office, batting her innocent eyes and asking for help. It seems her brother is falling in with bad companions. Can Mr. Tracy's help? Then she lets it slip that the thugs in question are the Stark gang, whoever they are. Tracy nearly jumps out of his chair. Yeah, he'll help, all right! He's reaching for his hat when Gwen hands him a letter to sign. It says, "The young lady says she is a cashier at a cafeteria but she is wearing Nuit Noir, a perfume which sells for 50 dollars an ounce." Tracy, along with the audience, is saved. We were just as gullible: The pretty girl was totally believable. Only Gwen saw through her.

It's always surprising that, with all the gadgets and scientific hardware on display, serials hold the scientists in very low regard. More often than not, they are played as unworldly buffoons who invent neat stuff. At one point, Tracy warns a scientist that the building in which he is delivering a lecture is about to blow up. Steadfastly, the old fart refuses to stop his lecture, choosing to bore his audience to death rather than letting the explosion kill them. "The rings around the planet Saturn are gaseous in nature," he drones on, while Tracy and his men

Hank Davis

195

Chapter 5 DEATH IN THE AIR

scramble to rescue the comatose audience.

Some notable moments to watch for: Chapter 12 includes a large-screen television mounted on the side of a truck. Even Tracy is a bit surprised. "I didn't think they had perfected a portable television set," he says. The railroad train cliffhanger at the end of Chapter 3 was so impressive that it ended up intact (and eventually colorized) 15 years later in Republic's *Zombies of the Stratosphere*. The take-out of the final chapter is an absolute cheat. Anyone who sat through chapter 14 knows that last week's cliffhanger just didn't happen that way. But who can complain? The energy level really picks up in the final chapter as Stark takes Tracy prisoner. Out of nowhere, Junior becomes an absolute super sleuth and saves the day. When things wind to a finish, the slow-witted, physically uncoordinated Mike McGurk catches an egg in the face and all the adults, as well as Junior, stand around laughing at him as the final credits roll.

At one point, Tracy eavesdrops on the bad guys and hears them say that "Zarkoff" will help them dispose of the contraband. Zarkoff? Are we suddenly in the middle of *Flash Gordon*? We already have Ming the Merciless (Charles Middleton) playing Pa Stark. All that's missing now are Flash and Dale. In any case, if the audience liked the team here, they'll really love them in the *Daredevils of the Red Circle*, shot 10 months later by Republic. *Daredevils* reunited directors Witney and English with stuntman David Sharpe (in an even more extended acting role), as well as resident bad guy Charles ("Ming") Middleton. What could be more fun?

1939
Buck Rogers

How successful was the original *Flash Gordon* serial? *Buck Rogers*, released in 1939 by Universal, is only one small piece of the answer. A fuller measure of *Flash*'s success can be attained by looking at Republic's *Undersea Kingdom* as well as the two *Flash Gordon* sequels released by Universal in 1938 and 1940. But before they were even finished filming sequels to *Flash Gordon*, Universal took the time to produce *Buck Rogers* as one more way to capitalize on their space-opera franchise.

It's just about impossible not to compare this serial to *Flash Gordon*. The similarities grab our attention at almost every level, starting at the core and spreading out to the most peripheral details. Flash and Buck are both space-age heroes battling evil despots in futuristic settings. Both characters are played by the same actor, Larry "Buster" Crabbe, and directed by Ford Beebe. Instead of Prince Barin in *Flash*, we have Prince Tallen in *Buck;* instead of Clay People we have Zuggs. And if the plot, setting, lead actor and director aren't enough, there's also the look and sound of the serials. *Buck* and the original *Flash* share an art director (Ralph DeLacy), who reused many of the same sets, props (like the bullet-shaped subway cars) and stock footage. And then there's the music. Serial fans might not leave the theater humming the background music, but those little themes and interludes often worm their way into our consciousness, just waiting to stir up old feelings and memories when they're recycled in later serials. *Buck* borrows its background music liberally from both of the previous *Flash* serials (which, in turn, cribbed many of their memorable themes from a series of earlier Universal features we detailed in our discussion of *Flash* in 1936). Even the forwards to each chapter of *Buck Rogers*, as they scroll upwards into infinity, are accompanied by the identical four-note theme that made the *Flash Gordon* chapter intros so memorable.

Constance Moore, Buck and Buddy with (left to right) Reed Howes, Carleton Young, Wheeler Oakman and Henry Brandon

The curious thing is, rather than reducing *Buck Rogers* to a poor man's *Flash Gordon*, this serial rises above its derivative status into wholly enjoyable entertainment. Certainly, the material was worth the attention. Since it first appeared as a comic strip in 1929, *Buck Rogers* has been a staple of American popular culture. Before this serial, *Buck* had turned up in comics and radio, and later years would include yet more radio (until 1947), television and feature movies. The cast of this movie, while perhaps not a Who's Who of serial moviemaking, is certainly chock full of familiar names, faces and voices. Actors like Ken Duncan, Wheeler Oakman, Stanley Price, Jack Mulhall, C. Montague Shaw and Henry Brandon are all familiar to cliffhanger fans. Stuntman David Sharpe bore an uncanny resemblance to Jackie Moran, the actor playing teenage Buddy Wade, and no doubt doubled him during the more demanding action scenes. Even producer Barney Sarecky had worked on the second *Flash* serial and went on to a productive career at Republic.

Chapter 1 of *Buck Rogers* gets things started off in style. A dirigible carrying Buck and Buddy crashes in a god-forsaken arctic waste, where it remains for 500 years until the year 2440, when our adventure begins. Note, by the way, that this is about the fifth serial plot we've encountered that involved dirigibles in some capacity. Remember that the *Hindenburg* crashed and burned in May 1937, considerably before this serial was filmed. It is thus odd to assume (a) that dirigibles were still viable forces in commercial aviation, but that (b) they would continue to be so in the year 2440. That's a lot of faith to place in a huge sausage full of hydrogen or helium or whatever they'd be using in the future. Fortunately, their ship contained some experimental Nirvano gas, which leaves our heroes in suspended animation for 500 years. A couple of guys on a routine space patrol (not in a dirigible!) uncover the old sausage and thaw it out. Buck and Buddy are carried outside and come back to life, leaning against their antique ship, while music from *The Bride of Frankenstein* swells in the background. Then the four characters take off in a vintage looking Flash Gordon ship on wires, spouting sparks as it flies. Buck and Buddy are welcomed by kindly Dr. Huer of the Hidden City and soon join forces in the fight against Killer Kane. And there is the plot, all 12 chapters' worth.

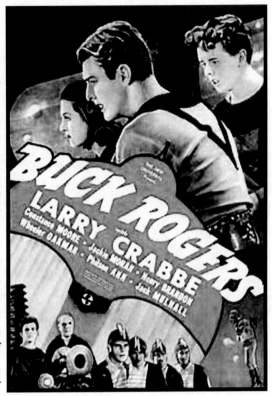

Perhaps *Buck Rogers'* biggest deficit—and it goes right to the heart of the serial—is the absence of an inspiring villain. To this day, no one can talk about any of the original *Flash Gordon* serials without mentioning Ming the Merciless, a role Charles Middleton made his own. The simple truth is that serials need memorable villains as much, if not more, than they need heroes. *Flash* had both. *Buck* only has the good guys going for it. Killer Kane might have been a wonderful comic strip character, but the version brought to the screen by actor Anthony Warde was hardly enough to get anybody's pulse racing. Warde is simply not up to the challenge. Unlike Ming, who seemed to take evil to a cosmic level, Killer Kane seems little more than an earthbound thug, modeled after characters portrayed by George Raft or Jimmy Cagney. Even his name sounds like a mob boss, not an interplanetary menace. He's a two-bit gangster who happens to live in the 25th century. With Kane at the center, we need Elliott Ness more than Buck Rogers. The one thing you can say for the casting of Kane is that his character looks and acts a lot like Adolf Hitler, another petty thug with ambitions of world domination. Although Hitler was only becoming a household name in America when this serial was released in 1939, the European management at Universal would have been more than familiar with the Nazi menace and quite pleased to tweak *der Fuhrer*'s moustache with this bit of social satire.

Buck (Buster Crabbe) and Buddy (Jackie Moran)

Those delightful forewords at the start of each episode may have been borrowed liberally by George Lucas for *Star Wars*, but they presented quite a challenge for youthful audiences. Kids more than 60 years ago could not have had an easy time as 26 lines of text went scrolling by at considerably more than a snail's pace. Columbia beat the problem in their serials by having a narrator read the summary. Republic, like Universal, stuck with the printed word, but within several years had shortened their summaries to one or two sentences—a far cry from the treatise-length intros offered in *Buck Rogers*.

Some bizarro moments to watch for:

An exchange between Captain Lasca, on board a spaceship, and Killer Kane:

"This is Captain Lasca reporting from Saturn."

Kane: "Never mind all that."

Huh? And then, for all you Wheeler Oakman fans, your hero is at it again with his unsquelchable Noo Yawk accent.

Oakman: "You're not on a course for Oith," he observes.

The pilot replies, "I'm not headed for Erth." It sounds like they're talking about two different planets.

And then, there's the noise. As in *Flash Gordon* serials, all *Buck Rogers* engines, whether elevators or space ships, make a sound like a cross between an electric razor and a buzz saw. Basic 1930s wisdom— electrical devices are loud. Period.

In his book *Science Fiction Serials* (McFarland), Roy Kinnard reports that a 13th episode of *Buck Rogers* containing little but recycled material from earlier chapters was originally planned but withdrawn by Universal. Even so, the 12-chapter serial is not immune to recycling its own footage. Chapters 9 and 11 both contain cost-cutting flashbacks lasting about three minutes.

Nostalgia alone would preclude calling *Buck* a better serial than the original *Flash Gordon*. But the truth is, in terms of sheer entertainment value, *Buck Rogers* probably eclipses both of the *Flash Gordon* sequels. Certainly, much of the dialogue here (for example, between Buck and the rulers of Saturn) is more adult and politically savvy than some of the tripe that Crabbe was forced to deliver in the beloved *Flash Gordon* trilogy.

In the final chapter, the Hidden City elders award young Buddy an honorary flight lieutenant's medal, "despite your age." In truth, it's the least they can do since this spunky, semi-annoying, 13-year-old has saved just about everyone in sight. And so, medal in hand, Buddy turns to the elder statesmen and utters that wonderful all-purpose 1930s reply: "Gosh, that's swell!"

Knowing what we do about the spread of popular culture, there's every chance that the kid has just infected the 25th century.

Daredevils of the Red Circle

Think of this serial as litmus paper. It has just about every endearing quality necessary to a cliffhanger rolled up into one spectacular package. Audiences who don't like *Daredevils of the Red Circle* may be more interested in the musical section of the local video store. Becasue action and adventure ain't gonna get any better than this.

Daredevils consistently appears on lists of all-time greatest serials and it's easy to see why. To begin with, Republic Pictures seems to have pulled out all stops in bringing this serial to the screen in 1939. Directed by William Witney and John English, the results just bristle with energy. Witney is considered by many to be the greatest serial director of all time. This was his ninth cliffhanger for Republic. Witney would go on to complete 15 more for the studio before his departure in 1943. But what makes *Daredevils* exceptional goes beyond its well-staged fistfights and car chases.

There is something absolutely inspired in the casting of the three lead

characters, played by Charles Quigley, Herman Brix and David Sharpe. These guys aren't just good actors; there is a chemistry between them that transcends the competence each of them brings to his role. This collective energy creates a warmth and humor that draws the viewer even more deeply into the weekly adventures. Using a trio of actors wasn't exactly new to the folks at Republic, who had a track record of successful Westerns featuring the Three Mesquiteers. It's just that such trios typically resided in the old West and hadn't spent much time in the realm of serials before.

Charles Quigley is the centerpiece. Ruggedly handsome, he has the presence of a young Cary Grant and clearly possesses the best social skills

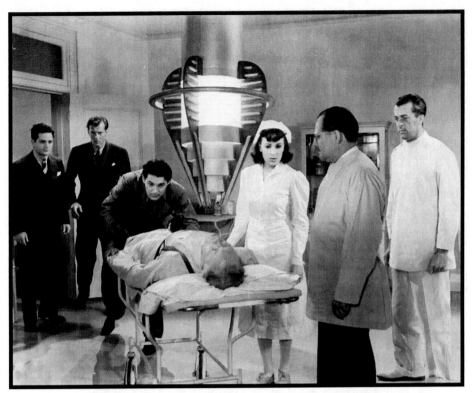

The Daredevils inadvertently expose the District Attorney to the Ray of Death.

of the three performers. Herman Brix, soon to be transformed into Bruce Bennett, was no stranger to the Republic casting list. He is the strong man of the trio, and by far the least talkative. Brix is the proverbial Chevy truck: like a rock, he is solid, uncommunicative and dependable. Like Quigley, he's also a hell of a good-looking guy. David Sharpe rounds out the trio. He, too, is a very appealing actor but different from the other two Daredevils. Sharpe projects a boyish image, full of boundless energy and enthusiasm. Although he appeared in two previous Republic serials, *Dick Tracy Returns* and *The Lone Ranger Rides Again*, Sharpe was best known for his prolific, usually uncredited work as a stuntman. Probably the only thing keeping him from movie stardom—other than his value performing stunts—was his unimposing speaking voice. No matter how strong or fearless a hero appears to be, it just won't work if he speaks his lines with a vocal apparatus in the adolescent range. But as one of the three Daredevils, David Sharpe was just perfect. In his autobiography, Director Witney describes the trio of Quigley, Brix and Sharpe as if they were a single entity, having the qualities of intelligence, strength and agility.

Charles Middleton plays the villain of the piece. Middleton is seen here without his customary stage makeup. His dour features may be fairly new to most of us, but his voice is unmistakable. The plot of *Daredevils* is ingenious.

Peril in the power plant: Brix and Sharpe tied back to back.

Middleton's character has broken out of prison after 15 years and vowed vengeance on Granville, the man whose testimony put him there. Most serials would stop there, but *Daredevils* takes it up a notch. Middleton's character (known only by his prison number—39013) kidnaps Granville and stashes him away in a cell in the basement of his own house. If that weren't bad enough, Middleton then impersonates Granville, using a disguise so perfect that no one—including Granville's own granddaughter (the alluring Carol Landis)—suspects anything. Each day, Middleton visits Granville in his basement cell and spends a few moments tormenting him. He's the perfect villainous host.

Granville (Miles Mander) is everything a serial prisoner should be: He frets, pleads, cajoles and does a generally fine job of fueling the twisted ego of his captor. Meanwhile, Middleton is intent on destroying Granville's financial empire. He spends most of the serial's 12 episodes plotting to destroy the real estate, oil and gas holdings that Granville has taken a lifetime to accumulate. Middleton's big mistake comes in the spectacular first episode. Although he succeeds in burning down an amusement park owned by a Granville, the fire claims the life of Quigley's small brother. It's rare that a little kid gets bumped off in a serial, but this mistake is going to cost the villain dearly. The immediate result is that the three Daredevils put their breathtaking circus act on hold and go to work full time unmasking the diabolical maniac responsible for setting this fire. For the

Classic Cliffhangers

Miles Mander (as Granville), along with the Daredevils and Carole Landis.

next 11 episodes, the chase is on, with Middleton barely staying one move ahead of the mentally and physically agile trio.

The first episode is an absolute stunner—one of the all-time highlights of serial moviemaking. Not only do we see the Daredevils' circus act and the awful amusement park fire that follows, but we also get to watch one of the most unique and exciting cliffhangers in serial history. Middleton has taunted the police by boasting that he will destroy Granville's brand new tunnel running between the mainland (Los Angeles) and a nearby island (Catalina). Nevertheless, plans are made to go ahead with the grand opening ceremony. Middleton all but wrings his hands in glee when it is decided to proceed with the ceremony, despite the danger. Now he can destroy the tunnel while everyone is watching. When Daredevil Quigley takes his motorcycle through the tunnel for a last minute security check, he hears some ominous noises coming through the walls. Within minutes, water has begun to leak through the ceiling tiles and the whole structure looks like it might give way. Scrambling for the exit, Quigley races his bike through the tunnel as a growing torrent of water sweeps along behind him, literally lapping at the wheels of his bike. The effect still packs a considerable wallop nearly 70 years after it was created.

With all the varied location work, this serial looks like it was shot on a very big budget. Obviously, nothing could be further from the truth. In fact, the serial was brought in a few bucks under budget at $126,118 on a one-month shooting

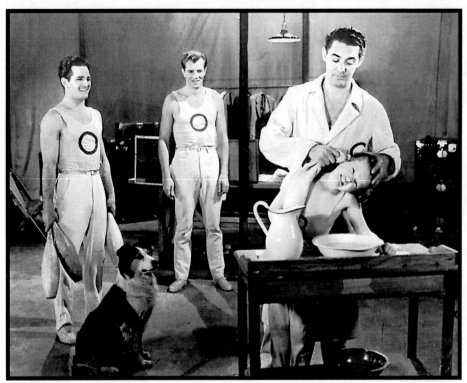

David Sharpe, Herman Brix and Charles Quigley (the Daredevils) scrub Quigley's kid brother, Robert Winkler.

schedule in April 1939. Nevertheless, *Daredevils of the Red Circle* makes the serial version of *Superman*—made nine years later—look like a home movie. Here are some highlights to watch for: David Sharpe's character (the "agility" third of the trio) is hilarious. He never walks around anything when he can jump on it or over it. No wonder he made his living as a stuntman. In fact, Sharpe's energy is contagious. Even the more reserved Quigley and the solid Brix hop in and out of cars and over rail fences. The Daredevils seem to be in a perpetual game of leapfrog. The energy level even extends to the machines around them. In episode 7, Quigley drives an old Woody station wagon up and down some desert terrain as if he were behind the wheel of a modern sport utility vehicle.

About the only downside to this marvelous classic serial is an occasional glimpse of 1930s racism. Fred "Snowflake" Toones makes Stepin Fetchit look like a role model for black pride. The world is just too complicated a place for him. We first encountered Toones in *Hawk of the Wilderness*. Granted, he offers a more restrained performance here, but it's still a pretty disturbing display. Toones is even outwitted by the Daredevils' pet dog, Tuffie. Note that Tuffie (who also appeared in *Hawk*) spelled his name with a "y" in that earlier appearance. This suggests what many of us have suspected for years: that dogs really don't care how you spell their names as long as you pronounce them correctly.

Classic Cliffhangers

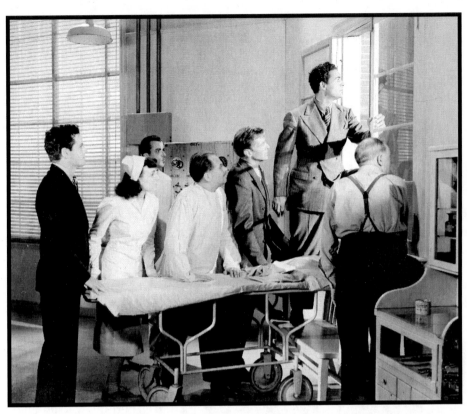

Sharpe, Brix and Quigley (in suits and ties) peer at peril beyond the window.

According to Witney, Toones ran the shoeshine stand at Republic Studios. It's another case of life imitating art: menial jobs all around. "We tried to write Snowflake into as many serials as we could," recalls Witney. What Witney doesn't tell us is that Toones appeared in nearly 150 films, in a career beginning in the late 1920s, including the 1931 Mascot serial *The Galloping Ghost*, and continuing into the 1950s. Toones' roles were almost always the typical 1930s stereotypes, including servant, butler, porter, cook, janitor, dice player and washroom attendant. If Fred Toones were alive today it is doubtful that he would keep a copy of this serial among his prized possessions. For the rest of us who can look past the racial intolerance of this era, *Daredevils Of The Red Circle* is certainly worth owning and prizing. It is as fine a movie serial as we are likely to see, made during the Golden Era by the studio renowned for taking the genre to the level of art form.

The Green Hornet

Try to imagine if *The Lone Ranger* was magically transported forward in time, leaving those "thrilling days of yesteryear" behind. And while we're at it, why not change the setting from the Old West to the modern East? In all likelihood the result would be the *Green Hornet*. It's no coincidence, of course, that both masked heroes originated during the 1930s at radio station WXYZ in Detroit. It also didn't hurt that George W. Trendle and scriptwriter Fran Striker were behind both projects.

Although not as iconic a figure as The Lone Ranger, the Green Hornet held his own as a radio star for nearly 17 years, first appearing in January 1936. Like the Lone Ranger, the Green Hornet announced himself each week with a signature piece of semi-classical music. Instead of the "William Tell Overture," the Green Hornet buzzed into living rooms to the strains of Rimsky-Korsakov's "Flight of the Bumble Bee." No one seemed to mind that bees and hornets are entirely different species. Stinging insects were a close enough match for most listeners.

The Green Hornet was in its fourth radio season when Universal secured

the rights to produce a movie serial version of the radio show. All things considered, the big-screen version stayed fairly close to its radio predecessor. It didn't hurt, of course, that Fran Striker remained on the set in the official role of "advisor" and received screen credit at the start of each episode. Rather then use Al Hodge, the radio voice of the Green Hornet, Universal chose to cast relative unknown Gordon Jones in the title role. You may remember Jones for his role as Mike the Cop in the Abbott & Costello TV show (1952-53). Hodge would have to wait for the emergence of television before he would bask in the weekly limelight as the star of *Captain Video*. Trivia buffs may know that

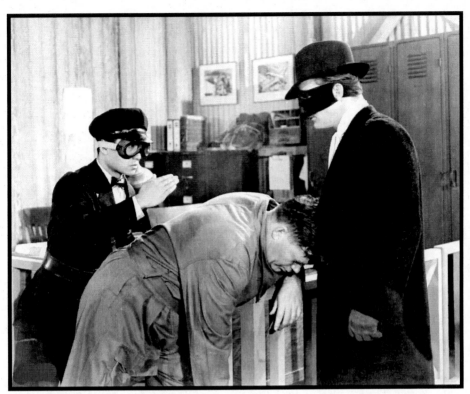

Keye Luke delivers a karate chop as Gordon Jones watches appreciatively.

an uncredited Al Hodge provided the voice of the Green Hornet when the character appeared on screen in the Hornet mask. Considering the fact that the Hornet's costume also hid the appearance of several stuntmen, it begins to appear as if Gordon Jones had relatively little screen time. In truth, his appearances were confined to moments when alter ego Britt Reid, publisher of the *Daily Sentinel*, appeared in a suit and tie.

Reid's ethnic-minority sidekick, Kato (not to be confused with Tonto), was played by Charlie Chan's number one son, Keye Luke. Kato's national identity has always been something of a mystery. Certainly, the WWII years were no time to feature a Japanese hero, so Kato remained a Filipino for most of his radio days. When Keye Luke was cast in the role for the serial, it was clear that viewers would not mistake him for a Filipino. And so, within minutes of the first chapter, we learn that Kato is actually a Korean. Ten years later, of course, even that decision may not have played well in the heartland, but in 1940 who knew anything about Korea? It was still safe to be a Korean good guy. We also learn quite a bit about the relationship between Britt Reid and Kato in the first chapter. In about 20 seconds we get everything we need to know about the loyalty between these two men, where they met, and Kato's role as confidant, valet and scientific colleague. But make no mistake: Kato is still in a subservient position. Just like a regulation issue Negro houseboy, he calls Reid "Mr. Britt."

Hank Davis

Another karate chop from Kato immobilizes two safecrackers as the Green Hornet watches with gun drawn.

Since they owned the copyright to the Lone Ranger, Trendle and Striker took the outrageous step of telling audiences that Britt Reid was actually related to the Lone Ranger. John Reid, the lone Texas Ranger who began wearing a mask and hanging out with Tonto, was actually the grand uncle of our hero, Britt Reid. The sense of *déjà vu* that swirls around the Green Hornet doesn't stop with The Lone Ranger. Like Batman's alter ego, Bruce Wayne, Britt Reid is a wealthy playboy who battles criminals under cover of night. And like Superman, the Green Hornet's alter ego has a close working relationship with a woman (Anne Nagel) who views him with some degree of disdain—just like Lois does Clark. But the Green Hornet's inner circle also includes the kind of annoying character that Batman, Superman or the Lone Ranger never had to endure. Michael Axford is a reporter on the daily *Sentinel*, but he is also something of a bodyguard, hovering around Reid to make sure he doesn't hurt himself. Played by Wade Boteler, Axford is clueless about Reid's secret identity. In fact, clueless doesn't begin to describe his character. The man is primarily there to provide ethnic humor, circa 1940. He is a slow-witted, loud-mouthed Irish buffoon, uttering phrases like "Suffering Mackerels!" On top of everything else, he hates the Green Hornet and does his utmost to slur this heroic character whenever he is with Britt Reid.

Although this serial is packed with action, snappy dialogue and perky direction by Ford Beebe and Ray Taylor, it falls far short of anyone's Top 10 list. One of its faults is the lack of any central plot. The Green Hornet is simply out to smash racketeers. The trouble is, they come in too many varieties. There are too many bad guys *du jour*. Movie serials really need a clear vision of evil, embodied in a central villain whose identity is concealed until the great unmasking in the final episode. That really doesn't happen here in any meaningful way. Instead, we have a parking lot racket one week, an air crash insurance scam the next, a bunch of trucking company thieves the next, etc.

The central mechanical prop, which comes directly from the *Green Hornet* radio show, is a super speedy car known as Black Beauty. This customized 1939 coupe makes a distinctive buzzing noise as it travels and is every bit as noisy as one of Flash Gordon's rocket ships speeding through outer space while suspended on a string. As one cop says to another, "Gone like a spook. I never saw a car move so fast." It seems odd that the Green Hornet tries to avoid cops at all costs, but drives around at twice normal speed with his hornet buzzer going full blast. So much for being inconspicuous. The same speeded-up footage of the Black Beauty careening around the Universal back lot is repeated throughout the serial.

Each chapter of this serial begins with an elaborate written Foreword that scrolls off into infinity. The technique is, of course, borrowed directly from Universal's highly successful *Flash Gordon* serials. And in case the similarity was missed, the music department uses the opening title theme from *Flash*. It's *déjà vu* all over again. Some of the day for night shooting is all too obvious. The continuity person, assuming Universal elected to use one on this serial, had good reason to scream bloody murder. Car chases start in broad daylight and cut seemingly randomly to nighttime road scenes and back again to broad daylight. The effect is so blatant that it almost becomes surreal.

The cliffhangers that appear during this 13-chapter serial are fairly standard issue, although one of the take-outs is worth mentioning. At the end of Chapter 2, we watch two trains headed for a certain collision. The crash will be horrendous. But at the start of Chapter 3, we see the two trains approaching each other and realize that what we experienced last week was all a problem of perspective. With the camera moved just a little bit to the left, we can see that the trains are on adjacent tracks and can pass each other harmlessly. This is not your everyday take-out.

Once again, Universal borrows disaster footage straight from its library of newsreels. The studio knew enough to leave work with miniatures to the pros at Republic. For a sample of the kind of miniature work Universal could do, look at the armored car cliffhanger in Chapter 10. It's laughable—a stark reminder of just how far Universal's miniature work lagged behind their competitors. The use of stock footage might be all right, if the inserted film appears to come from the same century as the feature. Unfortunately, the fire truck inserts in Chapter 11 look like they come from a silent Mack Sennett movie, and indeed they might have.

Chapter 12 is called "Terror at the Zoo" and borrows heavily from an unidentified earlier film about the circus. Watching all those lions, tigers, chimps

"FLYING COFFINS"

Chapter 3

THE GREEN HORNET

A NEW UNIVERSAL PICTURE

and elephants, not to mention crowds of people stampeding in terror, could lead us to believe that this was a big-budget serial. In truth, it's a low-budget 1939-made serial with access to Universal's considerable film vault. There's even some footage in there that looks like it was shot at carnival time in Rio. The crowds are immense, although the owner of the Cooper Zoo claims he is not making any money because his customers have been frightened away. He uses this reasoning to refused to pay blackmailers the princely sum of $5,000. Again, where were the folks from Continuity when you need them?

Spoiler alert: There's a great conclusion to Chapter 13. The four remaining racketeers manage to shoot each other. Somehow, things are staged so that the four of them just keep shooting until all of them are dead. What a slick way to wrap up the story with not a drop of blood falling on the hands of Kato or The Green Hornet. And it's a good bet that our man's identity remains a secret at the end. It's just what we need for a sequel, which is precisely what Universal had in mind. *The Green Hornet Strikes Again* appeared months later in 1940, making it the fastest sequel to hit the screen in movie serial history. Warren Hull replaced Gordon Jones in the title role, and also on hand were Keye Luke, Anne Nagel and Wade Boteler. Once again, poor Al Hodge was rejected for the role he continued to play on the radio.

Mandrake The Magician

Like many stars of the movie serials, *Mandrake the Magician* began life as a comic strip hero. His character first appeared as a daily feature in 1934 and caught on almost immediately. Within a year, Mandrake was a staple of the Sunday papers.

The debonair magician was probably modeled after his creator, Lee Falk—also a suave, well-dressed character. By 1938, Columbia pictures had negotiated with King Features for the rights to bring Mandrake to the big screen. Their 12-episode serial hit the theaters in 1939. The ad line was "Black Magic conjures up a flaming holocaust of thrills." A line like that could only have appeared prior to WWII.

Mandrake The Magician features Warren Hull in the title role and Al Kikume as Lothar, Mandrake's trusty African sidekick/servant/flunky. It's really not clear what's going on between these two guys. Originally, Lothar was supposed to be the King of a mysterious African tribe. Whatever status Lothar might have had in the old country (which was plainly *north* of the Sahara, by the way) has not traveled well across the Atlantic. Here, Lothar drives the boss's car, punches bad guys and says, "Yes, Master" a lot.

Mandrake, too, is a curiosity. In the comic strip, the character began life with supernatural powers. Those didn't last long and Mandrake gradually began to depend upon his intelligence and moxie. In the serial, Mandrake is just a regular well-dressed guy. He is not above a little parlor magic, although there isn't too much of it on display. Early on, Mandrake does his whole act—including a rope trick—for an upscale audience in a club. In later episodes, he is reduced to throwing some wiffle dust (exploding powder) or pulling the occasional quarter out of someone's ear.

The serial is old looking. Mostly, it's the cars. The 1938

Mandrake (Warren Hull) and Lothar (Al Kikume)

roadsters were big, noisy clunkers that didn't corner well and weren't built for speed. A 10-year-old car today was built in the 1990s and still looks new to most of us. Here, 10 year old cars have the look of Model T Fords and plainly belong to the silent movie era. The trucks are even more eye-catching. They look like they belong in a transportation museum. Along with the cars, the wardrobe really dates this serial. It isn't so much the cut of the clothes; it's the fact that all the guys wear suits, ties and hats no matter what they're doing. In the middle of a fight scene or a car chase, someone stops to adjust his hat. These are *thugs* for cryin' out loud, but they're all dressed for a debutante ball. Even the serial's villain "The Wasp" wears a 1930s hat as he sits there barking out orders in his cape and mask. When the bad guys go out to dig in the mud for some "platenite" to fuel the much-contested radium machine, they wear suits, ties and hats. It doesn't stop with the adults. The mandatory annoying kid wearing a suit and tie (a clone of "Junior" in Dick Tracy) hangs around Mandrake's house. If he ever went outside, somebody from props would no doubt slap a hat on his 10-year-old head.

There are a couple of howlers—wonderful moments of sheer serial lunacy. In Episode 8, a bad guy blows up a mountain and sends it crashing down on Mandrake's car. The car simply plows right through 40 million tons of rock and gravel. Mandrake turns to his servant and says, "Swell driving." Technology is always good for a few laughs. When the bad guys want to spy on Mandrake,

Mandrake and Lothar have Sam Ash all tied up.

they place an office Dictaphone in his house. When gizmos like microphones or telephones are supposed to give off death-dealing rays, the effect is created by wiggly zap marks that have been scratched directly on the film negative.

Once again, Columbia Studios uses their odd cliffhanger technique that doesn't quite work as well as Universal's or Republic's approach. In all fairness, it was the Columbia cliffhanger style that was directly copied during the 1960s when TV's *Batman* series ushered in a wave of high camp entertainment. Columbia serials are famous for the Walter Winchell–sounding voiceovers by Knox Manning. We see the action on the screen, and we hear the newsman's voice saying, "Racing for his life, Mandrake and his car are hurtled to certain death. WILL... HE... ESCAPE?" This wouldn't be so bad; in fact it adds to the campy pleasure of the cliffhanger, but Columbia ruins the suspense by teasing us not to be concerned about what we've just seen, but to worry about what's going to happen *next* week! We were still wondering about how (or whether) Mandrake would get out of the car. Meanwhile the voice tells us "In the next episode, you will see Mandrake trapped in a room full of poison gas. WILL...HE...ESCAPE?" Well, wait a minute. Why should I care about *that*? I haven't even seen it happen yet. And now you've ruined the suspense about the car crash, since I already *know* Mandrake survived it long enough to get himself into a room full of poison gas. Jeez, I ain't coming back to *this* theater next week. But, of course, we always did.

A brief word about two of the supporting cast members: Doris Weston played Betty Houston, as close to a female lead as this serial offers. Weston never had much of a career. She appeared in nine films, all of them between 1937-1939. She was 22 years old when she appeared in *Mandrake*. She died before her 43rd birthday. Al Kikume had more of a career, almost all of it in B-movies. Kikume paid his dues in a bunch of Charlie Chan and Mr. Moto movies, but also appeared in other serials, including *The Adventures of Captain Marvel* (1941) and *Perils of Nyoka* (1942)—both of which are covered in Volume II of *Classic Cliffhangers*. His credits also include the immortal *Bela Lugosi Meets a Brooklyn Gorilla* (1952).

Warren Hull

Kikume often played exotics, although he was born in Kansas.

For many viewers, Warren Hull may seem an odd choice for a swashbuckling hero. Those who were around for daytime television in the 1950s will remember Hull as the host of a TV show called *Strike It Rich*. On these daily episodes, Hull introduced down-on-their-luck guests who were designed to make *anyone* feel good about their lives by comparison. It was an ironic way to reach national prominence for an actor who had defeated the Wasp and saved humanity as Mandrake, as well as playing the title role in the 1938 Columbia serial *The Spider's Web*. Hull also starred in *The Green Hornet Strikes Again* (1940). As for Mandrake, he never left popular culture for very long. Continuing as a comic strip, Mandrake also appeared in a brief television series in 1954 and was the star of a TV movie in 1979. As you're reading this, there is every chance that someone is hatching plans to bring Mandrake back to the silver screen. If they succeed, the results can't possibly look more bizarre than this delightful vintage serial.

The Phantom Creeps

As a kid, I had trouble understanding the title of this 1939 Universal serial. Was it about a bunch of *phantom* Creeps, as opposed to *real* ones? It took a while to figure out that this was a story about a Phantom (Bela Lugosi) who did a lot of creeping around.

I admit that I enjoy this serial more than many critics. Certainly, it's deliciously clear that neither the story nor its ambiguous title will withstand rational analysis. *The Phantom Creeps* is easily one of the most enjoyable serials with a hint of the bizarre and surreal this side of *The Lost City*. Most of its loopiness owes directly to the presence of Lugosi in the title role, along with his army of secret weapons and gadgets. In many ways, this is the perfect role for Bela, who appears here in his fifth and by far his juiciest sound serial. I mentioned earlier that *The Whispering Shadow* (1933) was also a showcase for Bela's unique persona. It was, but, by comparison, Bela was a lot more dignified in that earlier film. There's nary a trace of dignity here. *The Phantom Creeps* simply offers Lugosi a golden opportunity to strut his campy, deranged stuff. And, believe me, strut he does. In fact, "The Phantom Struts" might have been a better title.

The plot is pretty simple. Dr. Zorka (Bela) is a brilliant scientist, once again bent on world domination. Fortunately for us, he is losing his grip as his accomplishments become more and more far-fetched and difficult to control. They include a permanently scowling robot, a Z-ray, some mechanical spiders that create suspended animation, an invisibility belt (called a "de-visualizer") and a piece of meteorite left over from his 1936 film *The Invisible Ray*. When Bela

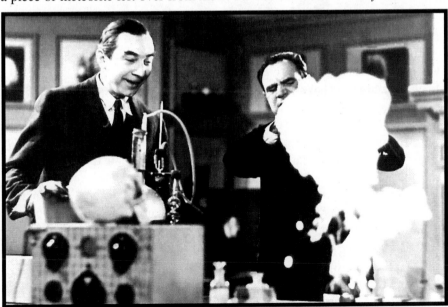

Dr. Zorka (Lugosi) and Monk (Jack C. Smith) play with fire.

Hank Davis

217

Bela and his loyal assistant Monk

accidentally kills his wife in Chapter 2, he loses what little remains of his sanity. For the next 10 chapters, it's a steady decline into madness as he battles with G-Men and enemy agents in his quest to conquer the world. It finally all unravels in Chapter 12, which deserves a paragraph of its own.

Bela's salary must have taken a chunk out of this serial's modest budget, forcing Universal to cobble the results together from pre-existing pieces. Serial and horror fans can enjoy trying to spot as many of these pirated sources as they can. Among the more obvious are: segments from the aforementioned *The Invisible Ray*; a brief clip and cliffhanger from *The Vanishing Shadow* that just happens to include actor Lee J. Cobb in his first film role; a healthy dollop of stock aerial footage; some stark and sweeping landscape footage from the *Frankenstein* films—used here under the opening credits for all 12 chapters; newsreel footage of a burning factory and a flaming train wreck; and substantial portions of the soundtrack from *The Bride of Frankenstein*. And look for Edward van Sloan (Professor van Helsing from the original *Dracula*), and don't miss a spunky reporter played by Dorothy Arnold, who later became Mrs. Joe DiMaggio.

Curiously, Universal did not reuse the robot they created three years earlier for *The Vanishing Shadow*. Instead, they designed an entirely new mechanical man (inhabited by actor Eddie Wolff). The extreme scowl on this robot's face virtually guaranteed it would not appear again. There's just no mistaking it for any robot in a film before or since. Bela is convinced that this robot will help him with his plans for world conquest, but the big guy is really quite a klutz. On those few occasions where Bela turns the robot loose on his enemies, all he does is flail his arms about and knock over furniture, allowing the agitated victims to scamper for the nearest exit. The little mechanical spiders do more damage than the scowling robot. The metal man's best scene comes in the final chapter when, just prior to his being blown up, he goes for a stroll in the garden. Robots are usually photographed indoors and it's easy to see why. It really is disconcerting to see this soulless lumbering creature out there amidst all the foliage.

Ford Beebe directed the serial, fresh from working on a trifecta of Buster Crabbe serials (*Flash Gordon's Trip To Mars, Red Barry, Buck Rogers*). If nothing else, the contrast in working with Lugosi must have been entertaining. The film seems to have a fixation on throwing bombs out of airplanes as a method of warfare. It isn't just Bela. Even the G-Men resort to it ("Just roll down the window, Jean, and toss a bomb at that car down there"). It's hard to imagine that anyone, even in the 1930s, saw this as a viable form of precision warfare.

The fire engine scene in Chapter 8 is quite startling. What might have been passable stock footage in 1939 is shocking today. The fire and its aftermath are real, and we know it. As the fire engines rush to their destination, there's not a car in those street scenes that was built after 1928. They look absolutely ancient. There are really convincing train wrecks at the end of Chapters 5 and 11. Like so many of these Universal cliffhangers it's easy to wonder if we are looking at unheralded work with miniatures or gruesome newsreel footage. Sadly, the verdict seems to be the latter. In fact, to check out how bad Universal's work with

Bela with his pride and joy

miniatures was, have a look at the final shot of Dr. Zorka's plane crashing into the sea in Chapter 12. The average 10 year old probably does more convincing work with toys in his backyard.

The final chapter has earned well-deserved cult status. Now completely over the top, Dr. Zorka climbs into a bi-plane to wreak vengeance on his enemies. We see Zorka sitting in the cockpit, laughing maniacally and tossing small bombs out the window. The film cuts back and forth between stock footage of a factory or a battleship blowing up and Zorka laughing like a fool. (Why battleships, by the way? What did *those* guys do to him?) Sometimes we don't even see the damage below. Instead a newspaper headline appears on-screen to describe the results ("Zorka destroys Federal Building"). Over and over: the laughing, the little toy bombs, the direct hits, more cackling. On one of those occasions, Zorka manages to take out the Hindenburg blimp. Presumably, his plane veered off course from destroying the Federal Building in Washington and found itself over Lakehurst, New Jersey, in time to destroy the German blimp. Once again, actual newsreel footage of the 1937 disaster is used. It's a bit hard to take. When seeing the flames and the people scampering around—well these sure weren't extras working for scale. Although it had been nearly two years since the actual disaster, it still seems a tad insensitive to use this footage to fatten a serial. (Can you imagine a producer today cutting corners by inserting footage of 9/11 into a film?) Incredibly, *The Phantom Creeps* was not even the first serial to use Hindenburg footage. That honor belongs to *Dick Tracy's G-Men*, released a few months earlier by Republic. In fact, the Tracy film turned the Hindenburg sequence into an entire cliffhanger. At least Zorka just destroyed the dirigible in passing.

Back around 1950, a 78-minute version of this 265 minute serial was released to television, then in its infancy and hungry for programming. It was no doubt that version that exposed a new generation of viewers, including myself, to such lunacy for the first time. Hopefully, these viewers have found their way back to the original serial by now. There are moments in the serial when Bela is off-screen for a few moments and the whole thing threatens to disintegrate into a routine WWII-era melodrama.

But then back he comes with his invisibility belt, mechanical spiders and giant mechanical man, blathering about taking over the world. And once again all is right in the magic world of serials.

1940
Deadwood Dick

Deadwood, South Dakota. Six simple syllables. That marvelous location continues to trigger interest and excitement in the hearts of Americans more than a hundred years after the Wild West was tamed. Nobody talks about Altoona Al or Mooseport Mike, but Deadwood Dick is a perfectly engaging title for a fictional hero.

Other than its picturesque name, Deadwood, South Dakota, continues to stir the imagination because of its legendary lawlessness. The town was, indeed, beyond the reach of justice. Originally settled on a tract of land stolen from the Sioux Indians, the U.S. government could recognize no settlement there and had no authority over the behavior of its settlers. Just imagine the appeal that that had to the sociopaths who flocked there in droves.

Although far tamer than the recent HBO series bearing the name *Deadwood*,

the 1940 Columbia serial lets it be known from the get-go that lawlessness is the order of the day. Things are so bad that the town council brings in Wild Bill Hickok to tame the local thugs who have the town in their grip. Famous or not, Wild Bill doesn't make it through the first episode before getting shot in the back. It was a small role for veteran actor Lane Chandler, appearing in his 15th serial to date, including *The Green Hornet, The Lone Ranger* and the second and third *Flash Gordon* serials. Chandler made five more serials after this, before packing it in in 1945. Taking some liberty with history, the Columbia scriptwriters and director James W. Horne claim that most of the bad guys are working for a super-villain known as The Skull. This caped and masked marauder has a

Lane Chandler (as Wild Bill Hickok) takes aim.

simple agenda—to keep the Dakota Territory from becoming a state. Only then can he be sure that his rein of terror will continue unabated. The Skull wants to be the "Dictator of Dakota," as the local residents complain, "We're battling organized crime."

If this plot sounds familiar, take some bonus points. It is, in fact, the exact duplicate of goings-on in Republic's *Zorro's Black Whip*. The main difference is that serial (which appeared four years after *Deadwood Dick*) took place in Idaho. Other than that, the backstory is the same. As usual, the villain is one of the town's leading citizens, although he pulls a Mr. Dress-up whenever he commits his crimes. The other serial that comes to mind is Republic's *The Crimson Ghost*, released in 1946. The idea of a villain in a skull mask may have originated here, but there's little doubt which serial did a better job of it. The Crimson Ghost was a genuinely scary-looking character that creeped out audiences week after week, long after they knew what to expect. The Skull in *Deadwood Dick* looks, depending on how it's photographed, like a really cheap Halloween mask or like a carved pumpkin head that's been on the shelf a few days past its prime. It's beginning to sag. As with most concealed identity villains, the character looks a lot more impressive in his cape and mask (such as they are) than he does when finally revealed as a middle aged, balding and paunchy businessman.

As in *Zorro's Black Whip*, the hero of *Deadwood Dick* carries out his one-man anti-crime wave in the disguise of the title character. When he isn't fighting the Skull, Deadwood Dick is known as Dick Stanley, publisher of the local

Don Douglas and Lorna Gray

newspaper. Dick doesn't mind sharing his secret identity with friends Calamity Jane, local beauty Ann Butler and Dave, the feisty typesetter. The character of Dave, incidentally, is the obvious role model for Tenpoint, another irascible typesetter, in *Zorro's Black Whip*. It's sort of funny that no one else can figure out Deadwood Dick's identity. He's the only guy in sight named Dick and his alter ego doesn't even take the trouble to change his name. His voice and general appearance remain the same, yet everyone around him remains clueless as to whom Deadwood Dick can be. Played by Don Douglas, Dick is not your typical serial hero. Although only 35 when cast in the role, Douglas looks more like a newspaper publisher than a swashbuckler. If anything, he reminds us of actor Dick Purcell, who played Captain America with similar middle-aged panache. Like Purcell (who died within weeks of playing Captain America), Douglas also left the movie world far too soon. He went for an emergency appendectomy and died of post-surgical complications on December 31, 1945.

Calamity Jane ("the boisterous tomboy of the West") was played by character actress Marin Sais. Appearing in nearly 150 films, including numerous silent serials, Sais found a home in Westerns. She had appeared in 73 films before 1920, and although she died on the same day of the year (December 31) as her co-star, Don Douglas, she lived until the age of 81. The lovely Ann Butler was played by

Newspaper publisher Dick Stanley and local beauty Ann Butler

the equally lovely Lorna Gray, known to serial fans under her later name, Adrian Booth. In this role, Ms. Gray is quite a scream queen, the very antithesis of the title character she played in Republic's 1946 *Daughter of Don Q* (see Volume II) and further yet from her most familiar role as Vultura in *Perils of Nyoka* (1942–also see Volume II).

Director James Horne does a decent job here, although *Deadwood Dick* is not his finest work. As is his trademark, director Horne comes closest to surrealism in his treatment of the Skull's henchmen. One finds the expected comedic touches, although the character of Dave (Harry Harvey, Sr.) is simply over the top. The director seems to have let veteran actor Harvey (with credits in nearly 300 films) have his way with the role of Dave. Harvey had a background in burlesque and minstrel shows and brings these skills to the screen here. His part was probably a training ground for the regular role he played as Sheriff Blodgett on the 1950s Roy Rogers TV show. Someone might have reminded both Horne and Harvey that comic relief works best when it offsets something else, like tension. This serial has far too much relief, and too little tension. Nevertheless, Horne does a good job with the action sequences (some excellent stunt work) and manages to keep the serial from looking cheap.

A couple of memorable moments to watch for: There's a very contemporary looking bottle of ketchup on the counter of the café about a half a century before such things would have existed. About 10 minutes into Chapter 4, there's an amazing unscripted moment. An imposter of Deadwood Dick creates a rein of terror, shooting up the town. In an outdoor scene, the fake title character shoots a rancher off his horse and rides away. As he does, his gun produces what might be the most perfect long range smoke ring ever captured on film. It's worth watching for.

The Skull keeps shooting his henchmen just before they can reveal his identity to the law. He plainly doesn't inspire much loyalty in his employees and, as usual, there seems to be an infinite supply of bad guys. Like field mice, you trap a few and there are 10 more waiting to take their place. The cliffhanger to Chapter 11 seems pretty definitive. The hero is thrown down a mineshaft. In case that doesn't kill him, the villains lean over the pit and empty their six-guns into him. Then a huge steel bucket is thrown down the shaft on top of him. Hey, why stop there? Why not throw in a few sticks of dynamite and a bushel of scorpions as well? Chapter 13 ends with our hero tied up on the railroad tracks in front of an onrushing train. Close your eyes and it's 1920!

If nothing else, *Deadwood Dick* reveals that Columbia was still making decent serials in 1940, five years before Sam Katzman took over the studio's serial unit and almost single-handedly destroyed their output and reputation. For the record, the interest in Deadwood did not begin or end with this Columbia serial. In March 2004, HBO premiered its all-star television series called *Deadwood*. Like the old Columbia serial, the TV series also matched real and fictional characters and included Wild Bill Hickok and Calamity Jane. To the disappointment of serial fans everywhere, the HBO version did not include anyone called "The Skull."

Drums of Fu Manchu

Although he has just about vanished off the radar screen, Fu Manchu was probably the most famous popular culture villain of the 20th century. Most teenagers today don't know who he is, but their parents do, and so do *their* parents. That's a lot of staying power for a character that began life in a 1912 magazine serial, and ended up appearing in movies, books, comics, magazine stories, as well as radio and television shows.

There were 13 Fu Manchu novels in all (written by British author Arthur Henry Sarsfield Ward, under the pen name Sax Rohmer). These novels were full of racism and all manner of politically incorrect dialogue. In fact, Rohmer was known to have boasted that he made his fortune on Fu Manchu without having any real knowledge of the Chinese, a blissful state of ignorance he plainly shared with his intrigued readership.

The idea to bring Fu Manchu to the silver screen neither began nor ended with this 1940 serial from Republic. There had been Fu Manchu movies—indeed,

Fu Manchu (Henry Brandon) greets (left to right) Olaf Hytten, Tom Chatterton, William Royle and Robert Kellard.

serials—dating all the way back to the silent era. Fu, himself, would go on to be played by a host of legendary actors, including Boris Karloff, Christopher Lee, Warner Oland (of Charlie Chan fame), John Carradine and Peter Sellers. However, this effort by what was arguably the best cliffhanger studio operating during its Golden Era was truly a match made in heaven. No fewer than six screenwriters were used to bring Rohmer's villain to life, and material from seven of the first nine Fu Manchu novels was employed. The only restriction Republic faced was to stay away from the seventh and eighth novels, which had already been commissioned to film. Other than that, Fu Manchu and all his disguises and schemes were at Republic's disposal.

The very atmospheric results, directed by the stellar team of William Witney and John English, were full of intrigue and surprisingly big-budget-looking action. In fact, the serial is so rich in ideas and detail that it has cliffhangers to spare; some of them appear midway through Chapters 9 and 10. Other serials would have been content to build up to events this diabolical. Here, they are almost throwaway ideas. The serial has an exotic feel even though most of it is set in the good old U. S. A. The location is plainly Los Angeles, although it is identified, for some reason, as San Angeles (an amalgam of California's two largest cities). Cy Feuer's musical score is both rousing and appropriately Asian sounding. The serial also benefits from acrobatic stunt work by Davey Sharpe,

Classic Cliffhangers

Fu Manchu (with cigarette holder), surrounded by fanged Dacoit, Loki (John Merton) and black-suited John Piccori.

a disciple of the "Never walk through a door when you can somersault through it" school of acting.

Henry Brandon is quite effective in the title role. His character—reed thin, tall as hell and sporting a pair of shoulder pads that would be the envy of Joan Crawford—*looks* great, although his voice takes a bit of getting used to. The facial close-ups are well lit and framed; Brandon must have spent time studying at the Bela Lugosi Institute, majoring in Evil Glares. His foe (Alan Parker), played by Robert Kellard, is less effective. Kellard's acting is wooden, even by movie serial standards.

The plot is quite straightforward. Fu Manchu is trying to conquer Asia. To this end, he needs the sacred scepter of Genghis Khan. The serial is basically a 15-chapter tug of war over this prize. In the course of all this plotting, we meet Sir Dennis Nayland Smith (William Royle), a Scotland Yard detective bent on hunting down Fu Manchu, and Nayland's Watson-like sidekick, known as Dr. John Petrie (Olaf Hytten). We also cross paths with Fu's daughter, the lovely and sinister Fah Lo Suee, played by Gloria Franklin. It is she who wins this serial's award for memorable dialogue by uttering the immortal line, "You have inhaled the incense of a beetle. Fu Manchu is your master."

Also noteworthy is a brief appearance by Dwight Frye, best remembered for his role as Renfield in the original *Dracula* (1931). Frye, who appears briefly in

Fu Manchu ponders a broken tablet.

Chapter 5, is nonetheless credited in the titles for all 15 chapters. Perhaps the most memorable characters are the Dacoits, Fu Manchu's zombie-like henchmen. Wearing latex skullcaps that render them bald and jaggedly scarred, these guys are appropriately creepy. Each Dacoit is supposed to be the result of Fu's patented brain surgery technique. At the rate these zombies get shot or thrown from buildings, Fu must spend half his waking hours in the operating room getting these guys ready for action. At the best of times Fu Manchu does not treat his failed henchmen any too well. As we see in Chapter 2, calling him "Illustrious One" and doing the humble shuffle won't save them from an encounter with a hungry octopus if the Big Guy thinks they've been slacking off. It's a case of "Do your job or there's a Dacoit who can." And Fu Manchu does not hesitate to use animals to dispatch his victims. Along with the octopus, Fu also keeps a room full of hungry rats. The man is an equal opportunity employer.

At one point, Fu Manchu brags, "I have a number of Oriental devices for extracting information from stubborn witnesses." This is, of course, a variant on the Nazi proclamation, "Vee haf vays of making you talk." Curiously, though, Fu bypasses all that exotic Asian technology and goes straight to Poe, as he unveils his Pit and the Pendulum apparatus. In this slightly low-budget version of Poe's original, the pendulum is not lowered onto the hero's body. Instead the table onto which the hero is strapped is raised toward the ceiling using a hand crank. Fu is apparently a cost-conscious villain.

In Chapter 12 the action shifts to one of the least convincing visions of India ever filmed. It sure looks a lot like southern California. When we hear the line "The hills are swarming with hostile Indians," it takes a moment to register. These aren't Apaches he's talking about! In Chapter 14 (called "Satan's Surgeon"), Fu threatens to turn Nayland Smith into a Dacoit using just "a slight operation." The line was last uttered by Moloch in the original *Dick Tracy* serial (Republic, 1937). It's a clever in-joke, but any humor disappears very quickly as the arch villain prepares to operate.

There are moments in the final chapter when over 50 actors (soldiers, tribal warriors) are on the screen at once. That would have been downright miraculous on Republic's total budget of $164,000. Even if this footage was taken from elsewhere, it remains pretty spectacular and is very deftly matched.

Actor Henry Brandon became a successful TV actor after his serial days were over. He worked continuously for 30 years, beginning in 1957. He has been seen in episodes of *Get Smart, Outer Limits, Mission Impossible* and *Gunsmoke*. Reflecting back on this serial, Brandon remembers watching kids at Saturday matinees cheering his performance as the diabolical Fu Manchu. It's no wonder. For all his evil, Fu has panache. His adversary, Alan Parker, is a flat character and Kellard isn't much of an actor. Worse yet, Parker's sidekick, Inspector Nayland Smith, is a British guy in his 50s. These heroes just didn't give that much to cheer for.

It's clear at the end of the serial that Fu Manchu is not dead, despite a spectacular car crash. He pledges that he will return, although he isn't specific about whether it will be in a Republic serial. In fact, the studio planned *Fu Manchu Strikes Back*, but events of WWII cast a new light on things. The Chinese government—our allies against Japan—were less than thrilled at this piece of anti-Chinese fiction, especially since most Americans weren't all that clear about the difference between Chinese and Japanese. With Pearl Harbor still ringing in their ears, audiences had plenty of Yellow Peril feelings and China wanted as little as possible of it directed their way.

In his autobiography William Witney identifies this serial as his and Republic's best work. We can consider that high praise since Witney was often self critical. In case there is any doubt, in 2001, Serial Squadron held a poll of its members, asking for their favorite all-time serial. *Drums of Fu Manchu* came in second, narrowly losing the contest to *Flash Gordon*.

The Shadow

The Shadow has been a staple of American popular culture for almost as long as the character has been around. In fact, as cartoonist Bob Kane freely admitted, The Shadow's influence on later crime fighters like Batman was anything but trivial. The basic idea was tremendously appealing: If criminals were going to be sneaky, what better plan than to have a hero, an *avenger,* who skulked around unseen in the shadows? A mysterious alter ego who could go after the bad guys on their own terms, unencumbered by bureaucracy and red tape.

The Shadow began life as a radio character in July 1930. Publishers Street & Smith issued their first quarterly *Shadow* magazine in April 1931. It rapidly became a monthly item, and when that didn't satisfy the public appetite, *The Shadow* magazine was released every two weeks. The public literally couldn't get enough of it. Novelist Maxwell Grant (writing under the pen name Walter Gibson) cranked out regular Shadow fare, writing a total of 282 pulp novels, many of which were later adapted for radio. Jim Harmon, author of *Radio Mystery and Adventure* (McFarland), describes *The Shadow* magazine as "an attractive and haunting thing on the newsstands. The covers were beautiful and frightening, like medieval paintings of scenes of the Black Death."

The earliest radio shows weren't quite up to that standard—indeed *The Shadow* first appeared as a sort of host/narrator, much in the fashion of Rod

The Shadow (Victor Jory), Margo Lane (Veda Ann Borg) and Jack Ingram

Serling on *The Twilight Zone*. Actually, we should be ashamed of ourselves for using a modern example like that. The Shadow was really a forerunner of other radio hosts like Raymond on *Inner Sanctum* or the host/narrator on *The Mysterious Traveler* or *The Whistler*. The radio show, at least initially, was there simply to promote sales of the magazine. In that far-off time, the pulps were seen as the primary sales medium. Indeed, it wasn't until 1937 that the show's sponsor, Blue Coal, agreed to follow the pulp's lead and let the Shadow character step into the stories and forego the role of narrator. It was a fateful decision. The radio show became an almost overnight hit and the dual character of Lamont Cranston/The Shadow was entrenched in popular culture. That mocking, filtered voice speaking the closing words, "The weed of crime bears bitter fruit. Crime does not pay! The Shadow knows!" was repeated in offices and schoolyards all over America.

During 1937-38, the radio lead was played by no less than Orson Welles, and his sidekick/partner Margo Lane was played by Agnes Moorehead. Indeed, during its first two-year radio run, Welles' Mercury Theatre group was largely responsible for the weekly radio broadcasts. During this period, the 22-year-old Welles prided himself on doing all of the radio broadcasts cold; without rehearsal. For $185 per week, his total commitment to the Shadow consisted of two hours per week, one of which was spent in limousines going to and from the studio. Many

Victor Jory as the Shadow's alter-ego, Lin Chang. That's Eddie Featherstone with the package.

of the weekly broadcasts were performed live at New York's Empire Theatre, in front of a packed house on Sunday afternoons. Actors working with Welles during those historic broadcasts laughingly remember the star commenting during off-air commercial breaks, "Hey, this is an interesting script. I wonder how it turns out!" Other performers followed Welles into the role of the Shadow, and today it is Bret Morrison who is best remembered. The tradition of live broadcasts in front of a theater audience continued for much of the series run, and it is not uncommon, especially on some early broadcasts, to hear audience response (amused laughter) erupting during inappropriate moments or commercials. For much of its run *The Shadow* appeared on Sundays at 5 p.m., prompting some observers to refer to the show as "The 5-o'clock Shadow." One way or another, *The Shadow* enjoyed a run on American radio for nearly a quarter of a century, an impressive feat in the ever-changing world of popular culture. Audiences were estimated at over 15 million listeners a week. Historians estimate that approximately 900 radio shows were broadcast, 700 of which featured The Shadow as Lamont Cranston's crime fighting alter ego.

Although the magazine and radio versions of *The Shadow* ran in parallel for many years, there was an important difference between them. The character in the pulp magazine was a caped, shadowy figure who punched and shot people. The radio version of *The Shadow*, which is by far the more famous one today, was a character that could achieve invisibility by "clouding men's minds." (Apparently, women also had trouble seeing him.) Curiously, it is the pulp version of *The Shadow* that appears in the 1940 Columbia serial. That means we never do get to hear the classic line, "Who knows what evil lurks in the hearts of men." We do hear the famous maniacal laugh, but it's not as effective when you can *see* the guy who's delivering it.

Two Poverty Row film adaptations of *The Shadow* appeared in 1937 and 1938 (*The Shadow Strikes* and *International Crime*). Both of these films based their character on the magazine version, although the radio series was not as well established when these films were made. In fact, there were several two-reeler shorts based on The Shadow character released in 1931, although those films obviously featured the Shadow as host/narrator rather than in his later role as mysterious crime fighter. Why Columbia would have also chosen the less sensational approach to the Shadow character in 1940 is unclear. Apparently, they knew that audiences were expecting some sort of invisibility and so the scriptwriters made the Black Tiger, the villain of the serial, invisible. The Black Tiger is committed to destroying and then taking over the country's transportation system. This makes for plenty of action in the form of explosions and peril—both staples of serial life.

The Shadow is yet another reminder that pre- Sam Katzman Columbia serials can really be fun. In fact, if Katzman had produced this serial, he might have had an invisible hero chasing an invisible villain all over town. Think of the money he could have saved! This serial is hyper-kinetic enough to remind viewers of vintage Republic product and, like Republic's best work, it somehow manages not to look cheap. Certainly one thing the studio did right was to cast Victor Jory in the central role. He is perfect in both voice and appearance. True to the pulp magazine version of his character, Jory runs around in a black hat and cape, quite visible to all. His opponent, as previously mentioned, is invisible. Watching The Black Tiger turn into a beam of light during the frequently seen transformation scenes is quite effective. His overwrought dialogue is far less so. Even in the context of over-the-top serial villains, this reading is a bit much.

As is typical for a James W. Horne-directed film, there are plenty of injections of comedy into the action. Many of the fights are staged as borderline Three Stooges routines. It really is pretty funny to see a bad guy punch a door by accident, although it's hard to sustain a feeling of menace when laughing at the bad guys.

Along with chewing the scenery in most of his scenes, Jory is also given the task of portraying several characters. This is, of course, an even cheaper special effect than invisibility. Jory masquerades as Ling Chan, a shady Chinese character. Jory's voice and pidgin English are really tacky, but true to the time of the serial. ("You don't *tlust* me?" he asks the thugs. They in turn refer to him as "The Chink.") It is essentially an Asian version of blackface comedy. If you like Amos & Andy, you'll love Ling Chan.

Although Jory was reportedly a real trooper about doing his own stunts, veteran stuntman George DeNormand covered many of the more demanding scenes.

DeNormand kept getting tangled up in the costume and often told interviewers that nobody in real life would wear a cape if he planned on getting into a fistfight.

As usual, the cops are of almost no use. Once into the spirit of this serial, it's clear that if the Black Tiger is to be stopped, it's going to have to be Cranston/The Shadow who does it. Within 10 minutes of the first reel, Cranston informs us that he is not going to let the cops in on his double identity because he doesn't trust them. A fine start—it's now *our* secret—just Victor Jory and two million kids. Since we know the truth, it's fun to watch the cops trip over their own feet trying to figure things out. At one point, they even suspect that *The Shadow* and the Black Tiger are the same person.

Some wonderful moments to watch for: When the Shadow calls the Police Commissioner, he does his maniacal laugh into the telephone, by way of greeting. "It's the Shadow," says the Commissioner. Chapter 5 is particular fun. There are lots of toy airplanes and a "rascal of destruction"—serial talk for a guy with a ray gun.

The official Columbia method of cliffhanger survival? Cranston simply walks away from last week's rubble, dusting off his cape. At least two buildings fall on him and his plane crashes in plain sight. No fuss, no problem. Six of the first 12 chapters end with exploding rooms, complete with ceiling beams and plaster dust. Again, just dust the old cape off and start the next adventure. And in true Columbia fashion, the voice over at the end of each episode teases us about the cliffhanger from the *next* episode, as if what we'd just seen wasn't enough to bring us back into the theater.

At the end, Jory looks right into the camera and tells the audience, "The Shadow doesn't exist. His work is done. I think I'll go on a long vacation." As it turns out, Jory didn't take much of a vacation. Within months he was back working on another Columbia Serial, *The Green Archer*. As for *The Shadow*, the character had about 15 more years of original radio programs, recycled into the present day, a series of books, magazines and comics that continue unabated, and a 1994 big-screen opus featuring Alec Baldwin.

Who knows what commercial potential lurks in the hearts of men? *The Shadow* apparently does.

King of the Royal Mounted

It's getting harder and harder these days for movie serials to stay "lost." Just when we think, "We'll never see that one again," along comes a new release on DVD making us wonder if anything can hide from collectors and cinephiles indefinitely. Fanboys can almost bet that the permafrost or some dusty warehouse or attic will still have secret treasures to yield.

So it is with *Zane Grey's King of the Royal Mounted* (the author's name is actually part of the serial's formal title). Sergeant King of the Canadian Royal Mounted Police had a 20-year run as a comic strip hero (from 1935-1955) and a brief career on the radio as well. While perhaps not as elusive as serials like *The Lone Ranger* and *The Vanishing Shadow* (both now available), *King of the Royal Mounted* has again joined the living, available in a meticulously restored print from VCI.

So now that we've got this 1940 serial in circulation again, how good is it? It depends on whom you ask. Many critics and collectors, including myself, think it's just fine—worthy of Republic's stellar Golden Age reputation. A conspicuous dissenting vote, however, comes from the serial's director, William Witney.

In his autobiography, Witney describes this serial as "another dud" (he also disliked his previous 1940 serial, *Red Ryder*.) The target of much of his disdain seems to be star Allan "Rocky" Lane. Both Witney and co-director John English developed a serious dislike for this actor whose ego, they believed, eclipsed his abilities. Witney also disliked the script of *King of the Royal Mounted*, which he described as "pure and simple propaganda."

There's certainly truth in that assessment, although it's worth remembering that America was on the brink of

Allan Lane feels a headache coming on.

entering WWII at the time. Not wanting to get ahead of historical events, Republic refused to identify the enemy as Germany, although the minimal clues were hard to miss. The head villain was named "Kettler" (as opposed to Hitler) and, in Chapter 1, his henchmen saluted a lot and said things like "For the Cause!" Republic sets the action in Canada, a Commonwealth nation that had already declared war against the Nazis. The plot leaves the U.S. out of things altogether. A Canadian scientist discovers "Compound X," a substance contained in pitchblende that can cure infantile paralysis. (Interestingly, no mention is made of either radium or uranium, the primary extracts of pitchblende.) Compound X also has properties that create magnetic mines, which are just what (the unnamed) German military needs to "blast the English fleet from the North Sea." The problem is, a team of enemy agents will have to sneak into Canada, where they can secretly mine the mysterious substance and smuggle it out of the country. Every action they take is followed closely by the Royal Mounted Police, who remain one step behind until the final chapter.

These days, American moviemakers routinely shoot in Canada to save money, letting cities like Toronto and Vancouver stand in for their American counterparts. In this serial, the opposite is true. Shot just north of Los Angeles at Big Bear Lake in the San Bernadino Mountains, this American location pretends to be Canadian. Within the first 10 minutes of Chapter 1, reference is made to Montreal, Ottawa and Winnipeg. The outdoor settings are really quite beautiful; in fact, if a serial ever cried out for color film, it is this one. Between the lush green forests and the red Mountie uniforms, the effect would have been stunning.

Sergeant King (Lane) gets bumped from his flight the hard way.

The mawkish patriotism that director Witney complained about runs fast and furious by the final chapter. Sergeant King and his sidekick Mountie Tom end up in a selfless battle over who will sacrifice his life to save peace-loving people of the world. It's pretty easy to guess who lives on to fight another foe. This "I'm not going to let you sacrifice yourself; I'll knock you out and go in your place" kind of selfless heroism turns up two years later in another Witney-directed wartime Republic serial, *Spy Smasher*.

Surprisingly, some of the miniature work here isn't up to Republic's usually lofty standards. Although they blew up buildings and cars better than anyone, Republic never was too good at submarines. Here, the grainy stock wartime footage intercut with studio miniatures just isn't convincing. Worse yet, within three minutes of the start of Chapter 1, we've got a little toy torpedo in a fish tank that has a string attached to it, as visible as a Flash Gordon spaceship.

There's plenty of action on display here, complete with a couple of plot twists and the usual movie serial lunacy. Cliffhangers include a forest fire, a train wreck, car, airplane and boat crashes, and a spectacular fire in a warehouse. In case that isn't enough, there's also a buzz saw, a bear trap, a boiling caldron, a roiling waterfall and a volley of gunshots. The fight scenes are spectacular with Republic's team of ace stuntmen performing to their usual high standard. In fact, this serial must set some kind of record for back flips; just about every fight contains at least one. The most visible among these prize fighter/acrobats is Davey Sharpe, who doubles the star, Allan Lane. Despite his acrobatics, Sharpe is not a good physical match for Lane and the facial differences between them are surprisingly obvious during fight scenes in Chapters 8 and 9.

A few of the secondary players are worth mentioning. Veteran actor Harry Cording plays the role of Garson, the lead henchman. Often described as a "burly bit-part actor," Cording, who appeared in over 250 films, is best known for his small roles in five Sherlock Holmes films made during the 1940s. He also had small roles in classic horror films *The Black Cat* (1934), *Son of Frankenstein, The*

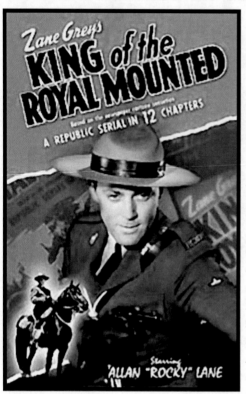

Wolf Man, The Ghost of Frankenstein and The Mummy's Tomb. In contrast, the leading lady (Linda Merritt) was played by actress Lita Conway, who appeared in a total of three films between 1940-41 before disappearing from the industry. Conway brought a disarming lack of glamour to her role, offering instead an engaging girl-next-door quality. The closest *King of the Royal Mounted* comes to comic relief is the character of Vinegar Smith, played by veteran actor Budd Buster (a.k.a. George Selk). Like Harry Cording, Buster had a long list of credits, appearing in nearly 300 films and many 1950s TV shows. Although Buster spent most of his time in the role of a grizzled cowpoke, he also appeared in *The Mummy's Curse* and *It Came From Outer Space.*

Two years after *King of the Royal Mounted* was released, Alan Lane appeared in another Witney-directed serial about the Mounties. This 1942 entry had the nearly identical title *King of the Mounties.* Needless to say, quite a bit of footage from the present serial was recycled into the subsequent release. The director re-used facial close-ups of Lane, even though the script was different. Witney argued there was no harm done since "Lane's expressions were all the same whether he was doing comedy or tragedy." Although director Witney had nary a good word to say about Lane, the actor does turn in a credible performance as Sgt. King. Four serial roles notwithstanding, Lane is best remembered as a cowboy star. Not many of his fans from Westerns or serials were aware that Lane was also the voice behind *Mr. Ed*, the famous talking horse of the 1950s television show. No doubt William Witney would have argued that Lane had finally found a role worthy of his talent.

The Green Archer

As we've already pointed out, Columbia serials have a pretty bad reputation. In some cases, their rep is well deserved, although most of it lies squarely at the feet of producer Sam Katzman. Before Katzman took over the helm of the serial unit in 1945 (which puts his output in the realm of Volume II of this book), Columbia turned out some pretty decent cliffhangers. Arguably the best of all of them was *The Green Archer*.

This 1940 entry isn't just good for a Columbia product, it's a fine serial by any reckoning. To begin with, the plot wasn't cobbled together in two days by studio hacks, who secretly longed for more serious assignments. The story of the mysterious costumed figure began life as an Edgar Wallace mystery novel. Its cinematic potential was obvious almost from the start. The first *Green Archer* adaptation was a 1925 Pathé serial featuring box-office stars Walter Miller and Allene Ray. After the Columbia serial version, the green costumed figure again appeared on the silver screen in a well-made 1960 German feature production (released a year later in America in dubbed form).

The plot is simple and engaging. The Bellamy Brothers (not to be confused with the country music stars of the 1980s) lay joint claim to Garr Castle—their family estate. Predictably, one brother is good and one is bad. (Ironically, in this adaptation, the bad one is named Abel.) Abel frames his brother, has him unjustly imprisoned and lays sole claim to Garr castle, which he turns into headquarters for his team of thieves. Along the way, Abel also lusts after his brother's wife and imprisons her in the dungeons below. What a guy! Meanwhile, ace insurance detective Spike Holland gets on the case and is aided by the shadowy *Green Archer* figure. It seems every time evil is poised to triumph over good, a well-placed arrow from the title avenger evens the playing field and bails out our hero. Will good finally triumph over evil? What is the identity of the masked figure? Those questions drive 15 energetic chapters and it's a great ride all the way.

Victor Jory restrains Constantine Romanoff, while Charles King watches with gun.

What elevates *The Green Archer* beyond ordinary serial fare is not just the plot, however. Director James W. Horne, whose career goes all the way back to the silent era, brings something extra to the party. There is a barely controlled element of farce here, and it isn't simply pitched to nine-year-olds. To this day, a sympathetic adult audience can sit through this serial with a minimum of squirming. The running joke is that the bad guys are incredibly stupid and the cops are no better. One of the thugs even wears his hat brim rolled up like Leo Gorcey of the Dead End Kids. Both cops and robbers are a bunch of physically and mentally challenged dolts. His henchmen and his foe, Spike Holland, constantly exasperate Abel, who is also thwarted by the cops who are supposed to be helping him. Inspector Thompson, the main policeman, isn't just a middle-aged, slow-moving, slow-thinking buffoon. He gets nearly everything wrong and has all the exasperated mannerisms of Oliver Hardy. It's pretty funny stuff at times, which is no real surprise since director Horne cut his teeth on Laurel & Hardy comedies, along with directing classic episodes of the Little Rascals.

Another of the serial's strengths is the performance of both lead characters. Victor Jory brings intelligence and class to his role as Spike Holland. He's not a conventional, good-looking leading man; in fact, Jory spent much of his 50-year film career playing heavies with a well-honed menace. Jory only appeared in one other serial—Columbia's *The Shadow*—earlier the same year. As his adversary, James Craven, is equally stellar, obviously enjoying himself immensely in the role. Craven went on to star in seven serials over a 10-year period, including

Captain Midnight, also for Columbia. In his role as Abel, Craven is both suave and demented, a challenging combination. Craven is also faced with a team of henchmen whose average IQ must be in the room temperature range—on a chilly day. Craven has great fun tormenting his deficient employees. "If your brain worked as fast as mine, I might be working for *you*." They are befuddled by nearly every assignment he gives them, and they pass the hours away playing tiddley winks, not poker.

There is plenty of action here. Each episode is chock full of chases through secret corridors and trap doors. Whenever things start to slack off, the director brings on the savage dogs. The sets are deliciously cheesy. What should be large stone blocks are obviously black lines painted on plywood walls. However, the special effects are surprisingly convincing. The car crashes look particularly good, as if the studio chose to total out real automobiles instead of using miniatures. Technology Marches On Department: In order to talk to their boss from the road, the bad guys have to pull their car over and use a radio set that fills up the entire trunk.

The serial might have been called "The Green Archer*s*." There are actually two of them. One is a well-meaning dorky guy employed by Abel. His job is made more complicated by the fact that the *real* Green Archer, whose identity we don't learn until the final chapter, keeps getting in his way. When the boss bangs his fists on the desk and tells his idiot servants to put an end to the Green Archer, they usually end up pummeling their own colleague by mistake. All these bows and arrows strike one sour note. In order to save Victor Jory at the start of Chapter 13, the Green Archer has to shoot two dogs. Although we're conditioned to see them as bad critters (the chapter is called "The Devil Dogs"), it's still a surprisingly inhumane touch.

The Columbia promotion machine must have been in danger of running out of breathless descriptions. Each chapter ends with a title card telling us to watch next week's thrilling episode while a voiceover implores us to see the next "shuddering" or "taunting" chapter. After 15 installments, that's a lot of adjectives.

Horne is also credited as one of the writers, which is not surprising. His spirit is all over this production. Larry Darmour acted as producer but, for some reason, received no screen credit. There is some irony in that since Sam Katzman, who received prominent screen credit on the serials he produced, cranked out products that were hardly a source of pride.

The final chapter is a real standout. The bad guys get their comeuppance, the Archer's identity is revealed and Jory and Iris Meredith, his comely co-star, finally look like they're ready to go find a room. But more than that, the episode is visually stunning and provides some genuine laughs. In what might have been an ad-lib, Jory grabs a shield off the castle wall and literally covers his ass as he walks by the Green Archer. To his credit, James W. Horne let that moment of inspired lunacy stand. Horne went on to direct a total of 10 serials for Columbia between 1940 and 1943. This is arguably his finest work.

Mysterious Dr. Satan

The years have been kind to *Mysterious Dr. Satan*. It is regarded by many as one of the best serials produced by Republic, the studio associated with the best in Classic Cliffhangers. However, those were hardly the sentiments that prevailed back in 1940 when the serial was released.

To begin with, *Dr. Satan* only went into production because, at the very last minute, it became clear that Republic was unable to secure the rights to *Superman*. An entire production team as well as a rough draft of the script was already in place, awaiting the go-ahead from studio exec Manny Goldstein. The nod never came, leaving the studio with a great big hole in its production schedule and a partially completed script that could no longer accommodate the Man of Steel. Director William Witney describes these events in delicious detail in his autobiography, although it's clear that he was no fan of this serial or the chaos surrounding its production. He disliked the script, which he considered hastily

Dr. Satan (Ciannelli), his robot and Ella Neal

cobbled together from re-written *Superman* scraps. Even more so, he hated the famous Republic robot, which he describes as a "man in a hot water heater."

Now, audiences might ask, who are we to disagree with a master of the genre? Well, with all due respect to Mr. Witney, that is exactly what we intend to do. Obviously, Witney saw *Mysterious Dr. Satan* in terms of what it might have been. Fortunately, we get to see it in terms of what it is, with no concern for behind-the-scenes intrigue. From that vantage point, there is a lot to love about this 1940 serial and its cobbled together script, hastily invented hero and wonderfully clunky robot. Whatever its checkered origins, *Mysterious Dr. Satan* has a lot going for it beyond mere nostalgia.

There is an undeniable dark side to this production, a fairly rare commodity in serials. Sure, there are plenty of fistfights and car chases, but there is something unusually somber and adult about the results. Part of it stems from 29-year old Cy Feuer's musical score, which creates palpable tension. Feuer was a master at this sort of thing, having just scored the last four Republic serials, including *Drums of Fu Manchu*. He would go on to add his deft musical touch to the next four Republic serials throughout 1941, including the studio's very next title, the landmark *Adventures of Captain Marvel* (see Volume II of this book). Cy Feuer died in May 2006, a well-respected man in his profession. Most of his fame was based not on these early Republic cliffhangers, but as the producer of Broadway

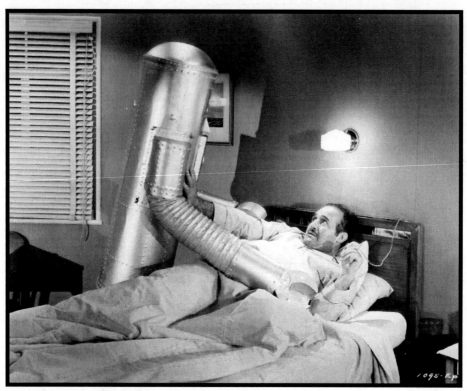

"You're not my nurse!" exclaims Bert LeBaron in vain.

musicals. Among his success stories were the New York productions of *Guys and Dolls, How to Succeed in Business Without Really Trying* and the discovery of Julie Andrews. Feuer was 95 when he died.

Along with Feuer's music, much of the tension here comes from the inspired casting of Eduardo Ciannelli in the title role. The producers had originally cast Henry Brandon to play the role of Doctor Satan. Brandon had previously impressed the Republic brass with his handling of the title role in *Drums of Fu Manchu*. When Brandon withdrew at the last minute, having secured a better paying job, Ciannelli was brought in as his replacement. It was a fortuitous change to say the least. Brandon was to have played the role in odd makeup, including rudimentary horns on his forehead. Cianelli played the role straight, using only his courtly manner and vaguely European accent to create an air of menace. There's no telling *how* crazy he is in those impeccably tailored suits. Even the goodly Dr. Scott, whom Dr. Satan kidnaps and forces to work on an army of robots, is courteous to his captor. You just can't help being civil to him. That air of sophistication and continental charm swirling around Eduardo Ciannelli was the real deal. The actor initially studied medicine, then trained to be an opera singer and actually performed arias on the European stage. However, such urbanity didn't get in the way of his playing roles like this or the high priest in Universal's *The Mummy's Hand* (1940).

David Sharpe (doubling Robert Wilcox as the Copperhead) leaps into action.

In the absence of Superman, the writers were forced to concoct another hero, although there would have to be some limits on the extent of his powers. They created Bob (not Bruce) Wayne, a typically good-looking man about town. His girlfriend is named Lois, which must have saved a few erasers when it came time to revise the *Superman* script. In Episode 1, Wayne (well played by Robert Wilcox) introduces his alter ego, "The Copperhead." Like his father before him, Wayne will don the metal mask and go to work against the bad guys. Lofty goals, to be sure, but not much of a disguise. It's sort of funny that nobody can figure out the identity of the Copperhead. He dresses in Wayne's clothes and talks in Wayne's voice, but even Bob's sidekick and his girlfriend Lois are clueless. The ruse is particularly laughable when Wayne (a.k.a. the Copperhead) telephones his home and Lois answers. "This is the Copperhead," he says in his normal voice. But because he's wearing the mask while telephoning, Lois has no idea who he is.

Only when Doctor Satan has been defeated in Episode 15 (at the hands of his own robot, of course) can Wayne reveal his identity and retire the copper headgear. Curiously, Republic closed the door to a sequel as the Copperhead blew his cover and, indeed, never returned to the screen in the next 15 years of serial production. Presumably, Doctor Satan was also damaged beyond repair by the time his robot (occasionally pronounced "rubbit" by Ciannelli) got through with him. In fact, only the robot survived this production. You just can't keep a good rubbit down. Our

MYSTERIOUS DOCTOR SATAN

A REPUBLIC SERIAL IN 15 CHAPTERS

EDWARD CIANNELLI
ROBERT WILCOX · WILLIAM NEWELL
C. MONTAGUE SHAW · ELLA NEAL
DOROTHY HERBERT
WILLIAM WITNEY and JOHN ENGLISH—Directors

Chapter 5 DOCTOR SATAN'S MAN of STEEL

friend in the "hot water heater" suit made another appearance in *Zombies of the Stratosphere*, a Republic serial produced in 1952. Robots have been a staple of serial production since the earliest silent movie days and continued to terrorize heroes and their girlfriends almost until the end. In fact, when Republic turned this serial into a feature film in 1966, they retitled it. In a somewhat revealing change of focus, the movie was called *Doctor Satan's Robot*.

There was something truly menacing about a stalking mechanical monster. Doctor Satan may have been evil but, cool and composed as he seemed, at least you knew he had a soul under those fancy suits. Maybe if talking to him long enough, he could be convinced not to conquer the universe. His rubbit, on the other hand, was pure hardware. Better to outrun him or short out his circuit board, because he sure wasn't going to be talked down.

Although William Witney had no love for this serial, it's hard not to marvel at the panache he and partner John English brought to directing it. The action scenes are particularly remarkable. There's enough location shooting to keep the viewer's interest, and the fight scenes involving stuntmen David Sharpe and Tom Steele are staged inventively throughout. These guys don't just stand still and punch in the manner of serials five and 10 years earlier. When they fight, it's like watching ballet. They run up walls and do back flips. You can tell that these displays have been thoughtfully choreographed with the viewer's excitement in mind.

Witney and English went on to co-direct 17 consecutive serials for Republic. It is difficult to overestimate the impact of their work on the industry and its future practitioners. Maybe it's just a coincidence, but one of Doctor Satan's henchmen is named "Gort." Ten years later that same odd moniker would surface as the name of the powerful robot in *The Day The Earth Stood Still*. It's hard to imagine that the folks involved in making that landmark science fiction thriller hadn't cut their teeth on *Mysterious Dr. Satan*.

INDEX

Classic Cliffhangers

About the Author

HANK DAVIS is a professor of psychology at the University of Guelph in Ontario, Canada, with an interest in evolutionary psychology and popular culture. He became hooked on movie serials when he was a kid growing up in New York. Hank has also written extensively about music and produced more than 100 boxed-sets and reissue albums of 1950s music, from Hank Williams to Sun Records stars like Johnny Cash, Jerry Lee Lewis and Charlie Rich. A lifetime baseball fan, Hank is also the author of *Small-Town Heroes*, a critically acclaimed behind-the-scenes look at minor league baseball, published by Bison Books. These two Volumes of *Classic Cliffhangers* are his first books about film.

Hank Davis

If you enjoyed this book
check out our other
film-related titles at
www.midmar.com
or call or write for a free catalog
Midnight Marquee Press, Inc.
9721 Britinay Lane
Baltimore, MD 21234
410-665-1198 (8 a.m. until 6 p.m. EST)
or MMarquee@aol.com